Reproductive
Technologies

Feminist Perspectives
Series editor: Michelle Stanworth

REPRODUCTIVE TECHNOLOGIES

Gender, Motherhood
and Medicine

Edited by
Michelle Stanworth

University of Minnesota Press,
Minneapolis

Chapter 1, 'Reproductive Technologies and the Deconstruction of Motherhood',
copyright © Michelle Stanworth. Chapter 2, 'From Walking Wombs to Test-
Tube Babies', copyright © Ann Oakley. Chapter 3, 'Foetal Images: The Power
of Visual Culture in the Politics of Reproduction', copyright © Rosalind Pollack
Petchesky. Chapter 4, 'Artificial Insemination, In-Vitro Fertilization and the
Stigma of Infertility', copyright © Naomi Pfeffer. Chapter 5, ' "There Is of
Course the Distinction Dictated by Nature": Law and the Problem of Paternity',
copyright © Carol Smart. Chapter 6, 'Surrogacy: Feminist Notions of
Motherhood Reconsidered', copyright © Juliette Zipper and Selma Sevenjuijsen.
Chapter 7, 'Human Embryos and the Law', copyright © Janet Gallagher.
Chapter 8, 'Victorian Values in the Test-Tube: the Politics of Reproductive
Science and Technology', copyright © Hilary Rose. Chapter 9, 'Infertility – a
Life Sentence? Women and the National Health Service', copyright
© Lesley Doyal.

Library of Congress Cataloging-in-Publication Data
Reproductive technologies.

   (Feminist perspectives).
   Bibliography: p.
   Includes index.
   1. Human reproduction——Technological innovations——
Social aspects. 2. Feminism. I. Stanworth, Michelle.
II. Series. [DNLM: 1. Reproduction. 2. Technology,
Medical. 3. Women's Rights. WQ 205 R4292]
QP251.R4447 1987   303.4′ 83   87–19021
ISBN 0–8166–1645–0
ISBN 0–8166–1646–9 (pbk.)

Published by the University of Minnesota Press
2037 University Avenue Southeast, Minneapolis MN 55414.
Published simultaneously in Canada
by Fitzhenry & Whiteside Limited, Markham.
Printed in Great Britain.

The University of Minnesota
is an equal-opportunity
educator and employer.

Contents

Preface

All worthwhile attempts to write and to do research intersect at some point with people's passions and personal concerns, as well as taxing their intellectual energies. This has been doubly so for me in the case of *Reproductive Technologies*, because the issues it raises touch upon so many experiences, painful and joyful, that mark my own biography as a woman. There are many people who have shared in the making of the project who deserve thanks – in particular, Gill Motley and Helen Pilgrim of Polity Press, Gillian Bromley and Katrina Robinson, John Thompson, who set the project in motion, and the authors of the book. But above all, I would like to give my thanks to David Held, who shared with me in the most generous possible way both the making of the book and the experiences that it recalls.

Michelle Stanworth
1987

Editor's Introduction

The birth in July 1978 of Louise Brown – the world's first 'test-tube baby' – marked the beginning of a decade of intense speculation about reproductive technologies. In a few short years, terms such as in-vitro fertilization, surrogate motherhood, genetic engineering, frozen embryos or egg donation have acquired the status of household words. Yet the meaning of these practices – for the patients who seek them out and the offspring who are created, and for the future of reproduction, sexuality, parenthood and the family – remains unclear.

These technologies claim to offer, on the one hand, a range of possibilities for extending the pleasures of parenthood to people who have been unable to realize their desire to have a child. They offer a chance for would-be parents to know, before a birth, about genetic or chromosomal abnormalities in their offspring and even – through gene therapy – eventually to eliminate some of these defects before conception takes place. Viewed from the vantage-point of these potential benefits, reproductive technologies validate the image of science as a realm of boundless progress, bringing triumph over natural obstacles for the satisfaction of human needs.

On the other hand, the new reproductive technologies extend the possibility of a medical and scientific practice that outreaches human understanding and public control. They bring dangers of new, unknown (and in the short term, unknowable) risks to patients exposed to these techniques and to babies born of them. They allow greater scope for the application of eugenic policies that would place a higher value on some human lives than on others. They appear to interfere with the 'naturalness' of the reproductive process and to turn the 'precious gift' of a baby into something that money can buy. When these dangers are placed in the forefront of discussion, the new technologies invoke the spectre of science-gone-mad, of a Frankensteinian world in which scientists manipulate – with unforeseeable consequences – the very foundations of life itself.

Such polarization of views is possible precisely because the new reproductive technologies open up to debate matters that formerly belonged in the realm of biological givens: in practices such as surrogacy, the gulf between 'biological motherhood' and 'social motherhood' is vividly exposed, provoking new personal and legal choices; fewer and fewer female and male infertilities are now 'final' in the physiological sense; fewer genetic abnormalities are undetectable. By altering the boundaries between the biological and the social – by demanding human decision where previously there was biological destiny – the new technologies politicize issues concerning sexuality, reproduction, parenthood and the family.

Whether commentators emphasize the positive or negative potential of reproductive technologies, they are agreed in identifying a range of social, ethical and legal questions raised by the new technologies. These questions tend, as other writers have pointed out, to fall into two categories. First there are those that focus on the ethical and practical problems arising from the manipulation of eggs, sperm and embryos outside the human body: Does scientific research on the human embryos generated by in-vitro fertilization undermine respect for the sanctity of human life? Should embryos be protected from commercial or scientific exploitation, and if so, would this be compatible with the provision of legal abortion? What will happen to the rest of us, with all our human imperfections, if scientists succeed in producing through genetic engineering 'the perfect child'? Secondly, there are those questions arising from the more complicated structure of parenthood that the new technologies entail: Who can claim the children produced from a donated egg or embryo? Who is the legal parent in the case of children born to a woman who is neither their genetic mother nor their social mother? Does in-vitro fertilization, or surrogate motherhood, threaten bonds between mothers and children and weaken the institution of motherhood itself?

It has been left to feminist writers to raise a third set of issues. In contemporary societies, where women not only bear children but are defined predominantly in terms of their reproductive capacities, what impact will changes in reproduction that may accompany the new technologies have on women's lives? What does it mean for women's health, safety and their choices about reproduction that the patients whose bodies will be the vehicles for the new technologies are overwhelmingly female, while the people who design, test, approve and apply the technologies – the embryologists, the molecular biologists, the obstetricians and gynaecologists, or 'the pharmacrats' as Gena Corea puts it – are overwhelmingly male? Armed with two substantial bodies of feminist critique – one documenting the indifference and even misogyny, that animates much scientific, obstetric and gynaecological practice towards women, and the other offering a philosophical re-examination of the masculinist nature of much of what passes for scientific objectivity and rationality – feminists have increasingly seen in the new reproductive technologies nothing less than an attempt to appropriate the reproductive capacities which have been, in the past, women's unique source of power.

The aim of this book is to offer a fresh appraisal of reproductive technologies – to evaluate their impact, to understand the often-ferocious debates that have arisen around them and to assist in formulating strategies for dealing with them. The book suggests that none of the three positions outlined above – the uncritical position which defers without question to the advances of science, the pessimistic position which predicts the downfall of civilization and the particular feminist reading which sees in these technologies an unmitigated attack on women – is, in itself, adequate. Although the three positions have very different starting-points, their arguments have features in common which the authors in this volume firmly reject.

In the first instance, reproductive technologies are not all of a piece: while there are similarities between them, deriving partly from the organization of science and medicine that underpins their application, there are also differences. Once attention is wrenched away from eye-catching conceptive technologies to 'routine' techniques for contraception, abortion, infertility treatment or antenatal care, the importance of these differences becomes transparent: while many of the routine technologies are severely flawed from the point of view of women on whom they might be used, many offer indispensable resources upon which women seek to draw according to their circumstances and priorities. With the newer technologies, as with the old, blanket acceptance or rejection is no substitute for informed and critical appraisal.

Secondly, no account of the reproductive technologies can be adequate that does not attend not only to the different relation of women and men to reproduction, but also to the differences among women. All women are subject, to greater or lesser degree, to social pressures to regard motherhood as the fulfilment of their lives; but these pressures have different impacts on women in different circumstances and women respond to them in varying ways, depending upon their social circumstances, their health and their fertility, and according to opportunities and meanings derived from ethnic and social class cultures. Thus, if it is misleading to assess reproductive technologies in the abstract, without distinguishing the different effects on women and men, it is also difficult to find a position on motherhood from which we can say clearly and unambiguously what women want or need.

Thirdly, reproductive technologies need to be put firmly in their place, as one dimension – but not necessarily the most important – of the forces that shape reproduction and the lives of women, men and children today. An overemphasis upon technology risks distracting attention from the politics and organization of health care in general, from the legal system which frames our rights over our bodies and our children, from political struggles over the nature of sexuality, parenthood and the family and from the impact of the varied material and cultural circumstances in which people create their personal lives. Fundamental social alternatives are not shaped by technologies alone, and technological determinism – whether of the variety that claims that scientific-technical progress provides the key to all social problems, or of the kind that seems to target technology as *the* obstacle to autonomy or freedom – will not do.

The opening chapter of *Reproductive Technologies* outlines the social and political context from which debates about these technologies emerge and hence sets the scene for the chapters that are to follow. The history of the development and the impact of the four major groups of reproductive technologies highlights the tension that lies at the centre of feminist concern: that, on the one hand, medical and scientific advances have offered women a greater chance to decide if, when and under what conditions to mother, while on the other, they have increased the potential for others to exercise an even greater control over women's lives. It is not ignorance and fear that make women wary of new developments in the area of reproduction, but knowledge and experience of the ambivalent effect of medical and scientific practice on women's reproductive lives. But this does not necessarily lead to the view that reproductive technologies represent a vehicle for men to wrest control of reproduction from women; on the contrary, this particular account of the impact of technology echoes too closely the very notions of science, of women and of motherhood that women have been attempting to transform. Against this background, Michelle Stanworth re-examines the intersection of reproductive technologies with the changing status of genetic parenthood, of family relations, of pregnancy and birth, and with the new eugenics. This analysis shows that the newer technologies are controversial (not only among feminists, but among a wider public) because they crystallize issues at the heart of contemporary social and political struggles over sexuality, reproduction, gender relations and the family – and that a concern for self-determination for women must engage above all with these struggles.

Feminist writers have expressed deep concern about forms of reproductive technologies which – in view of lack of solid evidence about safety and effectiveness – might properly be regarded as 'experimental' (Kaufert and McKinlay, 1985; Faulder, 1985; Corea, 1985a). In-vitro fertilization has been a particular focus of concern (Corea, 1985a chapter 8; Cripps, 1984). In chapter 2, Ann Oakley extends this line of enquiry to encompass technologies for viewing the interior of the womb. The marked enthusiasm of medical practitioners in the early decades of the twentieth century for the routine use of X-rays to diagnose pregnancy and to monitor the development of the foetus has a parallel, she suggests, in professional attitudes to the routine use of ultrasound today; in both cases, the technology has been widely applied before its safety and effectiveness have been evaluated properly. Oakley's concise and powerful outline of the recent history of medical care for pregnant and birthing women focuses on relations of power between medical practitioners and their female patients, relations that increasingly, in her view, reduce women to the status of reproductive objects.

The impact of ultrasound extends beyond its medical risks or benefits for individual women, for it is significant also in presenting a powerful visual image – the image of the foetus as free-floating, self-sufficient, independent of the woman who carries it. In chapter 3, Ros Petchesky shows how the meanings ascribed to the foetus, in a culture that equates visual imagery with objective reality, are a key part of the historical context of the routine use of ultrasound. She demonstrates how ultrasound images mesh with the attempts of anti-abortion campaigners to make the foetus, through video films like *The Silent Scream*, a public presence. Petchesky examines the impulse to 'see inside', and asks why it has come to dominate ways of knowing about pregnancy. Like Oakley, Petchesky affirms that ultrasound tends to discredit women's felt experience of pregnancy in favour of 'objective' data. But she argues compellingly that to reduce such technologies to a mere weapon in a male war against the womb is to submerge women's own responses to their pregnancies in male fantasies of power. Petchesky's analysis of the pleasure and comfort that some women derive from 'the chance to see my baby' suggests that the difficult questions about how women ought to use reproductive technologies cannot be answered from the standpoint of a common reproductive consciousness.

Concern for people who are infertile figures prominently in debates about conceptive technologies. The promoters of in-vitro fertilization validate their clinical practice by reference to the desperate desire of infertile women and men to have a child; feminist and other critics of these technologies fear that it is precisely the desperation of the infertile that will make them ready prey to experimentation and to techniques that are ethically suspect. In an original assessment of these claims, Naomi Pfeffer in chapter 4 draws attention to the complex social processes that shape the experience of infertility. Through a discussion of the range of techniques available for the diagnosis and treatment of infertility, she shows precisely what 'infertility specialists' stood to gain from the introduction of in-vitro fertilization. Her historical analysis draws out striking parallels between the ferocious debates over artificial insemination by donor in earlier decades of this century, and debates today around in-vitro fertilization. It shows, more importantly, that the refusal by both supporters and opponents of reproductive technologies to acknowledge the heterogeneity of infertility, or to recognize that the failure to conceive by no means rules out rational assessment of options and priorities, has had the effect of further stigmatizing infertile women and men, and of preventing exploration into the causes and consequences of infertility.

The focus of the next three chapters is a range of legal issues with which reproductive technologies intersect. In chapter 5, Carol Smart reminds us that the new conceptive technologies emerge at a point in history when there is a re-emphasis on fatherhood, and growing demands from anti-feminist men's groups for greater control over children. She establishes that movements today to strengthen the legal relationship between biological fathers and their children do not reflect a long-standing tradition in law; on the contrary, in the English legal system paternity has traditionally been based not on biological fatherhood but on marriage. The law has been as reluctant to allow married men to disavow the children of the marriage (even when there is clearly no genetic connection) as it has been hesitant to require men to take responsibility for their biological, but illegitimate, offspring. In recent legal opinion – concerning children born after artificial insemination by donor, custody decisions following divorce and the children of unmarried women – Smart discerns conflicting trends about the claims of biological fathers. What these opinions have in common is a reluctance to allow mothers alone to exercise parental rights. One of the greatest dangers to women from the new reproductive technologies is that the anxieties they engender will provide the rationale for an extension of the legal concept of paternity, and that the power of the state to restrict autonomous motherhood will thereby be enhanced.

In chapter 6 Juliette Zipper and Selma Sevenhuijsen consider the troubling phenomenon of surrogate motherhood, and the debates that have arisen around surrogacy in Western Europe. Why, they ask, is surrogacy – especially commercial surrogacy – almost universally condemned, and what implications does this have for the legal regulation of parenthood? To explain current attitudes towards surrogacy, they draw upon the history of feminist campaigns around motherhood and sexuality in the late nineteenth and early twentieth centuries. Their analysis of feminist thinking on motherhood traces the way in which the recognition of social motherhood as a political construction in the 1960s has yielded to a view, in the 1980s, of 'natural' motherhood as the apotheosis of feminist values. Zipper and Sevenhuijsen's critical and informed examination of proposals that have emerged in Western Europe for the regulation of surrogacy shows the concerns that lay behind these proposals – concerns above all with the credibility and the validity of the motivations of women. Current attempts to exert control over the phenomenon of surrogacy, they argue, not only overlook the ways in which surrogacy escapes surveillance and regulation; they also risk letting concern for the problematical and delicate outcome of exceptional cases be used as a rationale for overturning the few legal protections that women already have.

In-vitro fertilization is controversial, not least because it provides a source of 'surplus' embryos and a technique for creating more. In chapter 7, Janet Gallagher explores in detail the current legal status of the embryo in Britain and the United States. In most contexts and in spite of variations in the law in different jurisdictions, the personhood of the foetus (and therefore of the embryo) is not accepted in law. But Gallagher documents recent cases in the United States that represent an alarming drive to reinterpret the status of the foetus in ways that would severely restrict the lives of pregnant women. With remarkable sensitivity, Gallagher analyses the sources of concern over embryos and the proposals that have been advanced to guard against an unregulated traffic in human gametes or embryos. She suggests that while total opposition to embryo research allies with claims to foetal rights that are dangerous to women, it is possible nevertheless to construct a strategy that does not result in the abandonment of embryos to medical or commercial exploitation.

In chapter 8, Hilary Rose counterposes an analysis of competing accounts of the history of science with a detailed examination of new developments in molecular biology. She concludes that anxieties about scientific developments that might occur – about the impact of male pregnancies, for example, or 'artificial wombs' – distract from the dangers of technologies that are currently within reach. Most significantly, the rapid accumulation of genetic knowledge feeds into proposals for preventive screening of all pregnant women. Mass screening, it is sometimes claimed, will eliminate serious disabilities and give would-be parents the technical information necessary to terminate a pregnancy where the foetus is abnormal; Rose explains why this argument is false on both counts. The chapter also considers other currently available techniques, including those that make it possible to 'select' the sex of a child; Rose takes issue with the particular feminist view that sees in these techniques the eventual extermination of women and their culture. In an authoritative review of analyses of science, Rose highlights the gender-specific concept of 'progress' that characterizes many of these accounts, but she warns, above all, that it will not do for women to reject science: the project of feminist critique is to create a science that can be used as a position from which women and their bodies can be defended.

The final chapter returns to the issue of infertility, setting it into the broader context of the provision of health care for women. Lesley Doyal examines the incidence of infertility in Britain and shows that – in spite of lip service to the importance of motherhood – infertility services in England and Wales are marked by sharp regional variations in provision, long waiting-lists for consultation and treatment, inadequate facilities in the majority of districts and services dependent upon the ability to pay. She highlights, in addition, the narrow physicalist approach to treatment and the astonishing lack of resources directed at prevention. Doyal demonstrates that the shortcomings of infertility services echo more general problems in the provision of adequate health care; for example, in spite of a comprehensive National Health Service in Britain, health inequalities between the affluent and those on low incomes have widened over the years and the gap in treatment is especially marked for services associated with fertility control. Her analysis indicates that acceptance or rejection of reproductive 'technology' is only a small part of current struggles to provide decent health care for all women and men, struggles that must involve not only the extension of access to specific health resources, but also transformation of the way that services are administered and controlled. While Doyal's analysis is focused on the British National Health Service, it recalls the history of the women's health movement in many countries, where the emphasis has been upon providing women with the resources and information that they need to use health facilities wisely, and upon reshaping the organization and politics of institutions through which these services are offered.

Reproductive Technologies is not a book that provides easy answers to the many problems raised by medical and scientific practice in the area of reproduction. But, by exploring the complexity of these issues, the authors hope to provide pointers to the development of new strategies around reproductive technologies – strategies that are alert to the differences between women as well as to what they have in common.

1
Reproductive Technologies and the Deconstruction of Motherhood

Michelle Stanworth

Technologies designed to intervene in the process of human reproduction fall, roughly speaking, into four groups. The first and most
familiar group includes those concerned with fertility control – with
preventing conception, frustrating implantation of an embryo, or
terminating pregnancy. According to the General Household Survey
(Office of Population Censuses and Statistics, 1985, p. 45) in Britain
three women out of four aged between eighteen and forty-four use
some form of contraception; just over 140,000 residents of England
and Wales underwent an abortion in 1985 (WRRIC, June–July
1986). Many of the technologies of fertility control – diaphragms,
intra-uterine devices, sterilization, abortion, even the newly visible
condom – have been known in some form for centuries (McLaren,
1984, chapter 3). Hormone-suppressing contraceptive drugs are one
of the few genuine innovations in contraceptive technology this
century (Gordon, 1977, chapter 2). Since by the late 1970s the market
for 'the pill' in many Western countries was saturated, pharmaceutical companies now devote much of their research efforts to
finding new ways of administering contraceptives that would open up
expanding markets in the 'Third World' (Bunkle, 1984).

A second group of reproductive technologies is concerned with the
'management' of labour and childbirth. In the course of the past 150
years in Europe and America, childbirth changed from a home-based
activity, undertaken primarily with the assistance of female healers
and friends, to an activity defined as the province of medical
professionals. The extent of the shift is illustrated by the rising proportion of British babies born in hospital – from 15 per cent in 1927
to 99 per cent in 1985 (see chapter 2; Office of Population Censuses
and Statistics, 1986b). In its wake, a range of technologies for
monitoring and controlling the progress of labour and delivery
– instruments to assist delivery, caesarian sections, ways of inducing

labour, episiotomies, techniques for measuring foetal heart-rate and movement – have been applied on an increasingly routine basis; the caesarian section rate in the United States, for example, rose from 4.5 per hundred in 1965 to 19 per 100 in 1982 (Pfeufer Kahn, 1984, p. 15). In many Western countries, the potential for effective intervention in the management of labour and childbirth is approaching saturation point, not only because of the high proportion of birthing women who are already subject to these techniques, but also because of objections to 'high-tech' deliveries from women themselves.

A current focus in terms of the development of reproductive technologies is upon extending obstetric services backwards into the antenatal period, through the use of more elaborate technologies and screening procedures for monitoring foetal development in the early stages of pregnancy (Farrant, 1985); at least one-third of all pregnant women in the United States now experience ultrasound (see chapter 3). The focus is also upon perfecting new techniques for neonatal care; and upon research that might eventually enable the modification of inborn 'defects' through human genetic engineering. In short, the third and one of the growth areas in reproductive technology is concerned with improving the health and the genetic characteristics of foetuses and of newborns – with the search for, as some have said, 'the perfect child'.

The fourth and perhaps most controversial group are the conceptive technologies, directed to the promotion of pregnancy through techniques for overcoming or bypassing infertility. Estimates for Britain suggest that 50,000 new cases of infertility present for treatment each year and the number of people requiring treatment at any one time may be as high as two million (see chapter 9). Yet for much of this century, the treatment of infertility has been relatively static; apart from the clinical introduction of artificial insemination in the 1930s and the 'fertility drugs' of the 1960s, no new technologies were introduced until in-vitro fertilization burst upon the scene in the late 1970s as a 'miracle cure' (see chapter 4). Most research in the area of infertility is now devoted to the refinement of in-vitro fertilization and to the development of new applications – through combination with, for example, egg donation, embryo donation, low-temperature storage of gametes and embryos, or surrogacy – rather than to alternative approaches to infertility. The conceptive technologies, often treated as if they were synonymous with 'high-tech' medicine, in fact are immensely varied; they range from surrogacy or artificial insemination – both of which can be and are practised in ways that require no medical intervention at all – to in-vitro fertilization, which involves very sophisticated medical, surgical and laboratory procedures.

As the history of reproductive technologies is gradually being written, we have come to know more about the range of groups or institutions that have an interest in their development. Women themselves, as consumers of services concerned with reproductive care, have, to be sure, 'demanded' techniques that would help them to control their fertility, their pregnancies, their experience of birth and the health of their children. Yet it is clear that there is no simple cause-and-effect relationship between the 'demands' made by women and the 'supply' of reproductive technologies. For one thing, the 'demands' of those who can afford to pay are likely to be catered for far more assiduously than the 'demands' of those with smaller resources; and the greater the proportion of total health costs that is met by individuals, the more powerfully such inequalities are likely to assert themselves. For another, part of the 'demand' for reproductive technologies comes from state-subsidized programmes, and the objectives of the state in providing resources for the introduction of some technologies and withholding funding from others are not likely to reflect women's wishes in any straightforward way. The state responds to women's demands in the area of reproductive care selectively, in terms of its own priorities with respect to population policy, health expenditure and political pay-off. So, for example, in the context of rigorous insistence on reduction of public expenditure over the past decade, in-vitro fertilization programmes have received virtually no public funding in Britain, while the Department of Health and Social Security viewed benignly – in hopes of saving money on the care of handicapped children – the possibility of mass programmes of antenatal screening.

There are other reasons too, why the demands of women for technologies to aid in reproductive care are insufficient to explain the technologies currently on offer. What we 'demand' (that is, what we are willing to tolerate) as consumers depends on the options available to us. Undoubtedly, the demand amongst heterosexual women who wished to avoid pregnancy for a 100 per cent reliable contraceptive technique that carried no risks to health or quality of life would be overwhelming; but in real life, women have to divide their 'demands', more or less grudgingly between a range of less-than-satisfactory options. Even our notions of what 'satisfactory' would be are shaped partly by our knowledge of existing or potential alternatives. If we come to believe that home births are dangerous (whether or not that belief is objectively 'true') we are unlikely to be able to articulate clearly our dissatisfactions with hospital confinements.

Many of the groups most directly responsible for developing and promoting reproductive technologies have an agenda in which women's 'demands' play only a small part. For obstetricians and gynaecologists, specific types of reproductive technologies may carry advantages quite separate from their impact on mothers and infants. Reproductive technologies often enhance the status of medical professionals and increase the funds they can command, by underpinning claims to specialized knowledge and by providing the basis for an extension of service. Such technologies may, in addition, help a profession in its attempts to dominate other competitors for control of an area of work; the application of new forms of technology has been one way that obstetricians have succeeded in reducing midwives to a subordinate status in the field of maternity services. Perhaps most significantly, new technologies help to establish that gynaecologists and obstetricians 'know more' about pregnancy and about women's bodies than women do themselves. When the majority of the profession is male, it is perhaps not surprising that medical practitioners have been attracted to techniques that enable them to brush aside a woman's own felt experience of menstruation, pregnancy and birth.

Medical practitioners are themselves dependent upon the research and development activities of pharmaceutical and medical supply companies, and many of these corporations have a vast financial interest in the manufacture and promotion of technologies concerned with reproductive care. The buoyant market for infertility treatment has attracted considerable private finance for research and development, but even this is probably outstripped by investment in the realm of genetic engineering. Feminists have raised troubling questions about the accountability and public scrutiny of reproductive technologies, the development of which is motored by private investment (Rowland, 1985a, p. 541; Bunkle, 1984).

Precisely because of the different and sometimes conflicting interests at stake in the application of reproductive technologies, women have not been content to leave the evaluation of the impact of technology to 'the experts', who are often the very people involved in their promotion. Instead, they have highlighted the ambivalent effects of reproductive technologies on the lives of women. Women in Western Europe and North America today, compared with their foremothers, have fewer pregnancies, bear fewer babies against their wishes, are less likely to die in childbirth and less often experience the death of their babies. This is no small matter – and it is due, in some part, to technologies for intervening in human reproduction. But the view that reproductive technologies have given women control over motherhood – and thereby over their own lives – simply will not do.

First, this view takes insufficient account of the impact of changing social definitions of motherhood. While women today spend less time in pregnancy and breast-feeding than in the recent past, the care of children has come to be defined in a far more rigorous way; mothering involves responsibility not only for the physical and emotional care of children, but for detailed attention to their psychological, social and intellectual development. Motherhood is seen, more than in the past, as a full-time occupation. Mothers may be expected now to lavish as much 'care' on two children as they might previously have provided for six. In short, the reproductive technologies address themselves to only a small part of the experience of motherhood.

Secondly, reproductive decisions continue to be constrained by the shortcomings of existing means of fertility control. For example, the pill and the intra-uterine contraceptive device – heralded in the 1960s as instruments of women's liberation – appear now to carry worrying health risks and a range of distressing side-effects. Some contraceptive techniques, including some of the most reliable for preventing pregnancy, appear also to increase the risk of infertility, creating a catch-22 situation for women who wish to control the timing of child-bearing. The failure to develop safer and more acceptable means of birth control is not simply a technical problem; in part, it reflects the low priority given to women's health and a tendency to disregard symptoms and issues that women themselves think are important (Weideger, 1978; Pollock, 1984).

Thirdly, the way that access to means of fertility control is managed indicates how women's options regarding child-bearing are linked to their location in the social structure. In Britain, the recent Gillick case represented an attempt to restrict through the courts the access of younger women to contraceptive information and supplies. Controversial contraceptives such as the injectable long-acting Depo-Provera, though considered unsuitable for the majority of women in Britain, have been used extensively on their Asian and Black compatriots (Rakusen, 1981; Bunkle, 1984). Although the 1967 Abortion Act entitles British women to legal abortion on medical and social grounds, access to safe abortion in many parts of the country – as in the United States – depends on ability to pay; the bulk of legal abortions in Britain today are performed outside the National Health Service (WRRIC, June–July 1986). Infertility, and especially the infections that lead to tubal closure, are particular problems for Black women and women on low incomes in Britain and the United

States, but these are precisely the women who have least access to new conceptive technologies like in-vitro fertilization (Wilkie, 1984; Behrman and Kistner, 1975)[1].

Fourthly, the technical possibility of fertility control coexists with a powerful ideology of motherhood – the belief that motherhood is the natural, desired and ultimate goal of all 'normal' women, and that women who deny their 'maternal instincts' are selfish, peculiar or disturbed. At a conference in Oxford in 1987, Patrick Steptoe, the obstetrician who is credited with 'creating' the first test-tube baby, declared: 'It is a fact that there is a biological drive to reproduce. Women who deny this drive, or in whom it is frustrated, show disturbances in other ways.'[2] Research suggests that many members of the medical profession share this view (Barrett and Roberts, 1978).

While many women wish to have children, the views of medical personnel are not simply a reflection of that fact. The idea of maternal instinct is sometimes used to override women's expressed wishes with regard to child-bearing – discouraging young married women from sterilization or abortion, for example, while denying single women the chance to have a child (Macintyre, 1977; Veevers, 1980, chapter 7). In other words, a belief in maternal instinct coexists with obstacles to autonomous motherhood – obstacles, that is, to motherhood for women who are not in a stable relationship to a man. According to ideologies of motherhood, all women *want* children; but single women, lesbian women (and disabled women) are often expected to forgo mothering 'in the interest of the child'.

Finally, technologies for 'managing' pregnancy and childbirth are often embedded in a medical frame of reference that defines pregnant women as 'patients', pregnancy as an illness and successful child-bearing in terms that de-emphasize the social and emotional dimensions. In some respects, reproductive technologies have made child-bearing safer for women and their infants, but they have also brought new dangers in their wake (see chapter 2; Hubbard, 1984; Wertz, 1983). Apart from medical risks and benefits, as the process of pregnancy and childbirth has come under the control of medical professionals, the majority of whom are men, many women are left with a sense of being mere onlookers in the important process of giving birth.

Thus, medical and scientific advances in the sphere of reproduction – so often hailed as the liberators of twentieth-century women – have, in fact, been a double-edged sword. On the one hand, they have offered women a greater technical possibility to decide if, when and under what conditions to have children; on the other, the domination of so much reproductive technology by the medical profession and by the state has enabled others to have an even greater capacity to exert control over women's lives. Moreover, the 'technical possibility' of choosing an oral contraceptive or in-vitro fertilization is only a small aspect of reproductive freedom (Petchesky, 1986). For some women, motherhood remains their only chance of creativity, while economic and social circumstances compel others to relinquish motherhood altogether.

The Deconstruction of Motherhood

Against the stark backcloth of the history of technologies for controlling fertility, pregnancy and birth, how are we to analyse the emergent technologies concerned with promoting conception and with eliminating 'defects' in the unborn? One powerful theoretical approach sees in these new techniques a means for men to wrest 'not only control of reproduction, but reproduction itself' from women (Raymond, 1985, p. 12). Following O'Brien (1983), it is suggested that men's alienation from reproduction – men's sense of disconnection from their seed during the process of conception, pregnancy and birth – has underpinned through the ages a relentless male desire to master nature, and to construct social institutions and cultural patterns that will not only subdue the waywardness of women but also give men an illusion of procreative continuity and power. New reproductive technologies are the vehicle that will turn men's illusions of reproductive power into a reality. By manipulating eggs and embryos, scientists will determine the sort of children who are born – will make themselves the fathers of humankind. By removing eggs and embryos from some women and implanting them in others, medical practitioners will gain unprecedented control over motherhood itself. Motherhood as a unified biological process will be effectively deconstructed: in place of 'mother', there will be ovarian mothers who supply eggs, uterine mothers who give birth to children and, presumably, social mothers who raise them. Through the eventual development of artificial wombs, the capacity will arise to make biological motherhood redundant. Whether or not women are eliminated, or merely reduced to the level of 'reproductive prostitutes',[3] the object and the effect of the emergent technologies is to deconstruct motherhood and to destroy the claim to reproduction that is the foundation of women's identity.[4]

The problem with this analysis is not that it is too radical, as some have claimed; rather, in seeking to protect women from the dangers of new technologies, it gives too much away. There is a tendency to echo the very views of scientific and medical practice, of women and of motherhood, which feminists have been seeking to transform. This analysis entails, in the first instance, an inflated view of science and medicine, the mirror image of that which scientists and medical practitioners often try themselves to promote. By emphasizing the continuities between technologies currently in clinical use, and those that exist merely in the fantasies of scientific commentators; by insisting that the practices involved in animal husbandry or in animal experimentation can unproblematically be transferred to human beings; by ignoring the ways in which women have resisted abuses of medical power and techniques they found unacceptable: by arguing this way, science and medicine have been portrayed as realms of boundless possibility, in the face of which mere human beings have no choices other than total rejection or capitulation. Any understanding of the constraints within which science and medicine operate, and of the way these can be shaped for the greater protection of women and men, is effectively erased.

Also integral to this approach is a view of women that comes uncomfortably close to that espoused by some members of the medical professions. Infertile women are too easily 'blinded by science' (Hanmer, 1985, p. 104); they are manipulated into 'full and total support of any technique which will produce those desired children' (Rowland, 1985b, p. 75); the choices they make and even their motivations to choose are controlled by men (Corea, 1985a, p. 3). In the case of doctors, it is the 'maternal instinct' that allows women's own assessments of what they want from their bodies or their pregnancies to be overlooked; in this analysis, it is patriarchal and pronatal conditioning that makes infertile women (and, by implication, all women) incapable of rationally grounded and authentic choice. I argued above that the ideology of motherhood attempts to press women in the direction of child-bearing, and that in this sense women's motivations are socially shaped. But 'shaped' is not the same as 'determined'; and a rejection of child-bearing (for infertile women or fertile) is not necessarily a more authentic choice. The very existence of a range of sanctions and rewards designed to entice women into marriage and motherhood indicates, not that conformity is guaranteed, but that avoidance of motherhood (and autonomous motherhood) are genuine options, which efforts are made to contain.[5]

Finally, this approach tends to suggest that anything 'less' than a natural process, from conception through to birth, represents the degradation of motherhood itself. The motherhood that men are attempting to usurp becomes a motherhood that is biologically defined, and to which all women are assumed to have the same relationship. While it is the case that the lives of all women are shaped by their biological selves, and by their assumed or actual capacity to bear children, our bodies do not impose upon us a common experience of reproduction; on the contrary, our bodies stand as powerful reminders of the differentiating effects of age, health, disability, strength and fertility history. There is, moreover, little reason to assume that the biological potential to give birth has an identical meaning for women, regardless of their social circumstances or their wishes with regard to child-bearing. How can the experience of women who have chosen to remain childfree be fitted into a framework that sees the continuous biological process that culminates in birth as the core of our identity as women? How can we make sense from this perspective of women (such as those interviewed by Luker, 1984, pp. 168–9) who value children and child-bearing highly, but who experience pregnancy itself as merely an unpleasant reality *en route* to raising children? How can we explain the fact that fewer working-class women in Britain attend antenatal clinics, demand natural childbirth or breast-feed their infants? Luker's analysis (ibid.) suggests the possibility that while for many middle-class women pregnancy may be a scarce resource – time out from a hectic professional life to enjoy the sensations of being a woman – for a greater proportion of working-class women pregnancy may be more a taken-for-granted prelude to social motherhood, not an experience to be cherished in itself. Far too many women have experienced the type of reproductive care that is insensitive to their own wishes and desires; but shared reaction against unsatisfactory medical treatment should not be allowed to mask differences in women's own sense of what authentic motherhood might be. Women may legitimately, as Rayna Rapp said, 'want other things from reproductive technology than merely to get it off our backs' (Rapp, 1985, p. 4).

Feminist critics of technologies have always and rightly insisted that technologies derive their meaning from the social and political context in which they emerge. But where the context that is invoked in connection with reproductive technologies is the universal victimization of women, then it is easy to underestimate the significance of political struggles concerning the future of reproduction which are currently being waged. I wish to argue in the following sections that reproductive technologies are controversial – not only amongst feminists, but among a wider public – because they crystallize issues at the heart of contemporary controversies over sexuality, parenthood, reproduction and the family; and that a concern for self-determination for women must engage, above all, with these struggles.

Reproductive Technologies and Genetic Parenthood

In the United States, a bioethicist warned the Ethics Advisory Board investigating in-vitro fertilization that this technique blurs the issue of genetic identity with potentially dire social consequences: 'Clarity about who your parents are, clarity in the lines of generation, clarity about who is whose, are the indispensable foundations of a sound family life, itself the sound foundation of civilized community' (Leon Kass, cited in Grobstein, 1981, p. 65).

In Britain, the Warnock Committee devoted a large portion of its report to weighing up the legal rights of genetic parents over children born with the help of conceptive technologies, and to considering whether such children should have the right to know about, or to inherit estates or titles from, their genetic forbears (Warnock, 1985). The mass media, too, have found a lively source of controversial news stories in the question, not only of claims over children, but also over embryos: the fate of the 'Rios twins' – two embryos stored at low temperature at Queen Victoria Hospital, Melbourne, after their parents had died in a plane crash – occupied Australian newspapers for a good two months (Albury, 1986).

The concern about inheritance, succession and rights in children by commissions appointed to inquire into reproductive technologies has been perceived sometimes as a side-issue, reflecting the preoccupation of the state with paternity and property. But it is much more than that. For reproductive technologies have become a battleground on which are being waged important campaigns about the significance of blood ties and of genetic parenthood.

These campaigns have their roots in current tensions of family life. Accelerating rates of divorce and remarriage in many western societies means that pressing questions about claims over children impinge directly on many people's lives. Between the late 1950s and early 1960s in Britain, the divorce rate increased fourfold; it trebled again between 1961 and 1971. Throughout the 1980s, for every three couples who married for the first time, two couples divorced (Central Statistical Office, 1986, p. 37–41). A high and increasing proportion of divorced women and an even higher proportion of divorced men rapidly remarry, often establishing step-families or reconstituted families. Divorce does not signify in any clear way the 'breakdown of the family', or of marriage as an institution. What it does signify, however, is a markedly greater uncertainty in the 1980s (compared with, say, the 1950s) about the ties that bind individual parents to individual children. Legal battles over custody and access are only part of the story: alongside these run uncounted numbers of households in which uncontested custody or access arrangements are nevertheless a source of anxiety, in which one parent or both have to be more self-conscious than before about the basis of their relationship with their child. And this experience is not confined to parents: other relatives – grandmothers and grandfathers, uncles and aunts – often discover in these circumstances that extra tact and effort is needed to sustain a relationship with children who are their kin. The concern about genetic parenthood that has greeted the arrival of new technologies – who will parent the offspring of surrogate mothers? – reflects these pre-existing tensions around claims on relationships to children. In the face of divorce, and rising rates of remarriage, the pressure to rethink the moral and legal basis of claims upon children is clearly intense.

Technologies such as in-vitro fertilization, egg donation, surrogacy and the like have crystallized these anxieties about relationships to children precisely because their relation to genetic parenthood is an ambivalent one. On the one hand, the conceptive technologies address in a powerful way people's desires, not merely to enjoy a life with children, but to have a child 'of their own'. Women whose oviducts have been damaged by pelvic inflammatory disease may, with in-vitro fertilization, give birth to a child conceived from their own egg and their partner's sperm. A women who is fertile, but who does not have a fertile male partner, may with artificial insemination, conceive and bear a child that is genetically her own. Through full surrogacy, women who are unable to bear children may yet raise a child conceived from their own egg and their partner's sperm. The market for conceptive technologies thrives on the yearning for genetic parenthood.

In the dominant culture of Western societies, the importance of blood ties is a powerful cultural theme. The family is often imagined as a biological unit, in which social relationships grow straightforwardly out of genetic ones, such that commitment to 'the family' and to 'blood ties' becomes inseparable in many people's minds; the overlapping responsibilities of mothers, fathers and children are filtered through a biological lens. The importance of blood ties is further underscored by scientific theories – from the very dubious accounts of intelligence as a largely genetic characteristic, to the equally contentious claims of biologically based prenatal bonding – which make it their business to explain human qualities and relationships in terms of biological inheritance.[6] Finally, the poignant publicity given in the past fifteen years to the search for genetic mothers and fathers by children born of artificial insemination by donor, or by adopted children, emphasizes the idea that genetic connection is an immutable and overriding element of identity.[7] Through these overlapping sets of ideas, blood ties have come to stand in our culture as a symbol of permanence in human relationships – and the more fragile and contingent other relationships seem to be, the more compelling that symbol's appeal:

> When depressed about the fragility and transience of friendships, or the inconstancies of lovers, it was the myth of a child, a blood relation and what it could bring me, which seemed to me the only real guarantee against loneliness and isolation, the only way of maintaining a connection to the rest of society. (Klepfisz, in Dowrick and Grundberg, 1980, p. 18)

If the conceptive technologies thrive on these powerful cultural pressures towards having a child 'of our own', it would not be true to say that they unambiguously strengthen the tendency to value genetic claims to relationships. For the same technologies that enable some infertile people to become genetic parents also place the whole notion of genetic parenthood in jeopardy. When embryologists and obstetricians are needed to bring about insemination and conception, genetic parenthood no longer seems a natural process, with all the positive connotations that 'natural' carries in the area of reproduction. Moreover, practices such as artificial insemination by donor, or egg donation or (some forms of) surrogacy, pose a highly visible challenge to the notion that genetic parenthood guarantees familial relationship; a women who donates an egg to aid her sister's attempts to become pregnant may be the genetic mother, but she no longer appears as the 'real' mother in any meaningful sense. Thus, reproductive technologies carry the threat (or the promise) of delegitimating genetic parenthood, and even of fracturing common-sense understandings of what 'the biological' is.

If many official and media commentaries on reproductive technologies take the yearning for genetic parenthood for granted, feminist writers have posed the question differently. They have pointed out that an emphasis upon blood ties is not a given, but is historically and culturally specific (Edholm, 1982; and see chapter 5); in other words, the significance accorded to genetic parenthood in establishing social relationships varies across time and from one culture or class to another. Within the American community known as the Flats, for example, family is as family does: a neighbour who stands by a woman and her children in hard times may be called 'sister', while the genetic father of those children – if he chooses to distance himself from them – will not be admitted to the status of kin (Stack, 1974).

Against the background of communities such as this, pertinent questions have been raised about the 'obsessive' desire of infertile people for a child of their own. But – apart from the fact that there are compelling practical reasons why people, infertile or fertile, might seek genetic parenthood rather than, say, adoption[8] – it is not the individual pursuit of genetic parenthood that is the most threatening aspect of new reproductive technologies. Rather, the real concern lies in the legal and political construction that may be placed on genetic ties.

Any attempt to rethink the legal and moral basis of claims to children must take into account the different relationship to parenthood of most women and men. While the promise of genetic parenthood is part of the appeal of the new conceptive technologies, this appeal may be to a degree gender-specific: it is stronger, I suspect, for men than for women. Some of the surveys conducted to assess public attitudes towards new technologies show that while people of both sexes are increasingly tolerant of the use of these techniques, women are more inclined towards adoption as a solution to involuntary childlessness than are men. This need not reflect an inherent male urge towards genetic paternity, as some would claim. Rather, the fact that women care for children in most households – and the very success of the women's movement in emphasizing that this care is not an effortless outpouring of maternal sentiment, but real labour that forges a strong relationship between women and their children – means that men are more likely than women to be anxious about the basis of relationships with children they intend to father.

Women's legal and moral claims to children rest on two bases: first, their day-to-day responsibility for the care of children, and secondly, the fact that children are born to them. The latter claim reflects not so much a mother's genetic input to the child as the commitment involved in pregnancy and birthing. Men cannot bear children, and current evidence on the division of labour in households shows clearly that few men are willing to take responsibility for their day-to-day care. Any trend towards enhancing the legal rights that flow from genetic parenthood, as opposed to real parental commitment, would work decisively to the detriment of women (see chapter 5). Our concern must be to see that, in the search for a secure incontestable basis for claims to children, the anxieties that new reproductive technologies crystallize do not become the basis for giving even greater legal priority to genetic claims (see chapter 6).

Sexuality, Parenting and the Family

To those who see sex, marriage and parenthood as an indissoluble triad, the conceptive technologies offer another dangerous precedent; they separate parenthood from 'the sexual act', and do not ensure that parenthood will be confined to marriage. This kind of objection has long been directed at artificial insemination by donor; one delegate to the Council of Europe in Strasbourg identified in the 'paganistic and atheistic' practice of artificial insemination 'a world campaign to undermine marriage and the family' (cited in Barrett and McIntosh, 1982, p. 11.). The objection has now extended to in-vitro fertilization. One commentator refers to in-vitro fertilization as 'the flip side of the pill': 'contraception permits sex without conception, IVF offers conception without sex' (Kramer, 1985, p. 38). Others see in these procedures 'grave assaults on marriage and family, to say nothing of the subtle devaluation of sexual intimacy' (Hellegers and McCormick, 1978, p. 77).

These objections might seem merely quaint to liberals or radicals on issues of sexuality, were it not for the way they resonate with campaigns waged by the new right, in Europe and the United States, to tie sexuality and parenting more closely to the family. The near-success of Victoria Gillick, crusader on behalf of family authority, in persuading the British courts to prohibit the provision of contraceptives to young women without parental consent; recent attempts to restrict the availability of abortion; vigorous campaigns against sex education in schools: all are underpinned by the aim of restricting sexual expression to the heterosexual family and tying intercourse to procreation. The 'Moral Right' in Britain, compared with its American counterpart, is a weaker movement. But its campaigns gain credibility, nonetheless, from a government that constantly invokes Victorian values and the rolling back of the Welfare State, in order that The Family can reign supreme.

Yet the vision of 'the family' which the New Right wishes to resurrect – a family proudly independent of public provision, with fathers as breadwinners and figures of authority and mothers fulfilled by children and home (David, 1985) – is sharply at odds with the majority experience of men, women and children in, for example, Britain today. Several trends have together effected a decisive change. Throughout the eighties, the proportion of all births that were conceived within marriage has steadily declined: in 1985, almost one live birth in five, and 65 per cent of the births to mothers aged under twenty, were to unmarried women (Central Statistical Office,

1987, p. 52; Office of Population Censuses and Statistics, 1986b, p. 13–14). One marriage in three currently ends in divorce; almost 60 per cent of these divorces are to couples with dependent children (David, 1985, p. 9). By the early 1980s, 14 per cent of families had a lone parent (usually a lone mother), and 55 per cent of these families lived in or on the margins of poverty (Graham, 1984).

The result of these changes is that the activity of raising children takes places less and less often in the context of a permanent heterosexual marriage. Moreover, fewer and fewer marriages follow the 'traditional' pattern: in 1980, only 39 per cent of married couples with dependent children consisted of a husband in employment and an 'economically inactive wife' (Rimmer and Popay, 1982, p. 257).

The New Right spots conspiracies against the traditional family in sex education, in abortion, in divorce, in homosexuality, in contraception for young people – and now, in reproductive technologies (Schapiro, 1985). But the truth is, that many parents, and particularly women, have sought and are seeking to combine their commitment to children with patterns of living less restrictive than those of the conventional family. The number of women who choose, or find themselves able, to 'go it alone' in raising children is the most powerful expression of this.

To the extent that the medical profession, official inquiries, the state and the mass media, have chosen to endorse the conceptive technologies, it is only by denying the force of this trend towards autonomous motherhood. A classic example of this position is to be found in the report of the Warnock Committee, set up to advise the government of the United Kingdom on reproductive technologies. The Committee members, in their own words

> were keenly aware that no expression of their own feelings would be a credible basis for recommendations, even if they all felt exactly alike . . . we have attempted in what follows to *argue* in favour of those positions we have adopted, and to give due weight to the counter-arguments, where they exist. (Warnock, 1985, p. 1)

It is noteworthy, then, that the Committee rejected the possibility of women without a male partner using these treatments in order to have a child with a single statement of belief:

> We believe that as a general rule, it is better for children to be born into a two-parent family, with both father and mother, although we recognise that is impossible to predict with any certainty how lasting such a relationship will be. (Warnock, 1985, p. 11–12)

Despite the difficulties of defining what is in the interests of a child (see chapter 6), no evidence or argument is offered in support of this belief. On the Committee's recommendation, in-vitro fertilization, egg donation, embryo donation and artificial insemination were to be restricted to stable, cohabiting heterosexual couples. Moreover, the use by married women of these technologies was also ruled out unless the patient was able to obtain written consent from her husband. Thus, the Committee – in explicit but unreasoned defiance of trends towards independent motherhood – tried to ensure that the conceptive technologies would not be available to women raising children on their own.

In a recent lecture,[9] Mary Warnock clarified the Committee's reasoning when she said that the fundamental conclusion of the Committee was that infertility is a condition deserving medical remedy. The problem here, however, is that infertility is not a condition that is confined to the married, or the cohabiting, or to stable heterosexual couples. The long-term effect of reproductive technologies – whether they give people more power to direct their own lives, or whether they serve merely as expensive instruments of population policy – depends partly on resisting such restrictions on their use.[10]

The Status of Pregnancy

New reproductive technologies also relate to struggles over the changing status of pregnancy and childbirth and women's capacity to control these events. Pregnancy and childbirth clearly mean different things to different women, depending on whether they are willing mothers or reluctant ones, healthy or ill, supported by friends or family or alone. But one thing most women would agree upon is that the pregnant woman is the central participant in the process, and that child-bearing is an experience that makes sense in the context of her biography as an whole person.

Not everyone sees it that way. Two prominent social scientists, Peter Berger and Brigitte Berger, begin a chapter of their book *The War over the Family* with this startling account of childbirth: 'When a child is born into this world, he seems to enter it in a natural, effortless fashion' (Berger and Berger, 1983, p. 149). In this description, the 'child' is taken as the focal point. Birth appears as a 'miraculous' process, magical and disembodied, owing more to 'nature' than to the commitment of a living woman. The claim that childbirth is effortless can make sense only from one vantage-point – the vantage-point of a gender for whom childbirth may, indeed, involve no labour and no pain. In Berger and Berger's account of birth, the agency of the mother – her efforts to sustain and nurture the pregnancy, her labour in the delivery room, her intimate connection with the foetus she has brought to the point of independent life – are totally eclipsed.

The eclipsing of the pregnant woman's part in child-bearing is also a striking feature of discussions of the new conceptive technologies. Indeed, the very terms that frame these discussions often efface the activities of the woman who is their intended beneficiary. Consider the curious term 'test-tube babies' – first used for the offspring of artificial insemination, but now reserved almost entirely for embryos fertilized in the laboratory. The phrase 'test-tube baby' conjures an odd image of a foetus growing independently of the body of a woman (a miracle, perhaps, but this time of science rather than of nature). The test-tube baby is not, of course, grown in a test-tube. It requires for the foreseeable future the womb and the willing participation of a woman, to nurture and sustain the early embryonic potential for life.

Or consider the placing of seminal fluid near a woman's cervix by a doctor. Why should this practice be known as 'artificial insemination'? The only thing artificial about it, as Farrell Smith noted (in Holmes, Hoskins and Gross, 1981, p. 255) is that the man who provides the ejaculate does not inseminate the woman by having intercourse with her. But a natural process of conception still occurs, if it occurs, within the woman's body; the mother still nurtures the foetus through her body and gives birth to it in the traditional way. Characterizing this practice as 'artificial' encourages an unwarranted emphasis in the reproductive process on the act of sexual intercourse alone.

Finally, why have we accepted so readily the term 'surrogate mother'? A woman who goes through a pregnancy, and gives birth to an infant, can only be a 'surrogate' if pregnancy itself does not count as an act of mothering. In all these instances, from test-tube babies to artificial insemination to surrogate motherhood, it is the involvement of a pregnant and birthing woman which makes the process of reproduction possible. And it is precisely the significance of her pregnancy which the terms of the discussion deny.

I am not saying that the technologies themselves demean motherhood; that's another issue altogether. What I am saying is that these technologies draw their meaning from the cultural and political climate in which they are embedded – from a climate in which there is considerable ambivalence about pregnancy, and a tendency to value the product of pregnancy and childbirth (the foetus, the infant) over the mother herself (see chapter 3). The focus of the new conceptive technologies is not really 'infertility' (as the restrictions on their use should make clear), nor is it even 'the family'. Ultimately, the focus is 'babies' and their precursors, foetuses.

Babies make news, in a way that pregnant women don't. Babies legitimate the use of new conceptive technologies in very powerful ways, often to the exclusion of questions about the impact of those technologies on women. Take the media reception of surrogacy. In 1978, Noel Keane, the lawyer who arranged the first American adoption of a baby acknowledged to be born by surrogacy, had a problem: the courts forbade payments to surrogate mothers where commissioning parents intended to adopt; few surrogate mothers were prepared to offer their services for free; and even a television appearance by three satisfied parties to an arrangement that involved a surrogate pregnancy had failed to reduce public hostility to the practice. Keane became disheartened – but not for long. Here's how he describes the second appearance of commissioning parents George and Debbie, and Debbie's friend Sue (the surrogate mother) on a national network television show:

Should I stop while I was ahead or should I continue charting previously undiscovered legal, moral and religious territories? The answer would be provided by a television show. In late March 1978, Debbie, Sue and George made a repeat performance on the Phil Donahue show. But this time they brought a guest – two-month-old Elizabeth Anne.

The format was the same. Donahue worked the jam-packed crowd of women and fielded call-in questions. Debbie, Sue and George sat down in front, the center of hundreds of eyes in the live studio audience and of millions across the country. But while their earlier appearance had prompted moral reservations and legal questions from the audience, this time there was only one focal point: Elizabeth Anne, blonde-haired, blue-eyed, and as real as a baby's yell . . . The show was one of Donahue's highest-rated ever, and the audience came down firmly on the side of what Debbie, Sue and George had done to bring Elizabeth Anne into the world. (Keane and Breo, 1981, pp. 95–6)

On their previous appearance on the Phil Donahue show, neither Debbie's sincere desire to have a child she could raise with George, nor Sue's wholehearted delight at the pregnancy she was undergoing for her friend, moved the audience. It was Elizabeth Anne, the baby, who turned the trick.

By the same token, the birth of Nicola Bell in October 1986 – to a twenty-four-year old woman thought to be brain-dead, but not tested for brain-death until after the birth – has been received in Britain by the media as a wholly positive event (for example, *The Guardian*, 20 and 21 October 1986). There has been copious sympathy for the father, who will have to raise the baby alone. But delight at the delivery of Nicola by caesarian section left room for scarcely a murmur of questioning about the ethics of using a woman's body in this way, without her prior consent. In this case, the maintenance of Deborah Bell on a life-support system occurred at the express wish of Ian Bell, her husband, who was also presumed to be the father of the child; in some similar cases in the United States deliveries of babies to brain-dead mothers have occurred against the wishes of next-of-kin and at the instigation of male lovers who claimed to be the fathers of the foetuses that the women were carrying.[11] The ethical issues in such cases are clearly complex and the birth of a baby is a cause for celebration. But the lack of debate, in Britain at least, about the integrity of women's bodies in such cases reflects a worrying tendency to privilege the foetus or the baby over the woman in whose body it is carried.

It is in this context that the reproductive technologies which enable doctors – and through them, the state – to have a more and more direct relationship with the foetus pose a danger to women (see chapter 7). It is not technology that creates this danger, but the politics of indifference to women's wishes with regard to pregnancy and birth.

The New Eugenics

The first American physician who admitted openly that he had assisted in establishing a 'surrogate pregnancy' justified his action in the language of eugenics. 'I performed the insemination', Dr Simonds wrote, 'because there are enough unwanted children and children of poor genetic background in the world' (Keane and Breo, 1981, p. 36). He is not alone. For much of this century, reproductive technologies have been seen by some as tools for encouraging the propagation of the 'superior', or for reducing the numbers of the hereditarily unfit. The feminist campaigner Margaret Sanger, in 1919, saw the chief issue of birth-control as 'More children from the fit, less from the unfit' (Gordon, 1977, p. 281). George Bernard Shaw was among those who, in the 1930s, were excited by the prospect of using artificial insemination as a means for multiplying the offspring of a gifted minority, not least himself:

When I, who have no children, and couldn't have been bothered with them, think of all the ova I might have inseminated!!! And of all the women who could not have tolerated me in the house for a day, but would have liked some of my qualities for their children!!! (Kevles, 1986, pp. 191–2).

The naivety of these views became cruelly apparent with the sterilization campaign launched by Hitler in June 1933. Aimed at mental deficients, schizophrenics, manic depressives, those with severe deformities and the hereditarily blind, deaf or alcoholic, it sterilized, in the first phase, some 350,000 individuals and paved the way for Auschwitz (Lifton, 1986). By the 1940s, even the popular press in Britain was alert to the sinister eugenic potential of practices such as artificial insemination by donor.[12]

Artificial insemination by donor has been in clinical use in Britain since the 1930s, with, as far as I know, little sign of the eugenic consequences that Shaw and his associates hoped for, or that others feared. What new ingredients have been added since the early post-war period to provoke the kind of anxiety about eugenics that surrounds discussion of reproductive technologies today?[13]

First, the advance in genetic knowledge since the forties – accelerating rapidly with the development of recombinant DNA techniques – has been remarkable. Scientists have identified some 3,000 distinct conditions that are transmitted genetically from parent to offspring (see chapter 8). These range from disorders that may threaten the life of a child, to others (such as male baldness or colour-blindness) which can be regarded, at worst, as minor afflictions. Clinical techniques for screening at the prenatal or post-natal stage (amniocentesis, chorionic villus sampling or the Guthrie test for phenylketonuria (PKU)) make it possible to detect the likely presence of some of these conditions in foetuses or newborn infants. A number of techniques also exist for identifying, among adults, people who do not themselves suffer from a genetic disorder but who, as carriers, might pass it on to their children. Hence, genetic knowledge gives the potential to recognize the genetic basis of inherited conditions and susceptibilities in an individual long before there is any outward sign.

Secondly, this increase in genetic knowledge has taken place against a backdrop of revived interest in the biological basis of human behaviour, and of renewed attempts to target less-privileged social groups as the source of society's ills. Rhodes Boyson, a member of the Conservative government in Britain, attributed the increase in single-parent families partly to artificial insemination, and blamed the procreative habits of single parents for 'violent crime, football hooliganism, mugging and inner city revolt' (*The Guardian*, 10 October, 1986). And on both sides of the Atlantic, the new right emphasis upon fiscal responsibility has allowed cuts in public expenditure for the unemployed, those on low incomes, the elderly, the chronically ill or the disabled to be cloaked in the mantle of 'economic realism'. The doctrine of survival of the fittest – which helped to inspire the growth of the eugenics movement in the late nineteenth century – has once again found fertile ground.

A short way behind the genuine interest in finding medical solutions to particular disabilities that bring suffering to some children and their families, runs a concern merely to reduce public responsibility. In Britain, a spokesperson on behalf of embryo research exemplifies the tendency to argue for preventative research into genetic disorders in ways that further stigmatize the handicapped: 'We feel strongly that the lives of handicapped children are severely blighted and that the care of them is a considerable burden to their parents and the State.' (Peter Thurnham, MP, quoted in Ferriman, 1985). More baldly, a former health-systems analyst in the office of the American Surgeon-General suggests that it is the existence of (genetically?) mentally deficient people that prevents the solution of other social problems: 'If we allow our genetic problems to get out of hand, we as a society run the risk of overcommitting ourselves to the care and maintenance of a large population of mentally deficient persons at the expense of other social problems' (cited in Kevles, 1986, p. 277). All these phenomena – the rolling back of welfare programmes; the return, in Britain, of some people with disabilities to 'community care' without the resources to protect their quality of life or that of their principal carers; the tendency to define handicap as a burden on the public purse – form the context in which attitudes to screening programmes develop. A large number of British Members of Parliament who are in favour of restricting women's rights to abortion, strongly support at the same time proposals for a national prenatal screening programme that would encourage the termination of more pregnancies on genetic grounds (Farrant, 1985, p. 105).

Genetic knowledge, and voluntary programmes of screening and counselling, offer would-be parents the chance to prepare for the care of a child with special needs, or to terminate a pregnancy with which they feel unable to cope. But the technical capacity to monitor individual genetic make-up also raises, particularly in the current political climate, a number of major questions. Genetic knowledge enables the identification of inborn or inherited disorders or suscep-tibilities, major and minor, many of which can be neither treated nor cured. Will money that goes into developing screening techniques to identify such problems substitute for funds that might be used to develop treatments, or to provide better support systems, for those who suffer the effects of such disorders? If no practical medical help can be offered to people who carry potentially disabling genes, then what will be the impact of such information on the carriers? More importantly, to what purposes might this information be put by others? In the absence of strong legal protections, screening might, in other words, provide a burden of genetic knowledge which could be used to limit the autonomy of individuals and groups, rather than extend it.

These issues have already been aired to an extent in the United States, where in the early 1970s compulsory programmes of genetic screening were introduced, and where black people were particularly affected by employment restrictions placed, for example, by major commercial airlines and by the Air Force Academy on carriers of sickle-cell trait. In Britain, however, discussion of the implications of screening programmes has been confined to a greater extent to medical and scientific constituencies, although there is some sign that this is now changing.

In thinking about reproductive technologies and eugenics, it is not the bizarre fantasies of people like Robert K. Graham – the Californian entrepreneur who aims to encourage the 'mating' of superior women with the sperm of Nobel prize-winning men – that deserve detailed attention. Rather, it is the organization of routine medical practice that needs scrutiny. A survey of consultant obstetricians in Britain found that 75 per cent of those questioned required women to agree to abortion of an affected foetus before they give amniocentesis; information that should be a resource for parents becomes, in these cases, an instrument of population control (Farrant, 1985, p. 113). It is not acceptable that the understandable desire of many women to have as healthy a baby as possible should become a duty, aimed at the welfare of the gene pool, rather than that of the parents or the child.[14]

Screening of adults for genetic conditions, or prenatal screening of foetuses, work by influencing the reproductive decisions of would-be parents. The choices presented by these programmes – to give birth or not to a foetus with a potentially serious abnormality, to turn to artificial insemination or some other 'safer' means of having a child, to forgo procreation altogether – are often grim. Eugenists such as Sinsheimer see a more rosy prospect in genetic engineering; if developments in biomedicine eventually enable scientists to replace problematic genes with more meritorious ones (in the newborn infant, or the embryo),[15] then the quality of the population could be improved not by the culling of the unfit, nor even by interfering with people's procreative freedom, but merely by 'the conversion of all the unfit to the highest genetic level' (Sinsheimer, in Kevles, 1986, p. 268). This, in essence, is the appeal of the 'new eugenics'.

Even if human genetic engineering is a science-fiction possibility at the current stage of development,[16] the concern that it evokes is understandable. There is a worry that the definition of 'unfit' will become a mask for prejudice and intolerance; that information about biochemical differences will become translated into judgements about the differential value of persons. That, in short, we will not distinguish finely enough between scientific questions and political ones. More immediately, there is a danger that genetic knowledge will be seen not as a tool of human advancement but as the tool: that research which might reduce the number of genetic defects will replace research to improve the prospects of people with disease or disability; that attempts to reduce genetic variability will be substituted for efforts to create an environment in which the range of human variability can flourish.

But just as genetic engineering must be put in its place, by challenging the notion that medical technique can provide a sufficient response to issues of disability and physical difference, so too in our resistance to eugenic policies it won't do to overrate the importance of reproductive technologies. In Britain, despite the existence of a 'comprehensive' National Health Service, the maternal mortality rate and the infant mortality rate for women in the 'unskilled' working class is nearly double that for women in professional and managerial groups – and the gap has scarcely narrowed since the 1930s (Townsend and Davidson, 1982, p. 70–71). This has little to do with eugenic policies or with new technologies, and everything to do with the routine effects of life in a society that is deeply stratified. To make resistance to reproductive technologies too central to a strategy for reproductive freedom plays into the hands of those who would equate 'family' welfare with the mere arrival of a child. The struggle for reproductive rights must be embedded in a broader programme to create the forms of support that will enable people in varying circumstances to build secure and healthy futures for themselves and their children.

Conclusions

In a lecture given in 1986, the chair of the Warnock Committee mentioned a survey conducted by a popular women's magazine, in which the overwhelming majority of respondents had said that they did not trust scientists to reveal the full truth about their research; Mary Warnock saw this as a reflection of appalling fear and ignorance about science.[17] But it is not fear and ignorance that makes women wary of scientific or medical innovations; it is knowledge and experience of the ambivalent effects of medical technologies on women's lives. Because of these ambivalent effects, and because of the hidden agenda of many of those who promote and apply these techniques, assessment of risks and benefits cannot be surrendered to the 'experts' (see chapter 2). We have no option but to ask (of in-vitro fertilization, of chorionic villus sampling, of ultrasound, of gene therapy): Does it work? Does it deliver what it promises? Does it involve risks to the health or well-being of the patient? – while insisting that there is no such thing as a purely technical answer to these questions. All assessments of the efficacy and safety of a technique contain a social dimension; what, after all, is 'an acceptable level of risk'? In trying to ensure that the criteria used for assessing technologies incorporate women's own priorities with regard to health, reproduction and well-being, we have no option but to engage with science. As Hilary Rose says in chapter 8, science is far too important to be left to men.

At the same time, we must remain firm that technical knowledge does not dictate human choices, or even make such choices clear-cut. Knowledge of a likely abnormality in a foetus, provided by prenatal screening, may be useful background information for would-be parents. But, as Rose argues, none of the very different decisions they may make in these circumstances can be 'read off' from the technical information provided by the geneticists.[18] And, most importantly, none of these decisions is properly one for a medical practitioner, as opposed to a parent, to make. In circumstances where parents, and particularly mothers, assume the overwhelming burden of material and emotional responsibility for the children they bear, it must be parents – and particularly mothers – who decide under what circumstances they are prepared to parent.

During the 1960s and early 1970s, campaigns around abortion provided an urgent focus for the women's movement. A great deal of energy went into exposing the 'motherhood mystique', and challeng-ing the social conditions that sometimes made childcare isolating and exhausting, rather than enriching. By contrast, relatively little atten-tion was given to physical aspects of reproduction: the experiences of conceiving, bearing and birthing children. Pregnancy and childbirth often seemed merely the brute biological backdrop to childcare, the physical rite of passage that signalled our individual entries into motherhood.

From the mid-1970s onwards, women have had the confidence to recognize pregnancy and childbirth as the accomplishments they are: to wrest them back from nature, to insist upon seeing them as part of a sphere of significant action as meaningful and as civilized as any of the accomplishments of men. This reclamation has not been a mere semantic exercise (if any semantic exercises are 'merely' that). It has involved campaigns to alter the conditions of reproduction and to ensure that women have the scope to develop the projects of pregnancy and childbirth, and relationships with children, in their own ways – as well as the freedom to refuse them altogether.

Since reproductive technologies so intimately affect women's bodies, our pregnancies, our children and our lives, we cannot avoid being actively involved in their appraisal. But the attempt to reclaim motherhood as a female accomplishment should not mean giving the natural priority over the technological – that pregnancy is natural and good, technology unnatural and bad. It is not at all clear what a 'natural' relationship to our fertility, our reproductive capacity, would look like. The early modern period in England – sometimes characterized as an era of 'natural fertility' – was a period when women and men (but especially women) were anything but *laissez-faire* where fertility was concerned (McLaren, 1984). They knew of, and drew upon, herbal, mechanical, dietary and behavioural remedies and safeguards in order to influence the timing of conceptions, the sex of a foetus, to prevent births or to ensure conceptions and they sought the services of midwives and other 'experts' to assist them in the application of these technologies. In today's world, the term 'natural' can hardly be applied to high rates of infertility exacerbated by potentially controllable infections, by occupational hazards and environmental pollutants, by medical and contraceptive mismanagement (Wilkie, 1984). If it is not clear what a 'natural' relation to our fertility would look like, it is even less clear that it would be desirable: fertility undermined by poor nutrition or by gonorrhoea, unchecked by medical intervention; high birth rates, with population growth limited only by high infant and adult mortality; abstinence from intercourse for heterosexual people except when pregnancy was the immediately desired result?

The thrust of feminist analysis has been to rescue pregnancy from the status of 'the natural' – to establish pregnancy and childbirth not as a natural condition, the parameters of which are set in advance, but as an accomplishment which we can actively shape according to our own ends (Lewin, 1985). To call 'natural' the energy and commitment involved in achieving a wanted pregnancy, in carrying it safely to term and in creating a sense of relationship with the child-that-will-be, is to deny the very human investment that some women make in 'my baby'. In the feminist critique of reproductive technologies, it is not technology as an '*artificial* invasion of the human body'[19] that is at issue – but whether we can create the political and cultural conditions in which such technologies can be employed by women to shape the experience of reproduction according to their own definitions.

2
From Walking Wombs to Test-Tube Babies
Ann Oakley

This chapter is concerned with the complex relationship between the social position of women as mothers on the one hand, and the growth of reproductive technologies on the other. The relationship between the two is, of course, mediated by developments in medical professionalization, and specifically by the evolution of obstetrics as a medical-technical speciality. Particular themes highlighted in the chapter are, first, the increasing historical emphasis within obstetrics on the mechanical model of women as mothers, and the collision that exists between this model and both 'scientific' and 'experiential' evidence about the social, economic and psychological implications of new reproductive technologies. The conflict between the two perspectives is characteristic of the relatively short time-period in which pregnancy has been subject to a centralized, technological mode of control.

A second theme concerns the extent to which it is true to say that the technological imperative within reproductive medicine is itself new; the historical evidence contradicts this, but it does show that today technology is developed and used in the 'management' of reproduction according to a logic that demands verifiable proof of effectiveness and safety. The fact that this logic is frequently breached (which it is) is therefore especially surprising. These themes are illustrated by considering technologies for viewing the interior life of the womb – X-rays and ultrasound scanning: what does the development of these technologies tell us about the relationship between medical professionals and women as mothers, and what can be deduced from it about the scientific status of the medical management of reproduction?

Reproduction: from Women's Experience to Medical Subject

These questions need to be located within the general historical context of changes in social definitions of childbirth. Broadly speaking, what has occurred over the last 150 years in Europe and North America is a profound shift in the control and management of child-bearing (both its promotion and its prevention). Before the rise of the modern medical profession, the main empirical healers available to the bulk of the population were lay women in the community. A close alliance existed between the work of women as unofficial healers and the aid they gave to other women wishing to avoid or achieve motherhood (Chamberlain 1981; Oakley 1976). Childbirth occurred at home. There was no systematic medical care during pregnancy. Institutions grouping pregnant and labouring women as 'patients' along with the sick did not exist.

In the eighteenth century the female community-based control of child-bearing began to be challenged by the emergence of technically minded male midwives, and by the establishment of lying-in hospitals where pregnant women could become objects of study for doctors and medical students (Versluysen, 1981). In the latter part of the nineteenth century and the early decades of the twentieth century, these developments were accelerated by an escalating concern on the part of the state with the quantity and quality of the population; with the deaths of enormous numbers of young children and women annually, either directly as a result of the process of child-bearing, or because of some other deficit of motherhood seen as being remedial through the efforts of central and local government (Inter-departmental Committee, 1904). Obstetrics and paediatrics became respectable specialities within medicine instead of aspects of women's domestic work, and rapidly acquired the covert status of being ways of controlling the roles and activities of women.

Integral to this process was the state registration of midwifery (Donnison, 1977), the development of a system of medical surveillance in pregnancy, and the increasing habit of hospital delivery (Oakley, 1984). The percentage of British babies born in hospitals or other institutions went from 15 per cent in 1927 to 24 per cent in 1932 to 64 per cent in 1954, reaching 91 per cent in 1972 and 98 per cent in 1980 (Oakley, 1984; Macfarlane and Mugford, 1984). Most recently there has also been a trend to situate more antenatal care in hospital rather than in the community, and to favour larger hospitals at the expense of smaller ones. Antenatal care, medical care during labour and delivery and the postpartum care of the baby, especially small, sick babies, have become increasingly technological, in the sense that specialized technical procedures occupy more and more of the space described by the heading 'medical care' (Macfarlane and Mugford, 1984).

These are the general developments. Of course there are exceptions and indeed, even signs of a move away from technology in certain areas (for example, Elliot and Flaherty, 1983). The technical and other professional developments within the medical world affecting reproduction have been accompanied by an emphasis on the status of women as objects within the reproductive process. They have also been characterized by a disjunction between the medical *claim* to therapeutic effectiveness and safety on the one hand, and relevant evidence of this on the other. Antenatal care as a mass screening service has never been evaluated, for example, and policies with respect to hospital delivery emerged piecemeal on the basis of arguments about existing trends and unsubstantiated claims about probable benefits (Enkin and Chalmers, 1982; Kitzinger and Davis, 1978).

Do Mothers Have Minds?

Bearing in mind this general context, two very specific facts about present-day reproductive technology and women provide a useful starting point for an historical explanation of the relationship between the way women are seen and the way in which reproductive technology develops. The first of these two facts is that you don't need a brain to have a baby. This has now become true in an absolutely literal sense. In the United States in 1983 a young woman who suffered a fatal seizure twenty-two weeks into a pregnancy was maintained on a life-support system for nine weeks, at the end of which time a live foetus was delivered by caesarian section. During this time the woman's brain was dead, but her body was not, although it developed many problems, including diabetes insipidus, Addison's disease and blood infections with which physicians were able to deal. After the baby was delivered, the woman was taken off the life-support apparatus, which had enabled her physically to support the life of a baby; she then stopped breathing and sustained a 'legal' death (Corea, 1985a, pp. 280–1).

The second fact comes from a recently published book by the medical sociologist, Barbara Katz Rothman. Rothman's book is called *The Tentative Pregnancy*, and it is concerned with the experiences of women having prenatal diagnosis. One of her findings concerned women's reactions to learning the sex of the foetus prenatally. In general, more maternal disappointment is expressed about daughters than sons, when the information about sex is acquired *at birth* (Williamson, 1976). Preference for men is a dominant cultural value. But Rothman found exactly the opposite during pregnancy. Of fifty women in her study who learnt the sex of their foetus as a result of amniocentesis, ten were disappointed. All ten were carrying boys. The explanation of this reversal of the usual reaction did not seem to be that the women in Rothman's sample were exceptional in any way – for instance in professing feminist beliefs (which are sometimes seen as the mark of exceptional women); on the contrary they seemed just as traditional in their social characteristics and attitudes as women in studies of post-birth reactions to the sex of infants. Rather, the explanation seems to be that as Rothman puts it, 'It is one thing to have given birth to a son. It is another thing to be told that the foetus growing inside your body is male. . . .To have a male growing in a female body is to contain your own antithesis. It makes of the foetus not a continuation and extension of self, but an "other" ' (Rothman, 1986, p. 144).

In other words, reproductive technologies such as amniocentesis have many implications, only some of which are capable of being anticipated within a straight medical or physicalist model of reproduction. That prenatal knowledge of foetal sex might bring about a whole historically new set of reactions in women and thus fundamentally affect parent-child relations, with all sorts of unknown consequences, is a fact presumably neither intended nor imagined by the pioneers of the technology in question.

These two facts – that women need only be bodies but are, on the other hand, much more than this – contradict one another. Reacting to foetal sex requires mental and emotional power. Acting as a mere life-support system for a foetus does not. And this contradiction between two definitions of women is not, as one might expect, apparent in exactly the same way throughout history. It is in many ways a recent invention. The specific reproductive definition of women as mindless mothers appears to have emerged simultaneously with the move towards a centralized technological control of pregnancy which has taken place over the last thirty years. This type of control insists on, and facilitates, a disregard for the intellectuality and emotionality of women. It has now become technologically possible to ignore the status of pregnant women as human beings. This is very different from the situation obtaining in the nineteenth century when it was quite impossible for doctors (for example) to forget that women were not simply bundles of reproductive apparatus. They knew women had minds as well; hence it was necessary for the doctors to produce arguments about the education of women causing their ovaries etc. to shrivel up, and to insist that combining biological femaleness with any kind of non-domestic pursuit was liable, at the very least, to drive women mad and at worst to destroy their husbands and children along with their ovaries (Bullough and Bullough, 1977). The point is that however patronizing, unscientific and plain nasty nineteenth-century doctors were in condemning women to what one

American feminist called 'the prison-house-of-the-home' (Gilman, 1903) – yet they had somehow to take on board women's humanity, their possession of minds and emotions and souls as well as ovaries and uterus. Today doctors have become much more subtle. They are increasingly devising ways of bypassing the need to stereotype women at all. This is one major effect of modern reproductive technology, and it began to be noted in the early decades of the twentieth century when mass surveillance of pregnant women in community and hospital clinics – otherwise known as 'antenatal care' – first got off the ground. One woman doctor anticipated the tone of many later twentieth-century criticisms when she said in 1934 that doctors needed to get their antenatal work into focus, remembering that 'the expectant mother is not an ambulant pelvis, but a woman with human needs, whose soul and body are closely interlocked (*Lancet*, 1934, p. 1204).

Reproductive Technology: What is it and is it New?

If this is the age of reproductive technology then, like the train, important questions must be asked about its appropriateness as a means of transporting human beings. What is 'technology', and how wide or narrow are the limits of the term 'reproduction'? Although talking about reproductive technology was made highly fashionable by the arrival of in-vitro fertilization, and the debate has thus come to be associated with the *promotion* of pregnancy, many important techniques in this field have to do with *preventing* pregnancy. In fact, historically and world-wide, preventing pregnancy has been much more important to women and men than promoting it. Thus, when we think about the relationship between women and reproductive technology, we must consider the impact on their lives of contraceptive devices and technologies as well as conceptive ones – and we must think about the fertility controllers, the family planners or 'preconception obstetricians' as they were recently dubbed (Modell, 1983), as much as we must think of men in their laboratories peering earnestly at embryonic cells dividing in glass dishes. Within this perspective it is immediately obvious that there is nothing new about reproductive technology as such. When the ancient Egyptians used crocodile dung to prevent conception, they knew what they were doing – it may not be pleasant but it works! (Himes, 1963). Other sorts of spermicides and mechanical plugs for the uterus – whether of camels or women – and the early animal condoms come into the same category. If necessity is the mother of invention, then needing to avoid motherhood has inspired many inventions.

Devices to promote fertility are also common. In traditional south Asian culture remedies for infertility include 'complex herbal compounds . . . prescribed according to instructions encoded in traditional medical songs' (McGilvray, 1982, p. 63). (The modern Western version of this would presumably be gynaecologists singing a prescription for the pill.) In the same culture male infertility is treated with honey, yoghurt, meat and eggs – which makes it sound like quite a good thing to have. The anthropologist reporting these recipes also noted that raw onion is regarded as highly effective in producing effective semen, and is therefore barred from the diet of students in the local mission hostel.

Such remedies may have been almost entirely useless in bringing about their desired objective. However, this is not really the point. If it were, we would have a similar response to in-vitro fertilization programmes, which are 80 per cent ineffective at best (Walters and Singer, 1982). The point is a different one. It is that the effectiveness of reproductive technologies is judged according to prevailing sets of values and beliefs. If you believe something works and is a good thing, then, in one important sense, whether it works or not is of little consequence. But what is remarkable about today's prevailing values is that they belong to a different paradigm from the one that operated in the days of crocodile dung. Today we are all rational creatures and are no longer willing to believe the evidence of our own senses without objective proof. Evidence about effectiveness is integral to the scientific world-view, it *ought* to matter and therefore it is even more surprising to find that it does not.

So far as technology goes then, it is also essential not to take too limited a view. We need to think not only about the techniques themselves, but also about their social location and meaning. Who operates them and who controls their use? Who is responsible for their evaluation? What kind of evaluation is it? These questions are now being asked quite widely about a range of scientific and industrial developments, but not quite the same spirit of enquiry exists in medicine. In particular, the extent to which questions about effectiveness, safety and social responsibility have been asked about reproductive technologies is severely limited. The major obstacle has been the status and organization of professionalized medicine. And there is no doubt that the major victims of this process have, indeed, been women.

A Womb of One's Own: or not?

How do these general considerations apply to one particular group of technologies, those for seeing into the interior life of pregnant women's wombs? And why are these technologies important, anyway?

Women, of course, cannot see into their own wombs, but on the other hand do generally have some idea what is going on in them. This applies both to the diagnosis and timing of pregnancy and to the growth, vitality and position of the foetus. These are the basic problems of knowledge that confront any would-be professional controllers of reproduction and inventors of reproductive technology, for if they do not know which women are pregnant, and can say nothing reliable about the condition and likely birth-date of the foetus, then why on earth are they pretending to be experts in the first place? In the nineteenth century the most cautious obstetricians said that the best thing to do in terms of diagnosing pregnancy was to wait until the baby was born (Blundell, 1834). Only then could you be sure that pregnancy was the correct diagnosis. The less cautious wrote chapters and textbooks on all those signs and symptoms of pregnancy they believed it was possible to detect – from abdominal enlargement and contractions to a funny look around the eyes (Tyler Smith, 1858) and 'an undue degree of despondency' in the woman herself (Playfair, 1898). Mistakes in diagnosis were obviously not uncommon, and very embarrassing for the doctor. The nineteenth-century 'obstetrician' Playfair, in his two-volume *Treatise on the Science and Practice of Midwifery* put his finger on a new motive for getting it right. 'The differential diagnosis of pregnancy,' said Playfair in 1876 'has of late years assumed much importance on account of the advance of abdominal surgery. The cases are so numerous,' he went on 'in which even the most experienced practitioners have fallen into error, and in which the abdomen has been laid open in ignorance of the fact that pregnancy existed, that the subject becomes one of the greatest consequence' (Playfair, 1898, p. 178). In other words the invention of technologies applied to reproduction was a process occurring dialectically with the growth of other medical technologies. Improved techniques and increased use of abdominal surgery made efficient diagnosis of pregnancy even more necessary if doctors were to hold onto their credibility.

It is important to put the nineteenth-century obstetricians' difficulties in perspective. First of all, very few pregnant women went to doctors at all. Most did nothing until labour started, when an 'untrained' but experienced local midwife would come to help with the delivery. Professional medical control of reproduction was therefore severely limited by a shortage of patients. Secondly, not only did doctors find it difficult to diagnose pregnancy, but they were not able to agree about how long pregnancy lasted, were wrong about when it started and could do virtually nothing about the common complications of pregnancy and childbirth aside from give dangerous purgatives and opiates, remove the patient's blood following the Galenic tradition, according to which pregnant women suffered from having too much blood in their bodies, and then leap in with their hands and forceps to extract unwilling babies from their mothers' wombs. A surgeon in Geneva reported hearing a foetal heart by accident through a corset in 1818, but even in the mid-century it was regarded by many doctors as quite improper to apply a stethoscope 'to the naked belly of a woman' (cited in Radcliffe, 1967, p. 71). (It is not clear whose propriety – their own or the woman's – the doctors were worrying about). However, it does seem as if keeping the patient and the doctor at a distance from one another was responsible for the development of the stethoscope with a long flexible tube attached to it, rather than the rigid one which required the doctor to lean over the patient in an intimate pose. This was especially difficult for obese doctors of whom there were apparently quite a lot around.

The development of the foetal stethoscope was shaped by prevailing social and cultural mores, in the same way as are all technologies. It was also part of a general shift in medicine from making a diagnosis on the basis of what the patient said, to making one on the basis of so-called 'objective' mechanically produced evidence. Indeed, Laennec, the French physician who invented the stethoscope, argued that technologies of physical examination (consultation, palpation and percussion) were superior to the traditional method of talking to the patient, who after all might be ignorant or prejudiced, or in fact, deliberately misleading (Reiser, 1978).

The demise of doctor–patient communication was further encouraged by the discovery in 1895 by the German physicist Röntgen of a species of rays that could penetrate or reveal the interior structures of opaque bodies. Röntgen's first X-ray was of his wife's hand – and it was taken to convince her that there really was a good reason why he came home so late from his laboratory night after night.[1] The first X-ray of a pregnant women was taken in 1896, and by the early 1900s there was a rising tide of enthusiasm for X-ray pelvimetry and also for using X-rays to diagnose pregnancy and monitor the growth of the foetus. It was said that the enlargement of the womb was obvious with X-rays at six weeks, though in order for the X-ray to be taken the patient had first to have a castor-oil enema and then lie on her back with between 1.5 and 2 litres of carbonic gas injected into her peritoneal cavity and a band tied tightly round the abdomen (Dorland and Hubeny, 1926). X-rays were regarded as particularly useful for charting foetal growth, since the different centres of ossification appeared in the foetal skeleton at standard times. By the 1920s some practitioners were arguing that every obstetric clinic should have an expert radiographer. A little later it was contended that antenatal work without the *routine* use of X-rays was 'no more justifiable than would be the treatment of fractures' (Reece, 1935, p. 489).

Although it is hard to tell from available statistics just how common X-rays were, one London hospital as late as 1954 was X-raying two-thirds of patients booked for delivery there. Even in the 1970s the incidence of foetal irradiation in some centres was still quite high – one in three in a group of British hospitals (Carmichael and Berry, 1978). This was of course some twenty years *after* the publication by Alice Stewart and her colleagues in Oxford of data showing an increased risk of childhood cancer following X-rays *in utero* (Stewart et al., 1956).

One way to follow the life and times of different technologies is to see what is said about them in print in the textbooks and other medical literature. This approach is useful in the case of X-rays, because it immediately enables one to see the close link between X-rays and another window on the womb, namely ultrasound scanning. In the well-known obstetric text, Browne's *Antenatal and Postnatal Care*, there is a separate chapter on antenatal X-rays from the second edition in 1937 to the ninth in 1960, which also carries a considerable note of caution about the hazards of X-rays following the publication of the Oxford findings. It is no accident that the next edition, in 1970, is the first to mention obstetric ultrasound (Browne, 1935 *et seq.*).

The basic technique of ultrasound was borrowed by medicine from a different field – that of warfare. During the First World War sound-waves were used to detect submarines, and after the war herring shoals and the architecture of the ocean floor were identified in the same way for the benefit of the shipping and fishing industries. The application to obstetrics came as an accident, almost, since the original idea, pioneered by Ian Donald and his colleagues in Scotland, was to use as diagnostic aids on mysterious tumours in the abdomens of women, the ultrasonic metal-flaw detectors used in industry. Their theory was that malignant tumours would look different from benign ones. Later it occurred to them that 'the commonest abdominal tumour in women is pregnancy', and additionally that there is not a lot of difference between a foetus *in utero* and a submarine at sea (Ian Donald, interview; Oakley, 1984, p. 161).

The early use of obstetric ultrasound occurred in the late 1950s. By 1965 pregnancy could be diagnosed with ultrasound as early as seven weeks and techniques for assessing foetal growth by measuring foetal heads had been worked out. A rash of papers appeared in print in the medical journals, and by 1966 the hospital in which the technique had been pioneered was scanning more than a quarter of all its patients. This is all very like what happened with X-rays and pregnancy. A decade later the same statements were being made about obstetric ultrasound as had been made about X-rays – it was said that modern obstetrics and gynaecology could not be practiced without ultrasound, and it was argued that this technique should 'be used to screen all pregnancies and should be regarded as an integral part of antenatal care' (Campbell and Little, 1980, p. 27). Today ultrasound has become a common method of foetal surveillance – a recent World Health Organization (WHO) survey of antenatal care in twenty-four European countries, found it in use in all twenty-two countries that gave information, with the most intensive pattern of use in countries with insurance-based health-care systems (WHO, 1985).

Some History Lessons

Four general points emerge from the history of X-rays and ultrasound as windows on pregnant women's wombs. First of all, it is possible to describe these histories without necessarily saying anything at all about the situation of women. Secondly, it is very hard to get accurate data about the extent of use of new (and old) technologies applied to the area of human reproduction. Thirdly, such techniques are introduced without having first had their effectiveness and safety evaluated. Fourthly, few people regard as at all problematic the question as to why new ways of managing and intervening in reproduction are in fact necessary – or whether they are so at all.

These points are quite intimately related. For example, the fact that technologies are not evaluated before becoming part of routine medical practice reflects the lack of any systematic public control of technology, and this in turn is partly responsible for the difficulty of finding out just who is using the technology, where, on whom, how often and to what effect. Medical practitioners in Britain today need to record only certain aspects of their practice. They have to say whether babies are delivered with instruments, for example, and they have been required since 1973 to note whether the mother had her perineum cut. But they do not have to record routinely whether or not ultrasound and X-rays were used during pregnancy, and doctors as a group often seem fairly unwilling to part with such information when asked for it. One survey of fellows of the American College of Obstetricians and Gynecologists in 1981 produced only a 28 per cent response rate. Nearly three-quarters of the obstetricians did not say how frequently they used ultrasound (Hohler and Platt, 1984).

Such mysteries in medicine are justified by the ethic of professionalization, which decrees that doctors are the exclusive owners of expert knowledge. They do not need to tell anyone else what they are doing or why. Indeed, retention of absolute control over technical procedures is clearly an absolute necessity for the survival of modern medical power (Zola, 1977). Simply, if lay people claim to know as much about a particular technology as the doctor, or even claim to some right of involvement in decisions about its use, they are seen to be challenging the heart of medical practice, which is that the doctor, by virtue of being the doctor, knows best. Seen in this way, doctors' control of information available to patients is part of the defence of expert professional knowledge – never a simple act of patronage or nastiness, but absolutely intrinsic to the claim of professionalization.

Challenges between doctor-knowledge and patient-knowledge are frequent today in the field of maternity care, and they centre on the two shortfalls of recent obstetric practice I mentioned earlier, namely the veiling of women's status as human beings within the category of obstetric patient and the consistent historical neglect of the need to evaluate medical technologies.

Within obstetric practice the idea may sometimes emerge painfully that women are people with rights and responsibilities and not just walking wombs. A woman in the last few weeks of her fourth pregnancy complains to a doctor in a hospital antenatal clinic about a symptom that is causing her anxiety:

> *Patient*: It's the tightening I keep worrying about.
> *Doctor*: It's normal in pregnancy. Your womb is supposed to tighten.
> *Patient*: I didn't have it with the other three.
> *Doctor*: Every pregnancy is different. Let's see you in one week.
> (Reading notes) You do seem to have put on a bit of weight.
> *Patient*: What does that mean?
> *Doctor*: It doesn't necessarily mean anything but you must take things easy.
> *Patient*: That's what my husband says. It's easy for men to say that.
> *Doctor*: You shouldn't blame us.
> *Patient*: I'm not blaming you. It's not your fault.
> *Doctor*: It's your set-up at home. You should have organized things better.
> *Patient*: Well, I've got three kids to look after.
> *Doctor*: Yes.

It is hard for the doctor to answer that one. The dialogue brings out several points. One, the 'patient's' own knowledge about how she feels (how her womb is behaving), is disregarded in favour of the doctor's expert overriding claim that 'every pregnancy is different'. (As a matter of fact the medical claim to superior expertise must be lodged on the opposite rule, that every pregnancy is the same, i.e., belongs to a category which can be known in non-subjective ways). Secondly, the verbal exchanges illustrate the intentional withholding of information: (*Doctor*: 'It doesn't necessarily mean anything'). Thirdly, the alliance between masculinity and medical control is referred to (by the woman herself). Fourthly, the mutual blaming that goes on reveals the 'patient' as a person with other responsibilities which the doctor is unwilling to authenticate as relevant or real. The problem of pregnancy management as he has defined it discounts the importance and wholeness of the person.

Such issues are today being taken into the limelight by women in consumer organizations, who are repeatedly saying both that they have rights as individuals and that doctors do not necessarily know best. These contentions are not the same as one another, but are often collated in the experience of receiving medical care. The power of the professional encounter both enables and requires a complex and internally reinforcing stereotyping of woman, such that (so that) it becomes difficult for women to respond simply to it, and this makes it difficult for women to respond at all, or at all effectively. The situation is made even more problematic because the weight of commercial interests often underlies medical ones. Thus the medical case for reproductive technologies such as ultrasound is supported by strong commercial interests, a point brought out when the Association for Improvements in the Maternity Services (AIMS) recently reported to the Advertising Standards Committee an advertisement for an ultrasound machine placed in the newspaper *The Observer* by the Japanese firm Toshiba. The advertisement said that the machine was absolutely safe. AIMS pointed out that this had not been proven, and the Advertising Standards Authority upheld their case (AIMS, 1983). We do not know how Toshiba reacted, behind the scenes, but the logic of the 'consumer' opposition to currently fashionable medical methods of managing reproduction targetting the industries that generate the technology is irrefutable. From another point of view, that of the desirability of evaluating technology, it is remarkable when challenges are put by the 'uneducated lay public' and not by the practitioners of science, i.e., the doctors using the technique.

Naturally, this reinforces the deceptive status of the idea that medicine is inherently in favour of evaluating itself. The most appropriate method of evaluating a technique such as ultrasound is that of the randomized controlled trial (RCT). It took over twenty years from the start of the technique for the first RCT of obstetric ultra-sound to be published. Yet even with this mode of evaluation, it is important to be realistic about what it can and cannot show – and absolute safety especially in the long-term, can never be proven. Even given these qualifications, it is important to note – because it is germane to the argument – that obstetrics and gynaeology is *not* one of the medical specialities that has practised the highest level of evaluation (Tyson et al., 1983).

This is one reason why the consumer organizations are raising questions about unevaluated medical technologies, but this level of involvement of women in their reproductive care in turn makes some doctors quite unhappy. One unhappy doctor is Mr Harold Francis, a consultant at Liverpool Maternity Hospital. Mr Francis wrote an article called 'Obstetrics: A Consumer Orientated Service? The Case Against', in the *Journal of Maternal and Child Health* last year (Francis, 1985). In this he complained that neurosurgeons do not have to contend with something called *The Good Neurosurgery Guide*, so why should obstetricians have to take the consequences of something called *The Good Birth Guide*? (The answer probably has something to do with the fact that birth is not quite the same process as neurosurgery). Mr Francis also states that from personal experience he knows that 'the Maoris in New Zealand, the Nomads of Iran and the Savannah dwellers of Sudan do not step behind a proverbial bush for a short time to emerge with the baby in the arm and nonchalantly swinging the placenta by the cord with the other' (ibid., p. 70). (It seems unlikely that anyone has suggested that they did.) Dismissing women who want 'a low-tech birth' as quite improperly affected by their own personal experience (which is presumably not as trustworthy as his own), he lists some alarming implications of avoiding medical care. Apparently undiagnosed ectopic pregnancy is likely to result from giving up the habit of being examined vaginally, and rejecting intrapartum foetal monitoring will result in a stillborn baby or a child with cerebral palsy. Even more alarming, Francis notes that 'A major in-vitro fertilization unit recently reported a stillbirth due to asphyxia during the second stage of labour in a woman who insisted on natural childbirth at home!' It is obviously difficult for some people to appreciate that some women care enough about motherhood and babies to use all available strategies both to get pregnant in the first place and then to ensure the best possible birth for the child. The only explanation Francis is able to find for this odd behaviour is that pregnant women are not only emotionally unstable but intensely egocentric, and that this combination of undesirable qualities was probably necessary for self-preservation 'when we lived in the caves'. (Mr Francis's history seems to be as bad as his obstetrics).

The case Mr Francis makes out is very interesting, because it draws out certain critical medical responses to the 'consumer' challenge. The irrelevance of choice – of the clients' rights to have a say in the kind of care they get – is not even stated, but assumed. A mythical and false golden age of natural childbirth is retrieved from nowhere, so that the protesting consumer can be caricatured as ridiculous. Then the danger of death and disability is held up as the price to be paid by women who assert the right to choose. Lastly the whole issue of women's fitness for motherhood and citizenship is called into question. If women do not really have the status of responsible individuals, then they can hardly be allowed to make choices and ask questions.

Far from defuelling the consumer revolt, such emotional archery would seem to call into question the intelligence and sensibility of men such as Mr Francis, and query their suitability for handling important matters of life and death. Certainly the nature of their response frames another crucial question: Why *do* medical practitioners adopt new technologies? It is much easier to answer the 'how' question attached to this, for the process whereby new technologies enter medical practice is surprisingly uniform, and there have also been some case-studies of what inspires some doctors and not others to pick up new ideas and practice them on their patients. John McKinlay's description of the 'seven stages in the career of a medical innovation' goes as follows: Stage 1 – when 'promising reports' begin to appear in the medical literature; Stage 2 – when professional organizations start to adopt the technique; Stage 3 – when the public begins to demand it; Stage 4 – when it becomes part of routine practice; Stage 5 – when there is some attempt to subject the technique to controlled experimental evaluation; Stage 6 – when the professionals themselves begin to denounce the technique, and lastly, Stage 7 – when discreditation sets in and a technique that was earlier hailed as the magic answer to everything is seen as appropriate in only a selected minority of cases (McKinlay, 1981).

The process is logical, if not exactly scientific. The most puzzling progression is from isolated reports to routine use, and it is this stage that some case-studies of medical practice have illuminated. In the United States, Coleman and his colleagues studied the use of a new drug and found that the most important stimulus for the physicians was knowing another physician who had started to use the drug.

Conversations on the golf-course appeared to be particularly important in determining prescribing patterns (Coleman et al., 1966). The history of reproductive technologies follows the same kind of pattern. It is not primarily a question of new technologies needing to be developed to save lives – or if it is, it is the need that is in question. Did women *need* to have new reproductive technologies invented? Did foetuses? Of course the conventional answer to these questions cites the fall in the reproductive mortalities that has occurred over the same period as technological management of childbirth has been introduced. And of course the sensible answer to this is that such correlations are not cause and effect – if they were we would be able to point to all kinds of interesting notions; we could say that industrial action in British schools is caused by the fashion for domestic video machines, or that British custard got yellower because air pollution in the inner cities decreased. Indeed, the human fallibility of the medical profession is proven by this very point – that it is difficult to prove beyond any doubt that the world benefits from its work.

Of course, it does need to be said that some new techniques for managing reproduction have been tremendously important in saving lives. Blood transfusion, antibiotic therapy and the prevention of deaths resulting from rhesus incompatibility are some medical activities that have undoubtedly decreased mortality.

Where do Babies Come From?

In other words, when you examine the evidence you see that the vast bulk of what doctors do in the name of furthering the success of human reproduction may be of benefit but equally it may not. It has been suggested that the underlying motive of obstetricians is an ungratified childhood curiosity about where babies come from – but I know of no evidence to support this statement. On the other hand, I can see quite a lot of evidence that the *effect*, if not the motive, of reproductive technology is to control the lives of women. The fact that one can talk about the history of reproductive technology without any reference to what was happening to women at the time merely underlines this point, because the situation of women feeds into the process of developing new methods of managing reproduction only in subtle, disguised and unacknowledged ways.

The American feminist Andrea Dworkin has described two different models of how women's reproductive capacities are controlled (Dworkin, 1983). Under the first – the 'farming model' – men plant women with their seed and then harvest the crop of babies. But the problem with this system is its inefficiency. There are too many uncontrollable elements – the women may be infertile, may produce defective babies, or may conspire to avoid conception altogether. The second model is called by Dworkin the 'reproductive brothel model'. According to this, women are collected together and held, are seen as interchangeable with one another and not as individual human beings. Just as sex can be a commodity when men and women exploit the idea that women are sexual objects for men, so reproduction becomes a commodity when women become reproductive objects.

Both 'farming' and 'reproductive brothel' models stress the treatment of women as objects, as biological systems manipulable in the interests of patriarchy, and only rarely themselves capable of manipulation. This is to underrate the capacities of women to act, initiate, assert and in overt and covert ways defeat the patriarchal plan. (A similar point was made by McNally [1979] about the exploitation of women temporary clerical workers – that very often such women could, and did, use the world of office-work to achieve their own ends.) It is also the case that what has happened to women has to some extent happened to people as patients – the medicalization described by Illich and others defrauds people of their autonomy and authenticity. Nevertheless, Dworkin's models do serve to illustrate the contrast between reproduction before the use of modern medical-technological management and after this system is established: centralized control by a powerful professional elite claiming expert technical knowledge is a more effective and total mode of control than a decentralized non-professional non-technological mode.

The move towards reducing women's reproductive status to that of objects (or object-containers) can be illustrated in several ways. One key example is that the routine use of ultrasound in pregnancy enables obstetricians to do without that classic piece of reproductive information – the date of the last menstrual period. Once it is believed that the machine is less fallible than the woman then the woman does not need to be asked any more. Accordingly, some practitioners no longer believe in asking women for their menstrual histories. This is in strong contrast to the message of the nineteenth-century textbooks which outlined a structure for the gynaecological examination in which the doctor was at least as dependent on the patient's information as the patient was on the doctor's. When we add to this change other information that can now be gained technologically (for example on when the foetus moves and whether it has got hiccups) we can see that there is less and less need for doctors to talk to women – unless they want to.

A second illustration of women's new status as reproductive objects is an organizational one. As was noted earlier, many modern health-care systems have been moving for some years towards the centralization of reproductive care in large hospitals. Following the Darwinian model this somewhat haphazard and unplanned evolution towards the centralization of birth in hospital is widely regarded as better – again, we must ask for whom? Routine hospitalized delivery has never been shown to be superior to routine home delivery so far as the safety of mother and child is concerned. But on the other hand it is much easier to control people when you have got them all in the same place (the sense behind the 'reproductive brothel' model). In the government reports on the maternity services published from the 1950s onward in Britain, the 'convenience' argument emerges more clearly as time goes on, and the argument about needing to pay attention to what women want and what their material conditions will facilitate becomes fainter and then finally disappears. In 1959 the Cranbrook Report said much more about the situation and rights of women as reproducers than did the 1980 Short Report – which may be progress for the profession and the policy-makers, but is not so for women. An even more recent report, the 1983 Proceedings of the Eleventh Study Group of the Royal College of Obstetricians and Gynaecologists does not mention the need to think about the social implications of techniques such as chorionic villus sampling until p. 381, and among its list of seventeen recommendations, none points to the need for research on the views and experiences of women as the people who are the prime receivers of the technique (Rodeck and Nicolaides, 1983).

This returns us to an earlier point, that reproductive technologies have profound personal and social implications, even if it is no longer strictly necessary for women as reproducers to possess minds at all. The social implications of technologies are always the last on the scene. Thus, it took some twenty years for the practitioners of obstetric ultrasound to wake up to the fact that seeing her foetus on the screen might change the way a woman felt about it. This elementary piece of wisdom was then translated into technical paediatric language and the notion of prenatal mother–child bonding was born. In his book *Power and the Profession of Obstetrics*, William Arney has argued that this language of bonding – whether pre- or post-natal – has been spoken by obstetricians in order to legitimize their response to the consumer revolt (Arney, 1982). They could not just respond by saying 'you're right', they had to respond by building into their practice a biologically approved need to institutionalize the emotional relations of mother and child. Children who are not bonded to their mothers (not so much is heard about the fate of mothers not bonded to their children), grow up, *à la* John Bowlby, into affectionless and socially disruptive adults. Accordingly this new responsibility of obstetrics to bond mother and child legitimizes such pseudo-radical procedures as talking to women in the antenatal clinic, putting wallpaper on the walls of delivery rooms and building delivery beds that look like what grandmother had in her log cabin, but convert at the touch of a button into a contraption neatly exposing the cartography of the mother's perineum to the determined and wilful gaze of the obstetrician.

A third obvious example of women's reproductive status as objects comes from the field that most people immediately think of when the phrase 'technology of human reproduction' is mentioned. The publication of the Warnock Report in 1984 rapidly introduced into everybody's language terms such as in-vitro fertilization, embryo transfer and surrogate motherhood. It also said quite a lot about ethical dimensions of these techniques, but in this respect was essentially conservative in referring decisions about the 'best interests' of women, babies and families to the judgement of the medical profession. It is unclear how one social group is able to make decisions about the best interests of another social group without at least asking them; what is clear is that when decisions about reproductive treatments are left to doctors, considerable social inequalities result. For example the percentage of abortions done under the aegis of the National Health Service (NHS) varies from 21 per cent to 88 per cent in different health authority regions (Fowkes et al., 1979). The reason for this variation is that the 'best interest' decisions of doctors depend on their own personal moralities. These are not evenly distributed geographically, and nor, of course, are they necessarily matched to the preferences of women. A naïve faith in medical wisdom is a vote for the reproductive subjection of women.

Another way to put this is to say that these particular technologies enable men to achieve what they have always wanted – proof of fatherhood. It is not possible to understand why new reproductive technologies happen or what their implications are without asking and answering the question 'What do men want'? Several well-respected anthropologists pointed out many years ago that a recurrent problem of civilization is to define the male role satisfactorily enough – for men (Mead, 1962). It has always been unsatisfactory for men that they have had to rely on women to know that they really are the fathers of their children. One reason is that sometimes they are not – one study that has been quoted quite widely found that 30 per cent of husbands in one town in the South-east of England could not have been the fathers of their children (Phillipp, 1973). Dramatically opposed to this picture of deception and uncertainty is a photograph in *The Guardian* last year that was drawn to my attention by a colleague. It shows Mr Ian Craft, described as Director of Gynaecology at Cromwell Hospital, surrounded by most of the mothers and fifty-eight test-tube babies born under his in-vitro fertilization programme. The photograph carries the byline 'FAST BREEDER' (*The Guardian*, 21 January 85).

Fast breeders may be slow or reluctant to appreciate one of the most difficult contradictions for women of the reproductive scene today – the split between reproduction and childcare. Reproducing the species does not stop on the mock-log-cabin delivery bed – you have to look after the baby as well. This rather obvious point escapes the bizarre logic of modern technology in two particular ways. On a societal level economic investment in expensive medical techniques must compete with other forms of investment, for example in forms of primary health care that support the indigenous ability of a community to care for itself. To take an extreme example, money spent on in-vitro fertilization programmes can be an alternative to investment in primary preventive health-care programmes aimed at eliminating major causes of infertility. Or money spent on the salvage of small babies via high-technology intensive care is money not spent on caring for handicapped children . . . and so on (Council for Science and Society, 1984). On the level of individual experience, the long-term task of parenting may be affected by reproductive technologies in many ways. Dissatisfaction with an unwanted caesarian delivery is not merely a luxury to be credited to the liberation of women, it may also be a primary obstacle to successful parenting – to a sense of positive confidence in motherhood as an authentic female achievement. The problem is that the health-care professionals and the policy-makers think about physical survival and physical mortality and techniques of physical intervention. They do not consider – much – the psychosocial or emotional dimensions of human experience, and so they are bound to have an incomplete picture.

Conclusion

The question is: why is it that in relation to any reproductive technology the recurrent medical question is *not* 'Why do women want it?' but 'Why *don't* women want it?' Unlike the stereotyping of women as patients, which has varied, medical puzzlement about some women's apparent lack of interest in the benefits of medicine is an early and consistent theme. In the latter part of the nineteenth century – and for some decades in this one too – many obstetricians were unable to understand why some women preferred to be cared for by midwives. Then, when antenatal care began during the First World War, the complaint immediately followed that any failure to achieve good results was due to the mothers not turning up for care. 'Most women desire as little examination as possible and do not realize how great a safeguard it may be' said a Ministry of Health report in 1927 (Campbell, 1927, p. 51), while the Short Report in 1980, 'whilst recognising that many women do not like assembly line antenatal care,' nevertheless asserted that 'every effort should be made to encourage women to attend as early as possible in their pregnancy for antenatal care' (Short Report, 1980, pp. 14–15). Between these dates, use of medical care by pregnant women had risen enormously, so the complaint is really not one about the statistics of attendance. It is instead two things. First it is the clamour of a professional group claiming what it sees as its rightful territory: thus the noise of the clamour is louder when the group in question feels the ground shifting under its feet, as bits of it are taken over by other specialities – for instance, paediatrics. But whether it is the contraceptive pill, or seeing the foetus on the ultrasound screen, or amniocentesis to detect handicap, or earlier in the process, pro- grammes of genetic counselling or preconceptual care or artificial modes of fertilization, many doctors do not seem to understand that what they have to offer are not universally desired goods.

The second agenda underlying the medical complaint about women's behaviour concerns obstetrical housework – doctors getting the state of the house in order. Andrea Dworkin, who I quoted earlier, once said that 'For a woman to be good she must be dead' (Dworkin 1975, p. 42). This is a slight exaggeration. But the historical evidence unmistakably points to a societal need to define the place of women and then keep them in it. Medical technology has played a role in this, just as science has been used to describe women's natures and social capabilities. In the early years of this century the women's movement drew attention – in the era before a national health service – to the sufferings of women consequent on their not having enough medical care. Now womens' sufferings are said to be due to too much medical care, whether it is pelvic infection due to an intra-uterine contraceptive device, too many antenatal examinations, or a one-in-nine risk of caesarian section. Somewhere in between the point at which they lacked sufficient care and the point at which they had too much – in fact probably somewhere in the 1950s – a balance was struck, but, as in so many other areas of life, the pursuit of an escalating and socially uncontrolled technology has converted a beneficent scene into a malignant one. In 1958 the social commentator Richard Titmuss noted that 'There is a danger of medicine becoming a technology. There is a danger of a new authoritarianism in medicine. . . . There is the problem of medical power in society; a problem which concerns much more of our national life than simply the organisation of medical care' (Titmuss, 1958, pp. 201–2). Thus the task, Titmuss concluded, was to integrate with medicine's attempt to become scientific, the goal of becoming more 'social', for it was only in this way that science and technology could be truly useful.

3
Foetal Images: the Power of Visual Culture in the Politics of Reproduction

Rosalind Pollack Petchesky

Now chimes the glass, a note of sweetest strength,
It clouds, it clears, my utmost hope it proves,
For there my longing eyes behold at length
A dapper form, that lives and breathes and moves.

Goethe, Faust

[Ultimately] the world of 'being' can function to the exclusion of the mother. No need for mother – provided that there is something of the maternal: and it is the father then who acts as – is – the mother. Either the woman is passive; or she doesn't exist. What is left is unthinkable, unthought of. She does not enter into the oppositions, she is not coupled with the father (who is coupled with the son).

Cixous, Sorties

In the mid-1980s, with the United States Congress still deadlocked over the abortion issue and the Supreme Court having twice reaffirmed 'a woman's right to choose,'[1] the political attack on abortion rights moved further into the terrain of mass culture and imagery. Not that the 'pro-life movement' has abandoned conventional political arenas; rather, its defeats there have hardened its commitment to a more long-term ideological struggle over the symbolic meanings of foetuses, dead or alive.

Anti-abortionists in both the United States and Britain have long applied the principle that a picture of a dead foetus is worth a thousand words. Chaste silhouettes of the foetal form, or voyeuristic-necrophilist photographs of its remains, litter the background of any abortion talk. These still images float like spirits through the courtrooms, where lawyers argue that foetuses can claim tort liability; through the hospitals and clinics, where physicians welcome them as 'patients'; and in front of all the abortion centers, legislative committees, bus terminals and other places that 'right-to-lifers' haunt. The strategy of anti-abortionists to make foetal personhood a self-fulfilling prophecy by making the foetus a *public presence* addresses a visually oriented culture. Meanwhile, finding 'positive' images and symbols of abortion hard to imagine, feminists and other pro-choice advocates have all too readily ceded the visual terrain.

Beginning with the 1984 presidential campaign, the neo-conservative Reagan administration and the Christian Right accelerated their use of television and video imagery to capture political discourse – and power (Erickson, 1985; Kalter, 1985). Along with a new series of 'Ron and Nancy' commercials, the Revd Pat Robertson's '700 Club' (a kind of right-wing talk show), and a resurgence of 'Good versus Evil' kiddie cartoons, American television and video viewers were bombarded with the newest 'pro-life' propaganda piece, *The Silent Scream*. *The Silent Scream* marked a dramatic shift in the contest over abortion imagery. With formidable cunning, it translated the still and by now stale images of foetus as 'baby' into real-time video, thus (1) giving those images an immediate interface with the electronic media; (2) transforming anti-abortion rhetoric from a mainly religious-mystical to a medical/technological mode; and (3) bringing the foetal image 'to life'. On major-network television the foetus rose to instant stardom, as *The Silent Scream* and its impresario, Dr Bernard Nathanson, were aired at least five different times in one month and one well-known reporter, holding up a foetus in a jar before ten million viewers, announced: 'This thing being aborted, this potential person, sure *looks like* a baby!'

This statement is more than just propaganda; it encapsulates the 'politics of style' dominating late capitalist culture, transforming 'surface impressions' into the 'whole message' (Ewen, 1984). The cult of appearances is not only the defining characteristic of national politics in the United States but is also nourished by the language and techniques of photo/video imagery. Aware of cultural trends, the current leadership of the anti-abortion movement has made a conscious strategic shift from religious discourses and authorities to medico-technical ones, in its effort to win over the courts, the legislatures and popular 'hearts and minds'. But the vehicle for this shift is not organized medicine directly but mass culture and its diffusion into reproductive technology through the video display terminal.

My interest in this chapter is to explore the overlapping boundaries between media spectacle and clinical experience when pregnancy becomes a moving picture. In what follows, I attempt to understand the cultural meanings and impact of images like those in *The Silent*

Scream. Then I examine the effect of routine ultrasound imaging of the foetus on not only the larger cultural climate of reproductive politics but the experience and consciousness of pregnant women. Finally, I shall consider some implications of 'foetal images' for feminist theory and practice.

Decoding *The Silent Scream*

Before dissecting its ideological message, I should perhaps describe *The Silent Scream* for readers who somehow missed it. The film's actual genesis seems to have been an article in the *New England Journal of Medicine* by a noted bioethicist and a physician, claiming that early foetal ultrasound tests resulted in 'maternal bonding' and possibly 'fewer abortions' (Fletcher and Evans, 1983). According to the authors, both affiliated with the National Institutes of Health, upon viewing an ultrasound image of the foetus 'parents [i.e., pregnant women] probably will experience a shock of recognition that the fetus belongs to them' and will *more likely resolve 'ambivalent' pregnancies 'in favor of the fetus'*. Such 'parental *recognition of the fetal form,'* they wrote, *'is a fundamental element in the later parent-child bond.'* Although based on two isolated cases, without controls or scientific experimentation, these assertions stimulated the imagination of Dr Bernard Nathanson and the National Right-to-Life Committee. The resulting video production was intended to reinforce the visual 'bonding' theory at the level of the clinic by bringing the live foetal image into everyone's living-rooms. Distributed not only to television networks but to schools, churches, state and federal legislators and anyone (including the opposition) who wants to rent it for $15, the video cassette provides a mass commodity form for the 'pro-life' message.

The Silent Scream purports to show a medical event, a real-time ultrasound imaging of a twelve-week-old foetus being aborted. What we see in fact is an image of an image of an image; or rather, three concentric frames: our television or video cassette recorder screen, which in turn frames the video screen of the filming studio, which in turn frames a shadowy, black-and-white, pulsating blob: the (alleged) foetus. Throughout, our response to this set of images is directed by the figure of Dr Bernard Nathanson – sober, bespectacled, leaning professorially against the desk – who functions as both medical expert and narrator to the drama. (Nathanson is in 'real life' a practicing Ob-Gyn, ex-abortionist, and well-known anti-abortion crusader.) In fact, as the film unfolds, we quickly realize that there are *two* texts being presented here simultaneously – a medical text, largely visual, and a moral text, largely verbal and auditory. Our medical narrator appears on the screen and announces that what we are about to see comes to us courtesy of the 'dazzling' new 'science of fetology' which 'exploded in the medical community' and now enables us to witness an abortion – 'from the victim's vantage point'. At the same time we hear strains of organ music in the background, ominous, the kind we associate with impending doom. As Nathanson guides his pointer along the video screen, 'explaining' the otherwise inscrutable movements of the image, the disjunction between the two texts becomes increasingly jarring. We *see* a recognizable apparatus of advanced medical technology, displaying a filmic image of vibrating light and shaded areas, interspersed with occasional scenes of an abortion clinic operating table (the only view of the pregnant woman we get). This action is moderated by someone who 'looks like' the paternal-medical authority figure of the proverbial aspirin commercial. He occasionally interrupts the filmed events to show us clinical models of embryos and foetuses at various stages of development. Meanwhile, however, what we *hear* is more like a medieval morality play, spoken in standard anti-abortion rhetoric: The form on the screen, we are told, is 'the living unborn child', 'another human being indistinguishable from any of us'. The suction cannula is 'moving violently' toward 'the child'; it is the 'lethal weapon' that will 'dismember, crush, destroy,' 'tear the child apart' until only 'shards' are left. The foetus *'does sense aggression in its sanctuary,'* attempts to 'escape' (indicating more rapid movements on the screen), and finally 'rears back its head' in 'a silent scream' – all to a feverish pitch of musical accompaniment. In case we question the nearly total absence of a pregnant woman or of clinic personnel in this scenario, Nathanson also 'informs' us that the woman who had this abortion was a 'feminist' who, like the young doctor who performed it, has vowed 'never again'; that women who get abortions are themselves exploited 'victims' and '*castrated*'; that many abortion clinics are '*run by the mobs*'. It is the verbal rhetoric, not of science, but of 'Miami Vice'.

Now, all of this raises important questions about what one means by 'evidence', or 'medical information', since the ultrasound image is presented as a *document* testifying that the foetus is 'alive, is 'human like you or me' and 'senses pain'. *The Silent Scream* has been sharply confronted on this level by panels of opposing medical experts, *New York Times* editorials, and a Planned Parenthood film. These show, for example, that at twelve weeks the foetus has no cerebral cortex to receive pain impulses; that no 'scream' is possible without air in the lungs; that foetal movements at this stage are reflexive and without purpose; that the image of rapid frantic movement was undoubtedly caused by speeding up the film (camera tricks); that the size of the image we see on the screen, along with the model that is continually displayed in front of the screen, is nearly twice the size of a normal twelve-week foetus, etc. (Planned Parenthood Federation of America, n.d.). Yet this literal kind of rebuttal is not very useful in helping us to understand the ideological power the film has despite its visual distortions and verbal fraud.

When we locate *The Silent Scream* where it belongs, in the realm of cultural representation rather than medical evidence, we see that it embeds ultrasound imaging of pregnancy in a moving picture show. Its appearance as a medical document both obscures and reinforces a coded set of messages that work as political signs and moral injunctions. (As we shall see, because of the cultural and political context in which they occur, this may be true of ultrasound images of pregnancy in general.) The purpose of the film is obviously didactic: to persuade individual women to abstain from having abortions and officials and judges to force them to do so.

As with any visual image, *The Silent Scream* relies on our predisposition to 'see' what it wants us to 'see' because of a range of influences that come out of the particular culture and history in which we live. The aura of medical authority, the allure of technology, the cumulative impact of a decade of foetal images – on billboards, in shopping-centre malls, in science-fiction blockbusters like *2001: A Space Odyssey* – all rescue the film from utter absurdity; they make it credible. 'The fetal form' itself has, within the larger culture, acquired a symbolic import that condenses within it a series of losses – from sexual innocence to compliant women to American imperial might. It is not the image of a baby at all but of a tiny man, a homunculus.

The most disturbing thing about how people receive *The Silent Scream*, and indeed all the dominant foetal imagery, is their apparent acceptance of the image itself as an accurate representation of a real foetus. The curled-up profile, with its enlarged head and fin-like arms, suspended in its balloon of amniotic fluid, is by now so familiar that not even most feminists question its authenticity (as opposed to its relevance). I went back to trace the earliest appearance of these photos in popular literature and found it in the June 1962 issue of *Look* (a major mass-circulation 'picture magazine' of the period). It was a story publicizing a new book, *The First Nine Months of Life*, and it featured the now-standard sequel of pictures at one day, one week, forty-four days, seven weeks, etc. In every picture the foetus is solitary, dangling in the air (or in its sac) with nothing to connect it to any life-support system but 'a clearly defined umbilical cord'. In every caption it is called 'the baby' and is referred to as 'he' – until the birth, that is, when 'he' turns out to be a girl. Nowhere is there any reference to the pregnant woman, except in a single photograph at the end showing the newborn baby lying next to the mother, both of them gazing off the page, allegedly at 'the father'. From their beginning, such photographs have represented the foetus as primary and autonomous, the woman as absent or peripheral.

Foetal imagery epitomizes the distortion inherent in all photo-graphic images: their tendency to slice up reality into tiny bits wrenched out of real space and time. The origins of photography lie in late-nineteenth-century Europe's cult of science, itself a by-product of industrial capitalism. Its rise linked it inextricably with positivism, that flawed epistemology that sees 'reality' as discrete bits of empirical data divorced from historical process or social relationships (Trachtenberg, 1980; Sontag, 1973, pp. 22–3). Likewise, foetal imagery replicates the essential paradox of photographs whether moving or still, their 'constitutive deception' as noted by post-modernist critics: the *appearance* of 'objectivity', of capturing 'literal reality.' As Roland Barthes puts it (1982, p. 196), the 'photographic message' appears to be 'a message without a code'. According to Barthes, the appearance of the photographic image as 'a mechanical analogue of reality', without art or artifice, obscures the fact that that image is heavily constructed, or 'coded'; it is grounded in a con-text of historical and cultural meanings.[2]

Yet the power of the visual apparatus' claim to be 'an unreasoning machine' that produces 'an unerring record' (the French word for 'lens' is '*l'objectif*') remains deeply embedded in Western culture (Eastlake, 1980, pp. 65–6; Berger, 1980, pp. 48–50; Bazin, 1980, p. 241). This power derives from the peculiar capacity of photo-graphic images to assume two distinct meanings, often simultaneously: an *empirical* (informational) and a *mythical* (or magical) meaning (Sekula, 1982, pp. 106–8). Historically, photographic imagery has served not only the uses of *scientific rationality*, as in medical diag-nostics and record-keeping; and the tools of *bureaucratic rationality*, in the political record-keeping and police surveillance of the state (Sekula, 1982, pp. 94–5; Sontag, 1973, pp. 5, 21). It has also, especially with the 'democratization' of the hand-held camera and the advent of the family album, become a magical source of fetishes that can resurrect the dead or preserve lost love. And it has con-structed the escape-fantasy of the movies. This older, symbolic and ritualistic (also religious?) function lies concealed within the more obvious rationalistic one.

The double text of *The Silent Scream*, noted earlier, recapitulates this historical paradox of photographic images: their simultaneous power as purveyors of fantasy and illusion yet also of 'objectivist "truth"' (Ewen and Ewen, 1982, p. 33). When Nathanson claims to be presenting an abortion 'from the vantage-point of the (foetus)', the image's appearance of seamless movement through real time – *and* the technologic allure of the video box, connoting at once 'advanced medicine' and 'the news' – render his claim 'true to life'. Yet he also purveys a myth, for the foetus – if it had any vantage-point – could not possibly experience itself as if dangling in space, without a woman's uterus and body and bloodstream to support it.

In fact, every image of a foetus we are shown, including *The Silent Scream*, is viewed from the standpoint neither of the foetus nor of the pregnant woman but of the camera. The foetus as we know it is a fetish. Barbara Katz Rothman observes (1986, p. 114): 'The fetus in utero has become a metaphor for "man" in space, floating free, attached only by the umbilical cord to the spaceship. But where is the mother in that metaphor? She has become empty space.' Inside the futurizing spacesuit, however, lies a much older image. For the autonomous, free-floating foetus merely extends to gestation the Hobbesian view of born human beings as disconnected, solitary individuals. It is this abstract individualism, effacing the pregnant woman and the foetus' dependence on her, that gives the foetal image its symbolic transparency, so that we can read in it our selves, our lost babies, our mythic secure past.

While such receptions of foetal images may help to recruit anti-abortion activists, among both men and women, denial of the womb has more deadly consequences. Zoe Sofia relates the film *2001: A Space Odyssey* to 'the New Right's cult of fetal personhood', arguing that: 'In science fiction culture particularly, technologies are perceived as modes of reproduction in themselves, according to perverse myths of fertility in which man replicates himself without the aid of woman' (Sofia, 1984, pp. 48–9). The 'Star Child' of *2001* is not a living organic being but 'a biomechanism . . . a cyborg capable of living unaided in space' (ibid., p. 52). This 'child' poses as the symbol of fertility and life but in fact is the creature of the same technologies that bring cosmic extermination, which it alone survives. Sofia sees the same irony in 'the right-wing movement to protect fetal life' while it plans for nuclear war. Like the foetal-baby in *2001*, 'the pro-life fetus may be a "special effect" of a cultural dreamwork which displaces attention from the tools of extermination and onto the fetal signifier of extinction itself' (ibid., p. 54).

If the foetus-as-spaceman has become inscribed in science fiction and popular fantasy, it is likely to affect the appearance of foetal images even in clinical contexts. The vantage-point of the male onlooker may perhaps change how women see their own foetuses on, and through, ultrasound imaging screens. *The Silent Scream* bridges these two arenas of cultural construction, video fantasyland and clinical biotechnics, enlisting medical imagery in the service of mythic-patriarchal messages. But neither arena, nor the film itself, meets a totally receptive field. Pregnant women respond to these images out of a variety of concrete situations and in a variety of complex ways.

Obstetrical Imaging and Masculine/Visual Culture

We have seen the dominant view of the foetus that appears in still and moving pictures across the mass-cultural landscape. It is one where the foetus is not only 'already a baby', but more – a 'baby man', an autonomous, atomized mini-space hero. This image has not supplanted the one of the foetus as a tiny, helpless, suffering creature but rather merged with it (in a way that reminds one uncomfortably of another famous immortal baby). We should not be surprised, then, to find the social relations of obstetrics – the site where ultrasound imaging of foetuses goes on daily – infiltrated by such widely diffused images.

Along with the external political and cultural pressures, traditional patterns endemic to the male-dominated practice of obstetrics help determine the current clinical view of the foetus as 'patient', separate and autonomous from the pregnant woman. These patterns direct the practical applications of new reproductive technologies more towards enlarging clinicians' control over reproductive processes than towards improving health (women's or infants'). Despite their benefits for individual women, amniocentesis, in-vitro fertilization, electronic foetal monitoring, routine caesarian deliveries, ultrasound and a range of heroic 'foetal therapies' (both *in utero* and *ex utero*) also have the effect of carving out more and more space/time for obstetrical 'management' of pregnancy. Meanwhile, they have not been shown to lower infant and perinatal mortality/morbidity, and they divert social resources from epidemiological research into the causes of foetal damage (Gold, 1984, pp. 240–1; Haverkamp and Orleans, 1982, p. 128; Hubbard, 1984, p. 341). But the presumption of foetal 'autonomy' ('patienthood' if not 'personhood') is not an inevitable requirement of the technologies. Rather, the technologies take on the meanings and uses they do because of the cultural climate of foetal images and the politics of hostility towards pregnant women and abortion. As a result, the pregnant woman is increasingly put in the position of adversary to her own pregnancy/foetus, either by having presented a 'hostile environment' to its development or by actively refusing some medically proposed intervention (for example, a caesarian section or treatment for a foetal 'defect') (Gallagher, 1984; Hubbard, 1984, p. 350; Fletcher, 1981, p. 772; and see chapter 7).

Similarly, the claim by anti-abortion polemicists that the foetus is becoming 'viable' at an earlier and earlier point seems to reinforce the notion that its treatment is a matter between a foetus and its doctor. In reality, most authorities agree that twenty-four weeks is the youngest a foetus is likely to survive outside the womb in the foreseeable future; meanwhile, over 90 per cent of pregnant women who get abortions in the United States do so in the first trimester, fewer than 1 per cent past the twentieth week (Grimes, 1984; Henshaw et al., 1985, pp. 90–2). Despite these facts, the *image* of younger and younger, tinier and tinier foetuses being 'saved'; the point of viability being 'pushed back' *indefinitely*; and untold aborted foetuses being 'born alive', has captured recent abortion discourse in the courts, the headlines and television drama.[3] Such images blur the boundary between foetus and baby; they reinforce the idea that the foetus' identity as separate and autonomous from the mother (the 'living, separate child') exists from the start. Obstetrical technologies of visualization and electronic/surgical intervention thus disrupt the very definition, as traditionally understood, of 'inside' and 'outside' a woman's body, of pregnancy as an 'interior' experience. Increasingly, 'who controls the interpretation of bodily boundaries in medical hermeneutics [becomes] a major feminist issue' (Haraway, 1985, p. 89). Like penetrating Cuban territory with reconnaissance satellites and Radio Marti, treating a foetus *as if it were* outside a woman's body, because it can be viewed, is a political act.

This background is necessary to an analysis that locates ultrasound imaging of foetuses within its historical and cultural context. Originating in sonar detectors for submarine warfare, ultrasound was not introduced into obstetrical practice until the early 1960s – some years after its accepted use in other medical diagnostic fields (Gold, 1984, p. 240; Graham, 1982, p. 39). The timing is significant, for it corresponds to the end of the baby boom and the rapid drop in fertility that would propel obstetricians and gynaecologists into new areas of discovery and fortune, a new 'patient population' to look at and treat. 'Looking' was mainly the point, since, as in many medical technologies (and technologies of visualization), physicians seem to have applied the technique before knowing precisely what they were *looking for*. In this technique, a transducer sends sound-waves through the amniotic fluid so they bounce off foetal structures and are reflected back, either as a still image (scan) or, more frequently, a real-time moving image 'similar to that of a motion picture' (as the American College of Obstetricians and Gynecologists put it, ACOG, 1981, p. 56).

While greatly hailed among physicians for its advantages over the dangers of X-ray, ultrasound imaging in pregnancy is currently steeped in controversy. A 1984 report by a joint National Institutes of Health/Food and Drug Administration panel in the United States found 'no clear benefit from routine use', specifically, 'no improvement in pregnancy outcome' (either for the foetus/infant or the woman) and no conclusive evidence either of its safety or harm. The panel recommended against 'routine use', including 'to view . . . or obtain a picture of the fetus' or 'for educational or commercial demonstrations without medical benefit to the patient' ('the patient' here, presumably, being the pregnant woman). Yet it approved of its use to 'estimate gestational age', thus qualifying its reservations with a major loophole (Shearer, 1984, pp. 25–6, 30; Gold, 1984, pp. 240–1). At least one-third of all pregnant women in the United States are now exposed to ultrasound imaging, and that would seem to be a growing figure. Anecdotal evidence suggests that many if not most pregnancies will soon include ultrasound scans and presentation of a sonogram photo 'for the baby album' (Gold, p. 240).

How can we understand the routinization of foetal imaging in obstetrics even though the profession's governing bodies admit the medical benefits are dubious? The reasons why ultrasound imaging in obstetrics has expanded so much are no doubt related to the reasons, economic and patriarchal, for the growth in electronic foetal monitoring, caesarian sections and other reproductive technologies. Practitioners and critics alike commonly trace the obstetrical technology boom to physicians' fear of malpractice suits. But the impulses behind ultrasound also arise from the codes of visual imagery and the construction of foetal images as 'cultural objects' with historical meanings.

From the standpoint of clinicians, at least three levels of meaning attach to ultrasound images of foetuses. These correspond to (1) a level of 'evidence' or 'report', which may or may not motivate diagnosis and/or therapeutic intervention; (2) a level of surveillance and potential social control; and (3) a level of fantasy or myth. (Not surprisingly, these connotations echo the textual structure of *The Silent Scream.*) In the first place, there is simply the impulse to 'view', to get a 'picture' of the foetus' 'anatomical structures' in motion; and here obstetrical ultrasound reflects the impact on new imaging technologies in all areas of medicine. One is struck by the lists of 'indications' for ultrasound imaging found in the *ACOG Technical Bulletin* and the *American Journal of Obstetrics and Gynecology* indexes. While including a few recognizable 'abnormal' conditions that might require a 'non-routine' intervention (for example, 'evaluation of ectopic pregnancy', or 'diagnosis of abnormal fetal position'), for the most part these consist of technical measurements, like a list of machine parts – 'crown rump length', 'gestational sac diameter', foetal sex organs, foetal weight – as well as estimation of gestational age. As one neonatologist told me, 'We can do an entire anatomical workup!' (Dr Alan Fleischman, personal communication). Of course, none of this viewing and measuring and recording of bits of anatomical data gives the slightest clue as to what *value* should be placed on this or any other foetus; whether it has a moral claim to heroic therapy or life at all; and who should decide (Petchesky, 1985, chapter 9). But the point is that the foetus, through visualization, is being treated as a patient already, is being given an ordinary check-up. Inferences about its 'personhood' (or 'babyhood') seem verified by sonographic 'evidence' that it kicks, spits, excretes, grows.

Evidentiary uses of photographic images are usually enlisted in the service of some kind of action – to monitor, control and possibly intervene. In the case of obstetrical medicine, ultrasound techniques, in conjunction with electronic foetal monitoring (EFM), have been used increasingly to diagnose 'foetal distress' and 'abnormal presentation' (leading to a prediction of 'prolonged labor' or 'breech birth'). These findings then become evidence indicating earlier delivery by caesarian section, evoking the correlation some researchers have observed between increased use of EFM and ultrasound and the threefold rise in the caesarian section rate in the last fifteen years (Sheehan, 1985; Haverkamp and Orleans, 1982, p. 127).

Complaints by feminist health advocates against unnecessary caesarians and excessive monitoring of pregnancy are undoubtedly justified. Even the profession's own guidelines suggest that the monitoring techniques may lead to misdiagnoses or may themselves be the cause of the 'stresses' they 'discover' (ACOG, 1981, p. 58). One might well question a tendency in obstetrics to 'discover' disorders where they previously did not exist because visualizing techniques compel 'discovery', or to apply techniques to wider and wider groups of cases (Thacker and Banta, 1982, p. 173). On the whole, however, diagnostic uses of ultrasound in obstetrics have benefited women more than they've done harm, making it possible to define the due date more accurately, to detect anomalies and to anticipate complications in delivery. My question is not about this level of medical applications but rather about the cultural assumptions underlying them. How do these assumptions both reflect and reinforce the larger culture of foetal images sketched above? Why has the impulse to 'see inside' come to dominate ways of knowing about pregnancy and foetuses, and what are the consequences for women's consciousness and reproductive power relations?

The 'prevalence of the gaze', or the privileging of the visual as the primary means to knowledge in Western scientific and philosophical traditions, has been the subect of a feminist inquiry by Evelyn Fox Keller and Christine Grontkowski. In their analysis, stretching from Plato to Bacon and Descartes, this emphasis on the visual has had a paradoxical function. For sight, in contrast to the other sense, has as its peculiar property the capacity for *detachment*, for *objectifying* the thing visualized by creating distance between knower and known. (In modern optics, the eye becomes a passive recorder, a camera obscura.) In this way, the elevation of the visual in a hierarchy of senses actually has the effect of *debasing* sensory experience, and relatedness, as modes of knowing: 'Vision connects us to truth as it distances us from the corporeal' (Keller and Grontkowski, 1983, pp. 207–18).

Some feminist cultural theorists in France, Britain and the United States have argued that visualization and objectification as privileged ways of knowing are *specifically masculine* (man the viewer, woman the spectacle: Irigaray, 1981, p. 101; Kuhn, 1982, pp. 60–5, 113; Mulvey, 1975; Kaplan, 1983, p. 324). Without falling into such essentialism, we may suppose that the language, perceptions and uses of visual information may be different for women, as pregnant subjects, than they are for men (or women) as physicians, researchers or reporters. And this difference will reflect the historical control by men over science, medicine and obstetrics in Western society; and the historical definitions of masculinity in Western culture. The deep gender-bias of science (including medicine), of its very ways of seeing problems, resonates, Keller argues, in its 'common rhetoric'. Mainly 'adversarial' and 'aggressive' in its stance towards what it studies, 'science can come to sound like a battlefield' (Keller, 1985, pp. 123–4). Likewise, presentations of scientific and medical 'conquests' in the mass media commonly appropriate this terrain into cold war culture and macho style. Consider this piece of text from *Life's* 1965 picture story on ultrasound in pregnancy. 'A Sonar "Look" at an Unborn Baby':

The astonishing medical machine resting on this pregnant woman's abdomen in a Philadelphia hospital is 'looking' at her unborn child in precisely the same way a Navy surface ship homes in on enemy sub-marines. Using the sonar principle, it is bombarding her with a beam of ultra-high-frequency sound waves that are inaudible to the human ear. Back come the echoes, bounding off the baby's head, to show up as a visual image on a viewing screen. (p. 45)

The militarization of obstetrical images is not implicit in the origin of the technology (most technologies in a militarized society either begin or end in the military); nor in its focus on reproduction (similar language constructs the 'war on cancer'). Might it then correspond to the very culture of medicine and science, its emphasis on visualization as a form of surveillance and 'attack'? For some obstetricians and gynaecologists, such visualization is patently voyeuristic; it generates erotic pleasure in the non-reciprocated, illicit 'look'. Interviewed in *Newsweek* after *The Silent Scream* was released, Nathanson boasted: 'With the aid of technology, *we stripped away the walls of the abdomen and uterus and looked into the womb*' ('America's Abortion Dilemma', 1985, p. 21 [emphasis added]). And here is Dr Michael Harrison writing in a respected medical journal about 'foetal management' through ultrasound:

The fetus could not be taken seriously as long as he (sic) remained a medical recluse in an opaque womb; and it was not until the last half of this century that *the prying eye of the ultrasonogram* . . . rendered the once opaque womb transparent, *stripping the veil of mystery from the dark inner sanctum*, and *letting the light of scientific observation fall on the shy and secretive fetus* . . . The sonographic voyeur, *spying on the unwary fetus*, finds him or her a surprisingly active little creature, and not at all the passive parasite we had imagined. (Quoted in Hubbard, 1984, p. 348) [emphasis added]

Whether or not voyeurism is a 'masculinist' form of looking, the 'siting' of the womb as a space to be conquered can only be had by one who stands outside it looking in. The view of the foetus as a 'shy', 'mysterious little creature', recalling a wildlife photographer tracking down a gazelle, indeed exemplifies the 'predatory nature of a photographic consciousness' (Haraway, 1985, p. 89; Sontag, 1973, pp. 13–14). It is hard to imagine a pregnant woman thinking about her foetus this way, whether she longs for a baby or wishes an abortion.

What we have here, from the clinician's standpoint, is a kind of *panoptics of the womb*, whose aim is 'to establish normative behaviour for the fetus at various gestational stages' and to maximize medical control over pregnancy (Hubbard, 1984, p. 349, quoting the Chief of Maternal and Fetal Medicine at a Boston hospital; cf.

Graham, 1982, pp. 49–50). Feminist critics emphasize the degrading impact that foetal imaging techniques have on the pregnant woman. She now becomes the 'maternal environment', the 'site' of the foetus, a passive spectator in her own pregnancy (Hubbard, 1984, p. 350; Rothman, 1986, pp. 113–15). Sonographic detailing of foetal anatomy completely displaces the markers of 'traditional' pregnancy, when 'feeling the baby move was a "definitive" diagnosis.' Now the woman's *felt* evidence about the pregnancy is discredited, in favour of the more 'objective' data on the video screen. We find her

> on the table with the ultrasound scanner to her belly, and on the other side of the technician or doctor, the fetus on the screen. The doctor . . . turns *away* from the mother to examine her baby. Even the heartbeat is heard over a speaker removed from the mother's body. The technology which makes the baby/fetus more 'visible' renders the woman invisible. (Rothman, 1986, p. 113)

Earlier I noted that ultrasound imaging of foetuses is constituted through three levels of meaning – not only the level of evidence (diagnosis) and the level of surveillance (intervention), but also that of fantasy or myth. 'Evidence' shades into fantasy when the foetus is visualized, albeit through electronic media, as though removed from the pregnant woman's body, as though suspended in space. This is a form of fetishization, and it occurs repeatedly in clinical settings whenever ultrasound images construct the foetus through 'indications' that sever its functions and parts from their organic connection to the pregnant woman. Fetishization, in turn, shades into surveillance when physicians, 'right-to-life' propagandists, legislatures, or courts impose ultrasound imaging on pregnant women in order 'to encourage "bonding"'. In some states, the use of compulsory ultrasound imaging as a weapon of intimidation against women seeking abortions has already begun (Gold, 1984, p. 242). Indeed, the very idea of 'bonding' based on a photographic image implies a fetish: the investment of erotic feelings in a fantasy. When an obstetrician presents his patient with a sonographic picture of the foetus 'for the baby album', it may be a manifestation of masculine desire to reproduce not only babies but motherhood.

Many feminists have explained masculine appropriation of the conditions and products of reproduction in psychoanalytic or psychological terms, associating it with men's fears of the body, their own mortality and the mother who bore them. According to one interpretation, 'the domination of women by the male gaze is part of men's strategy to contain the threat that the mother embodies [of infantile dependence and male impotence]' (Kaplan, 1983, p. 324; cf.

Benjamin, 1983, p. 295). Nancy Hartsock, in a passage reminiscent of Simone de Beauvoir's earlier insights, links patriarchal control over reproduction to the masculine quest for immortality through immortal works: 'because to be born means that one will die, reproduction and generation are either understood in terms of death or are appropriated by men in disembodied form' (Hartsock, 1983b, p. 253). In Mary O'Brien's analysis of the 'dialectics of reproduction', 'the alienation of the male seed in the copulative act' separates men 'from genetic continuity'. Men therefore try to 'annul' this separation by appropriating children, wives, principles of legitimacy and inheritance, estates and empires. (With her usual irony, O'Brien calls this male fear of female procreativity 'the dead core of impotence in the potency principle'.) (O'Brien, 1983, pp. 29–37, 50, 60–1, 139). Other, more historically grounded feminist writers have extended this theme to the appropriation of obstetrics in Britain and the United States. Attempts by male practitioners to disconnect the foetus from women's wombs – whether physically, through forceps, caesarian delivery, in-vitro fertilization, or foetal surgery; or visually, through ultrasound imaging – are specific forms of the ancient masculine impulse 'to confine and limit and curb the creativity and potentially polluting power of female procreation' (Oakley, 1976, p. 57; cf. Corea, 1985a p. 303 and chapter 16; Rich, 1976, chapter 6; Ehrenrich and English, 1978; and Oakley, 1980).

But feminist critiques of 'the war against the womb' often suffer from certain tendencies towards reductionism. First, they confuse masculine rhetoric and fantasies with actual power relations, thereby submerging women's own responses to reproductive situations in the dominant (and victimizing) masculine text. Secondly, if they do consider women's responses, those responses are compressed into Everywoman's Reproductive Consciousness, undifferentiated by particular historical and social circumstances; biology itself becomes a universal rather than an individual, particular set of conditions. To correct this myopia, I shall return to the study of foetal images through a different lens, that of pregnant women as viewers.

Picturing the Baby – Women's Responses

The scenario of the voyeuristic ultrasound instrument/technician, with the pregnant woman displaced to one side passively staring at her objectified foetus, has a certain phenomenological truth. At the same time, anecdotal evidence gives us another, quite different scenario when it comes to the subjective understanding of pregnant women themselves. Far from feeling victimized or pacified, they frequently express a sense of elation and *direct participation* in the imaging process, claiming it 'makes the baby more real', 'more our baby'; that visualizing the foetus creates a feeling of intimacy and belonging, as well as a reassuring sense of predictability and control (Hubbard, 1984, p. 335; Rothman, 1986, pp. 202, 212–13; author's private conversations with recent mothers). (I am speaking here of women whose pregnancies are wanted, of course, not those seeking an abortion.) Some women even talk about themselves as having 'bonded' with the foetus through viewing its image on the screen (Rothman, 1986, pp. 113–14). Like amniocentesis, in-vitro fertilization, voluntary sterilization and other 'male-dominated' reproductive technologies, ultrasound imaging in pregnancy seems to evoke in many women a sense of greater control and self-empowerment than they would have if left to 'traditional' methods or 'nature'. How are we to understand this contradiction between the feminist decoding of male 'cultural dreamworks' and (some) women's actual experience of reproductive techniques and images?

Current feminist writings about reproductive technology are not very helpful in answering this kind of question. Works such as Corea's *The Mother Machine* and most articles in the anthology, *Test-Tube Women*, portray women as the perennial victims of an omnivorous male plot to take over their reproductive capacities. The specific forms taken by male strategies of reproductive control, while admittedly varying across times and cultures, are reduced to a pervasive, transhistorical 'need'. Meanwhile, women's own resistance to this control, often successful, as well as their complicity in it, are ignored; women in this view, have no role as agents of their reproductive destinies.

But historical and sociological research shows that women are not just passive victims of 'male' reproductive technologies and the doctors who wield them. Because of their shared reproductive situation and needs, women throughout the nineteenth and twentieth centuries have often *generated* demands for such technologies (for example, birth control, childbirth anaesthesia, or infertility treatments), or welcomed them as benefits (which is not to say that the technologies offered always met the needs) Gordon, 1977; McLaren, 1978; Lewis, 1980, chapter 4; Petchesky, 1981; Petchesky, 1985, chapter 1 and 5). We have to understand the 'market' for the pill, sterilization, IVF, amniocentesis and high-tech pregnancy monitoring as a more complex phenomenon than either the victimization or the male-womb-envy thesis allows.

At the same time, theories of a 'feminist standpoint' or 'reproductive consciousness' that would restore pregnant women to active
historical agency and unify their responses to reproductive images
and techniques are complicated by two sets of circumstances
(O'Brien, 1983, chapter 1; Hartsock, 1983b, chapter 10). First, we do
not simply imbibe our reproductive experience raw. The dominant
images and codes that mediate the material conditions of pregnancy,
abortion, etc., determine what exactly women 'know' about these
events in their lives, their *meaning* as lived experience. Thus, women
may see in foetal images what they are told they ought to see. John
Berger distinguishes between 'photographs which belong to private
experience' and thus connect to our lives in some intimate way, and
'public photographs', which excise bits of information 'from all lived
experience' (Berger, 1980, p. 51). This distinction helps indicate
important differences between the meanings of foetal images when
they are viewed as 'the foetus' and when they are viewed as 'my
baby'. Women's ways of seeing ultrasound images of foetuses, even
their own, may be affected by the cumulative array of 'public'
representations, from *Life* magazine to *The Silent Scream*. It
possibly means that some of them will be intimidated from getting
abortions – although as yet we have little empirical information to
verify this. When young women seeking abortions are coerced or
manipulated into seeing pictures of foetuses, their own or others, it is
the 'public foetus' as moral abstraction that they are being made to
view.

A second problem for 'standpoint theory', in dialectical tension
with the first, is that women's relationship to reproductive
technologies and images differs depending on social differences such
as class, race and sexual preference, and biological ones such as age,
physical disability and personal fertility history. Their 'reproductive
consciousness' is constituted out of these complex elements, and cannot easily be generalized or, unfortunately, vested with a privileged
insight. The reception and meanings of foetal images derive not only
from representations but also from the particular circumstances of
the woman as viewer. These circumstances may belie a model of
women as victims of reproductive technologies. Above all, the
meanings of foetal images will differ depending on whether a woman
wishes to be pregnant or not. With regard to wanted pregnancies,
women with very diverse political values may respond positively to
images that present their foetus as if detached, their own body as if
absent from the scene. The reasons are a complex weave of socio-
economic position, gender psychology and biology. At one end of
the spectrum, the 'pro-life' women whom Kristin Luker interviewed,

identified 'the foetus' strongly with their own recent, or frequent, pregnancies; it became 'my little guy'. Their circumstances as 'devout, traditional women who valued motherhood highly' were those of married women with children, mostly unemployed outside the home, and remarkably isolated from any social or community activities. That 'little guy' was indeed their primary source of gratification and self-esteem. Moreover – and this fact links them with many women whose abortion politics and life-styles lie at the opposite end of the spectrum – a disproportionate number of them seems to have undergone a history of pregnancy loss or child loss (Luker, 1984, pp. 132, 138–9, 150–1).

If we look at the women who comprise the market for high-tech obstetrics, they are primarily those who can afford these expensive procedures and who have access to the private medical offices where they are offered. Socially and demographically, they are not only apt to be among the professional, educated, 'late-child-bearing' cohort who face greater risks because of age (although the average age of amniocentesis and ultrasound recipients seems to be moving down rapidly). More importantly, whatever their age or risk category, they are likely to be products of a middle-class culture that values planning, control and predictability in the interests of a 'quality' baby (Fine and Asch, 1985, pp. 8–9; Hubbard, 1984, p. 336). These values pre-date technologies of visualization and 'baby engineering' and create a predisposition towards their acceptance. The fear of 'non-quality' – that is, disability – and the pressure on parents, particularly mothers, to produce foetuses that score high on their 'stress test' (like infants who score high on their Apgar test and children who score high on their Scholastic Aptitude Tests), is a cultural as well as a class phenomenon. Indeed, the 'perfect baby' syndrome that creates a welcoming climate for ultrasound imaging may also be oppressive for women, in so far as they are still the ones who bear primary responsibility – and guilt – for how the baby turns out (Hubbard, 1984, p. 344). Despite this, 'listening to women's voices' leads to the unmistakable conclusion that, as with birth-control generally, many women prefer predictability and will do what they can to have it.

Women's responses to foetal picture-taking may have another side as well, rooted in their traditional position in the production of family photographs. If photographs accommodate 'aesthetic consumerism', becoming instruments of 'appropriation' and 'possession', this is nowhere truer than within family life – particularly middle-class family life (Sontag, 1982, p. 8). 'Family albums' originated to chronicle the continuity of Victorian bourgeois kin-networks. The advent of 'home movies' in the 1940s and 1950s paralleled the move to the suburbs and backyard barbecues (Zimmerman, 1986). Likewise, the presentation of a sonogram photo to the dying grandfather, even before his grandchild's birth (Rothman, 1986, p. 125), is a 1980s way of affirming patriarchal lineage. In other words, far from the intrusion of an alien and alienating technology, it may be that ultrasonography is becoming enmeshed in a familiar language of 'private' images.

Significantly, in each of these cases it is the woman, the mother, who acts as custodian of the image – keeping up the album, taking the movies, presenting the sonogram. The specific relationship of women to photographic images, especially those of children, may help to explain the attraction of pregnant women to ultrasound images of their own foetus (as opposed to 'public' ones). Rather than being surprised that some women experience 'bonding' with their foetus after viewing its image on a screen (or in a sonographic 'photo'), perhaps we should understand this as a culturally embedded component of desire. If it is a form of 'objectifying' the foetus (and the pregnant woman herself as detached from the foetus), perhaps such objectification and detachment are necessary for her to feel erotic pleasure in it (Weir and Casey, 1984, pp. 144–5). If with the ultrasound image she first recognizes the foetus as 'real', as 'out there', this means that she first experiences it as an object she can possess.

Evelyn Keller proposes that feminists re-evaluate the concept of 'objectivity'. In so doing they may discover that the process of 'objectification' they have identified as 'masculinist' takes different forms, some which detach the viewer from the viewed and some which make possible both erotic and intellectual attachment (Keller, 1985, pp. 70–3, 98–100, 117–20). To suggest that the timing of maternal–foetus or maternal–infant attachment is a biological given (for example, at 'quickening' or at birth), or that 'feeling' is somehow more 'natural' than 'seeing', contradicts women's changing historical experience (cf. Rothman, 1986, pp. 41–2). On the other hand, to acknowledge that 'bonding' is a historically and culturally shaped process is not to deny its reality. That women develop powerful feelings of attachment to their ('private') foetuses, especially the ones they want, complicates the politics of foetal images.

Consider a recent case in a New York court that denied a woman damages when her twenty week foetus was stillborn, following an apparently botched amniocentesis. The majority held that, since the woman did not 'witness' the death or injury directly, and was not in the immediate 'zone of danger' herself, she could not recover damages for any emotional pain or loss she suffered as a result of the foetus' death. As one dissenting judge argued, the court 'rendered the woman a bystander to medical procedures performed upon her own body', denying her any rights based on the emotional and 'biological bond' she had with the foetus (Margolick, 1985). In so doing, the majority implicitly sanctioned the image of foetal autonomy and maternal oblivion.

As a feminist used to resisting women's reduction to biology, I find it awkward to defend their biological connection to the foetus. But the patent absurdity and cruelty of this decision underscore the need for feminist analyses of reproduction to address biology. A true biological perspective does not lead us to determinism but rather to infinite *variation*, which is to say that it is historical (cf. Riley, 1983, p. 17 and chapters 1–2). Particular lives are lived in particular bodies – not only 'women's bodies', but just as relevantly, ageing, ill, disabled, or infertile ones. The material circumstances that differentiate women's responses to obstetrical ultrasound and other technologies include their own biological history, which may be experienced as one of limits and defeats. In fact, the most significant divider between pregnant women who welcome the information from ultrasound and other monitoring techniques and those who resent the machines or wish to postpone 'knowing' may be personal fertility history. A recent study of women's psychological responses to the use of electronic foetal monitors during labour

> found that those women who had previously experienced the loss of a baby tended to react positively to the monitor, feeling it to be a reassuring presence, a substitute for the physician, an aid to communication. Those women who had not previously suffered difficult or traumatic births . . . tended to regard the monitor with hostility, as a distraction, a competitor. (Bates and Turner, 1985)

To recite such conditions does not mean we have to retreat into a reductionist or dualist view of biology. Infertility, pregnancy losses and women's feelings of 'desperation' about 'childlessness' have many sources, including cultural pressures, environmental hazards and medical misdiagnosis or neglect (Albury, 1984, pp. 57–8). Whatever the sources, however, a history of repeated miscarriages, infertility, ectopic pregnancy, or loss of a child is likely to dispose a pregnant woman favourably to techniques which allow her to visualize the pregnancy and *possibly* to gain some control over its outcome.[4] Pregnancy – as biosocial experience – acts on women's bodies in different ways, with the result that the relation of their bodies, and consciousness, to reproductive technologies may also differ.

Attachment of pregnant women to their foetuses at earlier stages in pregnancy becomes an issue, not because it is cemented through 'sight' rather than 'feel', but when and if it is used to obstruct or harass an abortion decision.[5] In fact, there is no reason why any woman's abortion decision should be tortured in this way, since there is no medical rationale for requiring her to view an image of her foetus. Responsible abortion clinics are doing ultrasound imaging in selected cases – *only* to determine foetal size or placement, where the date of the woman's last menstrual period is unknown, the pregnancy is beyond the first trimester, or there is a history of problems; or to diagnose an ectopic pregnancy. But in such cases the woman herself does not see the image, since the monitor is placed outside her range of vision and clinic protocols refrain from showing her the picture unless she specifically requests it.[6] In the current historical context, to consciously limit the use of foetal images in abortion clinics is to take a political stance, to resist the message of *The Silent Scream*. This reminds us that the politics of reproductive technologies are constructed contextually, out of who uses them, how and for what purposes.

The view that 'reproductive engineering' is imposed on 'women as a class' rather than being sought by them as a means towards greater 'choice' (Corea, 1985a, p. 313) obscures the particular reality, not only of women with fertility problems and losses, but also of other groups. For lesbians who utilize sperm banks and artificial insemination to achieve biological pregnancy without heterosexual sex, such technologies are a critical tool of reproductive freedom. Are lesbians to be told that wanting their 'own biological children' generated through their own bodies is somehow wrong for them but not for fertile heterosexual couples? (cf. Fine and Asch, 1985). The majority of poor and working-class women in the United States and Britain still have no access to amniocentesis, IVF and the rest, although they (particularly women of colour) have the highest rates of infertility and foetal impairment. It would be wrong to ignore their lack of access to these techniques on the ground that worrying about how babies turn out, or wanting to have 'your own', is only a middle-class (or eugenic) prejudice.

In Europe, Australia and North America feminists are currently engaged in heated debate over whether new reproductive technologies present a threat or an opportunity for women. Do they simply reinforce the age-old pressures on women to bear children, and to bear them to certain specifications, or do they give women more control? What sort of control do we require in order to have reproductive freedom, and are there/should there be any limits on our control? (Gorovitz, 1982, p. 1). What is the meaning of reproductive technologies that tailor-make infants, in a context where childcare remains the private responsibility of women and many women are growing increasingly poor? Individual women, especially middle-class women, are choosing to utilize high-tech obstetrics, and their choices may not always be ones we like. It may be that chorionic villus sampling, the new first trimester prenatal diagnostic technique, will increase the use of selective abortion for sex. Moreover, the bias against disability that underlies the quest for the 'perfect child' seems undeniable. Newer methods of prenatal diagnosis may mean that more and more abortions become 'selective', so that more women decide 'to abort the particular fetus [they] are carrying in hopes of coming up with a "better" one next time' (Hubbard, 1984, p. 334). Are these choices moral? Do we have a right to judge them? Can we even say they are 'free'?

On the other hand, techniques for imaging foetuses and pregnancies may, depending on their cultural contexts and uses, offer means for empowering women, both individually and collectively. We need to examine these possibilities and to recognize that, at the present stage in history, feminists have no common standpoint about how women ought to use this power.

Conclusion

Images by themselves lack 'objective' meanings; meanings come from the interlocking fields of context, communication, application and reception. If we removed from the ultrasound image of *the Silent Scream* its title, its text, its sound narrative, Dr Nathanson, the media and distribution networks and the whole anti-abortion political climate, what would remain? But of course, the question is absurd, since no image dangles in a cultural void, just as no foetus floats in a space capsule. The problem clearly becomes, then, how do we change the contexts, media and consciousnesses through which foetal images are defined? Here are some proposals, both modest and Utopian.

First, we have to restore women to a central place in the pregnancy scene. To do this, we must create new images that recontextualize the foetus: that place it back into the uterus, and the uterus back into the woman's body and her body back into its social space. Contexts do not neatly condense into symbols; they must be told through stories that give them mass and dimension. For example, a brief prepared from thousands of letters received in an abortion rights campaign and presented to the United States Supreme Court in its most recent abortion case, translates women's abortion stories into a legal text. Boldly filing a procession of real women before the court's eyes, it materializes them in not only their bodies but their jobs, families, school-work, health problems, young age, poverty, race/ethnic identity and dreams of a better life (Paltrow, 1986).

Secondly, we need to separate the power relations within which reproductive technologies, including ultrasound imaging, are applied from the technologies themselves. If women were truly empowered in the clinic setting, as practitioners and patients, would we discard the technologies? Or would we use them differently, integrating them into a more holistic clinical dialogue between women's felt knowledge and the technical information 'discovered' in the test-tube or on the screen? Before attacking reproductive technology, we need to demand that all women have access to the knowledge and resources to judge its uses and to use it wisely, in keeping with their own particular needs.

Finally, we should pursue the discourse now begun towards developing a feminist ethic of reproductive freedom that complements feminist politics. What ought we to choose if we became genuinely free to choose? Are some choices unacceptable on moral grounds, and does this mean under any circumstances, or only under some? Can feminism reconstruct a joyful sense of childbearing and maternity without capitulating to ideologies that reduce women to a maternal essence? Can we talk about morality in reproductive decision-making without invoking the spectre of maternal duty? On some level, the struggle to demystify foetal images is fraught with danger, since it involves *re-embodying* the foetus, thus representing women as (wanting-to-be or not-wanting-to-be) pregnant persons. One way out of this danger is to image the pregnant woman, not as an abstraction, but within her total framework of relationships, economic and health needs and desires. Once we have pictured the social conditions of her freedom, however, we have not dissolved the contradictions in how she might use it.

Acknowledgements

The following people have given valuable help in the research and revision of the manuscript for this chapter, but are in no way responsible for its outcome: Fina Bathrick, Rayna Rapp, Ellen Ross,

Michelle Stanworth and Sharon Thompson. I would also like to thank the Institute for Policy Studies, the Barnard College Scholar and the Feminist Conference 1986 and *Ms Magazine* for opportunities to present pieces of it in progress.

4
Artificial Insemination, In-vitro Fertilization and the Stigma of Infertility
Naomi Pfeffer

The recent controversy over the new methods of overcoming involuntary childlessness has focused on the ethical aspects of the technique. On one side of the debate are those who claim that the new techniques are the beneficent outcome of scientific and medical progress administered by sympathetic and enlightened medical practitioners. As one Member of Parliament put it during the debate on Enoch Powell's *Unborn Child Protection Bill:*

> The object of our interest in medical research into embryology and human fertilisation is to help humanity. It is to help those who are infertile and to help control infertility. . . . The researchers are not monsters, but scientists. They are medical scientists working in response to a great human need. We should be proud of them. The infertile parents who have been helped are grateful to them. (House of Commons Debates, 1984–5, 73, column 654)

Opposing this view are those who see these means of treating infertility as misguided and unethical because they see them as meddling with the secrets of life itself. This technology, they argue, 'promises benefits perhaps, but [it] could end by destroying the essential humanity of man. . . . The technology that promised a paradise now shows signs of delivering a hell' (ibid., column 649). Furthermore, the much-vaunted potential benefits of these techniques are, they claim, simply the exonerations of the self-seeking. As another Member of Parliament put it, 'Necessity is undoubtedly the argument of those who do not wish to be constrained by ethics or even doubts as to where their monstrous techniques for freezing, cloning, manipulating and killing human embryos are leading medical ethics' (ibid., column 664).

A focus on ethical considerations effectively excludes any discussion of the social and historical context of the condition of infertility.

Consequently, none of the many different and often opposing reasons given for the recent interest in new techniques to overcome infertility can be challenged persuasively. Furthermore, this absence of a social and historical context has had an unfortunate consequence for infertile men and women, which is that in the course of considerable public exposure given to infertility, the stigma of infertility has been compounded. Providing a social context has therefore another and to me a more important purpose; that purpose is to deconstruct the stigma of infertility. This chapter examines three separate issues; first, the social processes that shape the experience of infertility; secondly, the recent history of the medical treatment of infertility; thirdly, the form and content of the public debates about different treatments of infertility which have taken place since the Second World War.

What causes infertility? This question is rarely addressed; the social factors that may cause infertility, such as environmental hazards, hormonal contraceptives or nutritional status are not examined. Instead it is implied that infertile men and women are struck down by a spontaneous idiopathic condition, a calamity hearkening back to biblical stories. The only statistics we are offered are unreliable estimates of the frequency with which various reproductive organs let their owner down; how many people can blame an ovary, testicle, fallopian tube or pituitary gland. But we are told little else about what sort of people become infertile. Are they rich or poor, working or unemployed, white- or blue-collar, happily or unhappily married, Black or white, Christian or Muslim? We are not told. Nor are we offered any explanation of why they want children, perhaps because having a child is treated as a natural outcome of marriage and normative heterosexual relationships. It seems that once you find yourself involuntarily childless, all other identifying marks are washed away. Of course, such transformations are not unusual; they are the hallmark of socially stigmatized conditions.

Besides their involuntary childlessness there is one characteristic which the infertile are said to share, that of desperation. The word desperation or some such synonym appears so frequently in conjunction with infertility that sometimes it appears that what troubles infertile men and women is not the absence of a child as such but some form of emotional disorder related to their failure. Desperation combined with infertility appears to produce a particularly potent mix; one that forces fecund women to lease their womb, sends infertile men and women scouring the world for orphans to adopt and incites some doctors into developing new techniques that subject people to many indignities.

Does infertility lead inevitably to unremitting desperation? Infertility is a very negative experience and at times most infertile men and woman probably will feel desperate. But desperation is only one of many different emotions that infertility can arouse, and not all of these are negative. There are positive aspects to childlessness which are rarely mentioned, or which are glossed as selfishness. Furthermore, desperation may not be a result of the condition of infertility but of the insensitive and humiliating treatment sometimes received at the hands of medical and other authorities, the very people who claim to be interested in rescuing the infertile from desperation. Focusing on desperation to the exclusion of all other emotions serves not to explain but to make a caricature of infertile men and women.

Physical infertility is not synonymous with involuntary childlessness. It is generally forgotten that some men and women are childless because of social and not physical impediments (Porter, 1984). The litmus test of physical fertility is conception and the safe delivery of a live baby. With few exceptions, no one knows in advance of trying to conceive whether they are fertile or not. Those people rendered sterile by their genes or through disease may not in fact want children; indeed, they may regret the loss of their fertility as a potential but they may not grieve the absence of a child. It is in the attempt to conceive that one discovers whether one is fertile or not. The decision to embark on parenthood, to undertake a major change in social status, antedates the attempt to conceive, particularly today when more effective means of fertility control are available. This decision is the result of processes that are shaped by social and historical forces, the impact of which are shared by the fertile and infertile alike; there is nothing peculiar about the motivation for parenthood of those who later find themselves infertile.

Scientists and doctors do not agree about what is the normal length of time it takes to get pregnant. Hence infertility is a self-imposed definition. At some point during an attempt at conception, frustration is acknowledged; a problem emerges that may require some sort of solution. Not everyone who acknowledges a fertility problem takes that problem to a doctor. Indeed, seeking medical advice is only one of the many options available. These options include denial, applying for a child to adopt or foster, changing partner, finding a new job, moving home, going on a long holiday or grieving the loss of a potential relationship, that of parent and child (Woollett, 1985). The choice of options is shaped by social factors such as class, gender, race, age, marital status, education, social isolation, etc., none of which feature in the discussion about the needs of the infertile.

There is no evidence that the involuntary childless who take their problem to a doctor are more desperate to have a child than those men and women who choose other solutions to their childlessness. The only factor that distinguishes them is their decision to seek a specifically medical solution to their infertility. It is often claimed that the problem of infertility is growing in scale so that it sometimes appears as though the cumulative desperation of the infertile threatens to engulf the fertile majority. It may be that the number of people seeking a medical solution to their infertility is on the increase but as statistics are not collected on such issues (and would be very difficult to collect) we have no way of knowing this for sure. Nevertheless,we cannot assume that once in the surgery these people will countenance uniformly the whole panoply of invasive investigations and treatments on offer. There is copious evidence which shows that not all patients concur with their doctors' recommendations (Stimson, 1975; Cartwright, 1967). Men and women have clear limits beyond which they will not venture. Some will not consider artificial insemination using donor semen, others refuse in-vitro fertilization whilst yet others reject adoption. Such limits are not evidence that some people's motivation for parenthood is insufficiently strong. Rather, these limits highlight the real social differences that exist amongst infertile women and men.

Fleshing out the real and complex experience of infertility leads us to ask who benefits from the pervasive caricature of the infertile as desperate people. Not the infertile themselves who cannot be helped by the reduction of a complex set of changing emotions and needs to a single negative word. Infertile women are not, I suggest, helped by a description of any distress they may feel as that of a 'barren woman's suffering' (Steptoe and Edwards, 1980, p. 47). These words are Robert Edwards's, the embryologist who, with his collaborator the gynaecologist Patrick Steptoe, pioneered the technique of in-vitro fertilization and embryo transfer.

Who then benefits from this caricature? There is a false assumption frequently made that professionals and their clients share the same goals. In this context, the professionals are the gynaecologists and embryologists and their clients are the infertile men and women who seek their help. For both, the aim is indeed the birth of a child, but their reasons for wanting this child clearly differ. Gynaecologists and embryologists who champion these new techniques have made their views known through articles in newspapers and television documentaries which portray them in heroic terms. We know that these doctors and scientists want to be able to continue to offer in-vitro fertilization and embryo transfer. These professionals have claimed that the new methods for assisting reproduction are indispensable in their endeavours to help their infertile patients. And we know from opinion research that a majority of the population of Britain wish them to be allowed to do so (*The Times*, 11 October 1982, p. 2). What we do not know is if this same desire is shared by the majority of men and women who are infertile, most of whom will *not* undergo in-vitro fertilization and embryo transfer.

Little information is available on what infertile people in general want. One survey (the only one of its kind and a little out of date) may provide us with some clues. In 1977, the members of the National Association of the Childless, a voluntary organization which offers support and advice to the infertile, were asked to state the single thing that they felt would most improve the medical treatment they had received. Admittedly, this survey was conducted before the birth of Louise Brown, the first test-tube baby. Nevertheless, its findings are of interest. Only 2 per cent of the respondents stated that more up-to-date techniques would have been beneficial. Of much greater importance to these infertile men and women were improvements in both the organization of the clinics they attended and in the attitude of the doctors they saw. Specifically, they complained about the length of time it took to reach some sort of diagnosis of their condition. This delay was caused by the infrequency of clinics which meant long gaps between each appointment, and when they did see a doctor, many complained of how difficult it was to get an adequate account of their problem. These difficulties in communication were compounded by patients rarely seeing the same doctor throughout the course of a treatment (Owens and Read, 1979).

These findings have an all-too-familiar ring about them; many patients, whatever their condition, level similar criticisms at their doctors. But in the recent debate about new approaches to the treatment of infertility, these well-rehearsed complaints have disappeared; the hearts and minds of even the most intransigent critics of doctors appear to have been won over. It is now common currency that those same doctors whose attitudes in the past provoked the complaints that I cited above are today concerned solely with the interests of their infertile patients. This is, I suggest, a simple and naïve rendering of an institution as complex as medicine, and it is to this institution that I shall now turn.

Professional Interest in In-vitro Fertilization

If doctors and scientists are not simply responding to the desperation of their infertile patients, why then do they support these new techniques? Considering what actually takes place in an infertility clinic may help to answer this question, for despite the tremendous amount of coverage given by the media to the birth of babies conceived in a petri dish and to multiple births caused by the drugs that stimulate ovulation, few people not initiated into the investigation and treatment of infertility know very much about its routine aspects.

The investigation and treatment of infertility has long been afforded low status in the medical hierarchy. The Warnock Report (1985, p. 14) deplored 'the tendency in some places for infertility patients to be given the lowest priority on waiting lists for both in-patient and out-patient treatment'. Infertility patients are alongside others included in the case-load of gynaecologists working in district general hospitals. It is only in the teaching hospitals or in the private medical sector that gynaecologists concentrate on infertility alone. The medical management of infertility has been unpopular with gynaecologists not only because of its intimate and sordid nature but because prior to the introduction of in-vitro fertilization and embryo transfer, those treating infertility could make few claims to special knowledge and treatment. Many of the procedures they used can be and are carried out by general practitioners.

The sordid and humiliating nature of the techniques used routinely to investigate and treat infertility are such that few people who go through them are prepared to discuss them in public. Doctors themselves share their patients' reticence perhaps because publicity would expose their role in these unsavoury proceedings. These investigations require men and women to lay bare their sexual selves for judgement and manipulation by the medical profession. The graphic but unexceptional example of the post-coital test should suffice to illustrate my point.

The post-coital test has played a key role in the diagnosis of infertility for more than sixty years and it is still very popular. One recent survey of the types of investigations received by infertile men and women found that over half of the respondents had been offered and accepted this test (Owens and Read, 1979, p. 50). Indeed, many infertile women submit to the post-coital test over and over again. The post-coital test is supposed to be a measure of both male and female fertility. In theory, it enables a doctor to assess the viability of sperm in the cervical canal to see whether the sperm are sufficiently vigorous to pass through that barrier or if that barrier itself is too heavily defended. The post-coital test is carried out in vivo. In vivo is the key to my point because one of the few ways in which sperm can reach the cervical canal is through sexual intercourse. Because the texture of a woman's cervical mucus changes during her menstrual cycle, the test should be carried out close to ovulation; unfortunately, gynaecologists' clinic times rarely coincide with their patients' menstrual cycles or with their libido. Consequently, this test dictates that patients have sexual intercourse at a time specified by their doctor and then rush to the hospital. There the woman undergoes a vaginal examination during which the fluids around her cervix are sucked out using a cannula, a sort of straw, so that they can be examined under a microscope. In contrast to the techniques of in-vitro fertilization and embryo transfer, using a straw to suck seminal fluid from a prostrate woman's vagina is most unlikely either to be shown step by step in a television documentary or to appear on the agenda of the meetings of government committees.

If those treating infertility have been dogged by procedures that do little to enhance their status, another difficulty has been the inability of gynaecologists to claim that a pregnancy in one of their patients came about through medical intervention alone; a gynaecologist who merely instructs a patient on when to have sexual intercourse can take little credit for a pregnancy that results. And because no one has been clear about what constituted an effective medical treatment, infertility and its solution have provided ample scope for all manner of myths, such as the magic effects on fertility of going on a holiday or of adopting a child. This state of affairs has been decried for many years in the textbooks and journals on research into and the treatment of infertility. In these pages can be found many disparaging references to the low standards and lack of scientific rigour that characterize the medical management of infertility. For example, despite its popularity and long history, the post-coital test cannot claim to conform to the criteria of science; as one textbook recently observed, 'there is still no uniformity in the way it is performed or the manner in which observations are evaluated' (Pepperell et al., 1980, p. 112).

The new techniques of in-vitro fertilization and embryo transfer overcome many of the dissatisfactions that have troubled gynaecologists treating infertility. These techniques provide them with an exciting, high-status area of research as well as a technically complex practice which only they can use; and on the very infrequent occasions when a pregnancy does occur, there can be no doubt who was responsible: science and medicine. Pictures of doctors and scientists actively engaged in harvesting human eggs and manipulating human embryos or holding up a baby as a trophy of their labour confirm *their* key role in the proceedings.

Job satisfaction is not the only carrot on offer; status and monetary reward are also in the bunch. In November 1982, a Working

Party of the Royal College of Obstetricians and Gynaecologists claimed that the body of knowledge and complexity of practice of obstetrics and gynaecology had expanded so much that the speciality should be carved up into four sub-specialities: gynaecological urology; gynaecological oncology; foetal medicine and reproductive medicine; the last would embrace the treatment of infertility.

Reproductive medicine covers disorders of menstruation, problems of the menopause as well as infertility. Feminists have demonstrated convincingly the low status afforded both research and treatment of disorders of menstruation and the menopause, derisively called 'female troubles'. In effect, prior to the introduction of the techniques of in-vitro fertilization (IVF) and embryo transfer, a gynaecologist hoping to specialize in reproductive medicine had little he could boast of. His knowledge of menstruation, menopause and infertility was little different from that of his colleague, the general practitioner, and save for surgery, both can and do offer the same tests and treatments. The only new treatment of infertility between the introduction of artificial insemination using donor semen in the 1930s, and the expansion of centres offering in-vitro fertilization and embryo transfer (which took place only after the report of the Working Party was published) was the use of drugs introduced in the early 1960s to stimulate ovulation.

The pressures towards sub-specialization within gynaecology and obstetrics, then, constitute another incentive for medical personnel involved in the treatment of infertility to lay claim to new areas of expertise. Official recognition of sub-specialization would attract financial reward for training and research. The techniques of in-vitro fertilization and embryo transfer, which involve complex procedures, require the assistance of an embryologist, and demand special equipment such as rapid radioimmune assays and real-time diagnostic ultrasound, would clearly demarcate the skills of the reproductive medical specialist from those of the general practitioner and the general obstetrician-gynaecologist.

Given the many ways in which gynaecologists stand to benefit from the widespread use of in-vitro fertilization and embryo transfer, it is not surprising that the provision of facilities for offering these treatments has expanded rapidly since 1984; according to the *First Report of the Voluntary Licensing Authority for Human In Vitro Fertilisation and Embryology*, there are now twenty-three centres in England and Scotland which offer these new techniques to patients. But the safety records and success rate of these new techniques leaves much to be desired. In-vitro fertilization and embryo transfer have been disappointing in terms of the number of pregnancies they produce; the procedure involves surgery to which a risk is always attached, and where embryo transfer succeeds, it is often with a multiple pregnancy. Multiple pregnancies increase the risks to the health of both mother and babies. Further experimentation by embryologists and gynaecologists is assumed to be necessary to overcome these technical problems and to reduce the risks of in-vitro fertilization and embryo transfer.

Yet how will this experimentation be monitored and controlled? The Voluntary Licensing Authority, sponsored jointly by the Medical Research Council and the Royal College of Obstetricians and Gynaecologists, has been set up in order to supervise standards of research into human embryos; it was, in fact, a direct response to attempts to outlaw such work. In stark contrast to concerted attempts to safeguard human embryos stands the neglect of the women who provide them and who subsequently may carry them to term. Concern for embryos has focused on their spiritual welfare as well as on the legal rights of human material which one day could lay claim to titles and estates. Little concern has been expressed for the welfare of the women involved. Such disregard is not unusual. In her book *Whose Baby Is It?* Carolyn Faulder points out that

> no one knows how many human beings in this country are annually involved in experimentation . . . [there is no] government department issuing forms and demanding that certain rules be followed. . . . There is no central registry recording the number and type of clinical trials in progress. . . . There is no law requiring that every proposal for a trial be notified. . . . No one knows how many research ethical committees there are. (Faulder, 1985, p. 95)

Furthermore, Carolyn Faulder illustrates how researchers skirt the issue of the ethics of their experiments by pandering to the false hopes of their patients. In this context, some infertile women are ready prey. One survey of patients undergoing in-vitro fertilization and embryo transfer found that their expectations of success were unrealistically high; some women rated their chances of having a baby as 50 per cent greater than reality (Johnston et al., 1984, p. 8). Embryologists as well as gynaecologists can and do justify these experiments by pointing to the needs and expectations of their desperate clients.

The ethics of medical experimentation on human subjects are supposed to be covered by the ethics of the doctor/patient relationship. But ethics here depend not only on fully informed consent of the patients concerned, whatever that may entail; they depend on a unity of interests between doctor and patient, a unity which I suggest does not exist. The risks and rewards are not the same for patients and doctors, especially in the private medical sector which has embraced these new techniques with such enthusiasm. The profit motive and the patient's best interests are often incompatible.

An expansion of opportunities for private practice has indeed been one of the rewards for gynaecologists of the new reproductive techniques. According to the *First Report of the Voluntary Licensing Authority for Human In Vitro Fertilisation and Embryology*, of the twenty-three centres offering in-vitro fertilization and embryo transfer, only one of these – St Mary's Hospital in Manchester – is supported by the National Health Service (NHS). Five are wholly in the private sector and as the Report of the Licensing Authority states, at present, these five centres are responsible for most IVF treatments in the United Kingdom. Although the remaining seventeen centres are housed within NHS hospitals (mostly teaching hospitals) and are supported indirectly by the NHS in that they use accommodation and certain other hospital facilities such as nurses and hospital porters, the 'major source of funding for IVF in the NHS sector is private practice' (Medical Research Council and Royal College of Obstetricians and Gynaecologists, 1986, p. 12). In some of these centres patients are asked for a specified donation for each treatment; in others, for example, the clinic run by Robert Winston of Hammersmith Hospital in London, the wealthier patients pay for their treatment and these fees are used to finance the programme.

Enthusiasm for in-vitro fertilization and embryo transfer has proceeded without much further work on establishing causes of infertility or improving other treatments. Over the past two years (besides the provision of in-vitro fertilization and embryo transfer) only one addition to established forms of treatment has been made; that was by a charitable organization which started a clinic held one night each week offering artificial insemination using donor semen. Ten centres have established research projects that utilize human embryos; in contrast, only two new research programmes into other aspects of infertility have been set up. The first is researching the problem of sperm/mucus hostility, a concept derived from the post-coital test. The second is investigating cases of infertility where no cause has been found. This five-year programme was sponsored by charitable donations from the infertile themselves and may be an indication of where their priorities lie.[1] In effect, in the absence of information about what sort of service infertile men and women want, there is a danger that those gynaecologists most enthusiastic about the new techniques will feel free to invest even more heavily in them to the detriment of existing facilities used to investigate and treat infertility. In some clinics, in-vitro fertilization and embryo transfer may become not the treatment of choice, but the only one available.

Infertile men and women tend not to be consulted about their treatment preferences. There is little discussion of the relevance of in-vitro fertilization and embryo transfer to current medical services for infertility. Nor are reliable statistics on success rates of the various treatments available. In such a context, the demand for support on the part of gynaecologists using these techniques could be interpreted as little more than a campaign for their right to clinical freedom and to feather their own nests with status and monetary rewards.[2] In such a campaign, the views of the infertile are superfluous; they could in fact prove counterproductive because they may contradict those of their doctor. What is required of the infertile is that they submit in silence to the claim that they are desperate.

'A brain-wave of Beelzebub': the Controversy Surrounding Insemination using Donor Semen (AID)

New medical solutions to alleviate infertility do not lead inevitably to a public outcry. When the drugs used to stimulate ovulation were first introduced into clinical practice in the early 1960s, few were troubled by the possible consequences. Following the publication of an article describing the conception and birth of a set of sextuplets, one doctor expressed his anxiety about the drugs contributing to a population explosion (Gullick, 1972, p. 111). And in the House of Lords, Lady Summerskill asked for reassurances of the drugs' safety in the light of the thalidomide tragedy (*Hansard*, 1965–6, 721, column 125). The medical press offered advice to doctors on how to handle the media whose excess enthusiasm for such events had disrupted hospitals. But no government enquiry was thought necessary. This might suggest that knowing that you came about as the product of a hormonal preparation along with several brothers and sisters of an identical age does not arouse the same ontological anxieties as knowing that either half of you was once frozen or that you were conceived on a petri dish through the endeavours of an embryologist.

In contrast to the lack of concern shown about the effects of these hormonal preparations, artificial insemination using donor semen has been the subject of numerous official and semi-official reports in its short but eventful life of less than fifty years.[3] The history of these investigations into artificial insemination using donor semen demonstrates the ways in which the public discussion of the medical management of infertility constructs the stigma of infertility. An analysis of these debates shows that when people talk about artificial insemination using donor semen they are talking about many different things; in effect, a number of different contemporary issues have been collapsed together in the debates. At an explicit level, the focus is on the technique alone; it is the technique that is the problem, not infertility. In the course of the debate about the technique, assumptions are made about the infertile which are detrimental to their image. The technique (which is seen as the trouble) and the needs of the infertile become welded together in the public mind. Thus what purports to alleviate in effect crystallizes and stigmatizes infertility, in the way that in-vitro fertilization and embryo transfer have become synonymous today with the needs of the desperate infertile. A brief history of the debates about artificial insemination using donor semen should clarify this complex argument about the construction of the stigma of infertility.

Artificial insemination using donor semen was first used in clinical practice as a treatment for infertility in England in the late 1930s. Although anxieties were expressed about its use, it did not become the subject of a major public outcry until 1945 when the gynaecologist Mary Barton, her husband the biologist Berthold Wiesner, and Kenneth Walker, the renowned urologist, sexologist and author of popular medical books, published a paper in the *British Medical Journal* which gave details of a number of their cases (Barton, Walker and Wiesner, 1945). Following the publication of this paper, the letters columns of the *British Medical Journal* (*BMJ*) were filled with expressions of revulsion. The correspondence on the subject was so voluminous that the editors were forced to declare that 'it ought to be wound up before the antagonists have torn each other to pieces' ('Editorial', 1945, p. 339). The revulsion expressed by the doctors who wrote to the *BMJ* was not exceptional; it was similar to that felt by some members of both Houses of Parliament and by journalists writing in newspapers. The Catholic Church restated its opposition to the technique. The Catholic Church has consistently forbidden the use of artificial insemination using donor semen both because it involves masturbation, a practice it condemns, and because it intervenes in the holy sacrament of marriage. Artificial insemination using donor semen was the subject of two specially convened conferences in 1946 and 1948. After listening to copious evidence both in favour of and against the technique, both conferences concluded that artificial insemination should be outlawed (Public Morality Council, 1947; Archbishop of Canterbury, 1948).

An article published in the *Sunday Despatch* in November 1945 articulated many of the contemporary concerns about artificial insemination using donor semen. It warned that 'a super-race of test-tube babies will become the guardians of atom-bomb secrets. . . . Fathers will be chosen by eugenic experts of the United Nations. The mothers will be hand-picked on their health and beauty records, family background and their achievements at school and university' (*Sunday Despatch*, 21 November 1945). Artificial insemination using donor semen had been promoted as a scientific solution to infertility. Science however had not been having a very good press, especially after the atomic bombs were dropped on Japan. Those who believed that science recognized no moral bounds took artificial insemination as further evidence that it would wreak havoc on society unless it was checked.

Another theme that worked against the image of artificial insemination using donor semen as a solution to male infertility was its recent use in agriculture. In 1943, the government through its agency the Agricultural Research Commission had introduced centres that offered high-quality bulls' semen for the insemination of cows. These centres were the corner-stone of the government's post-war reconstruction campaign to improve livestock numbers and quality and thereby increase the supply of dairy products and meat (Public Records Office/Ministry of Agriculture and Fisheries, 124/1). Numbers and quality of human beings were the goals of some who rallied in support of artificial insemination using donor semen in human beings. Eugenists and pronatalists defended donor semen as a solution to male infertility although the alleviation of infertility was not their first concern. Pronatalists who were still anxious about the declining birth-rate favoured artificial insemination using donor semen as a means of substituting for the procreative powers of men killed during the Second World War. There were women to whom conception through donor semen would be acceptable because, they claimed, these women 'would like to have children without marrying and without sinning' (*British Medical Journal*, 2, 1943, p. 219). The eugenists had long advocated the selective use of donor semen as a means of improving the quality of the nation's stock, a procedure they called eutelegenesis. Little wonder then that one of the correspondents to the *British Medical Journal* declaimed, 'Men are not cattle . . . man has a mind . . . and I think before plunging into human stud farming this must be taken into account' (Bendit, 1943, p. 404).

What sort of woman would contemplate using a veterinary technique which so many condemned when used on people? As one doctor argued, 'any women I have spoken to is revolted at the idea of artificial methods being used; they feel it violates something sacrosanct as between them and their husbands . . . I have yet to meet anyone to whom the idea of insemination by a stranger is not anathema' (Bendit, 1943, p. 404). It is hard to imagine what these women might be like especially as the recipients of donor semen would not identify themselves in public. Consequently, their characters proved fertile ground for prejudiced speculations and they became stigmatized.

Anxieties about artificial insemination using donor semen resurfaced during the 1950s after a divorce court was asked to decide whether its use by a wife without her husband's consent constituted adultery (*MacLennan* v. *MacLennan*, 1958). A debate in the House of Lords in February 1959 ended with the announcement that the government had decided to set up a committee of enquiry chaired by the Earl of Feversham which would enquire into the legal aspects of a practice which one Lord had dubbed 'a brainwave of Beelzebub' (House of Lords Debates, 1957–8, 207, column 956).

The social issue articulated in the context of the debate about artificial insemination using donor semen in the 1950s was the question of legitimacy. As Lord Brabazon of Tara put it, 'When we come down to brass tacks, the whole thing revolves on whether the child should be a bastard or not' (House of Lord Debates, 1957–8, 207, column 967). Bastardy was perceived as a growing threat; since the Second World War the number of illegitimate births had been rising steadily and the state was providing some support, albeit less than generous, for the single mother and her dependants. Divorce had become more common. Furthermore, it was clear that social mores were changing; the seeds of the sexual revolution of the 1960s had been sown. To many it appeared that the institution of the family, which they believed underpinned Western civilization, was under threat. Children conceived through donor semen represented a conscious effort to bring forth an illegitimate child within marriage. Recourse to artificial insemination using donor semen thereby constituted a very subversive act and a direct challenge to the family. Some supporters of the family appear to have seen this debate about donor semen as an opportunity to mount a last stand in its defence. The Earl of Feversham for one was fearful that artificial insemination would be used by the greedy and unscrupulous to defeat claims to titles and estates not rightly theirs. And not only was patrimony threatened; paternity itself was in jeopardy. For as the Feversham Committee warned, 'knowledge that there is uncertainty about the fatherhood of some is a potential threat to the security of all' (Home Office, 1960, p. 66).

Taking a leaf out of the *Report of the Committee on Homosexual Offences and Prostitution* (the Wolfenden Report) which had been published in 1957, the Feversham Committee concluded that whilst it could not condone the practice of artificial insemination using donor semen because clearly it was immoral, it could not prevent it from taking place between consenting adults. Thus the wives of infertile men who were inseminated with donor semen became stigmatized because according to the Feversham Committee, they were indulging in an unnatural act in order to conceive a bastard within the institution of marriage.[4]

The Hidden Agenda of the Current Debate

The debate over IVF and other reproductive technologies which surfaced in the 1980s has rather different undercurrents from those that characterized the earlier controversy about AID; but again, there is a hidden agenda to the current debate, and again, this hidden agenda sets the terms in which infertility is viewed.

The Committee established in 1982 and chaired by Mary Warnock considered the ethics of a range of techniques which it described as 'new processes of assisted reproduction' (Warnock Report, 1985, p. 4). It is therefore surprising to find the long-established technique of artificial insemination using donor semen included for consideration alongside techniques such as ectogenesis and parthenogenesis which as yet are a reality only in the pages of science fiction. The Warnock Report claims that what these techniques of assisted reproduction have in common is 'the anxiety they generated in the public mind' (ibid., p. 4). Thus, the problem of infertility is not included in the Committee's brief. Nor are the unfettered proclivities of science because two of the techniques included, surrogacy and artificial insemination using donor semen, do not require the intervention of science at all. It is these anomalies in the range of techniques that the Committee discussed which provide clues about the deeper issues that make up the hidden agenda of the current debate.

The one common factor shared by the range of techniques scrutinized by the Warnock Report is that they all entail the manipulation of human gametes and embryos. Handling human gametes and embryos outside of the body raised the problem of moral responsibility and legal ownership. It is not surprising therefore to find that very many of the recommendations of the Warnock Report are about their ownership, supply and disposal. In many ways the Warnock Report recapitulates the anxieties about adoption of children current in the 1920s. Then adoption was not regulated by the law; it could be and was exploited as a source of cheap child labour or even, it was feared, used as a front for traffic in children by white-slave traders. Such anxieties were common currency then and were even the subject of international investigations, conferences and conventions by the League of Nations (League of Nations, 1927). Similar anxieties are present today although they are articulated less explicitly. Instead of a traffic in children we have a trade in human gametes and embryos, and in place of white-slave traders, in the public imagination are *desperate* infertile men and women and unscrupulous doctors and scientists. In this context, the reasons for the inclusion of artificial insemination using donor semen and surrogacy for consideration by the Committee chaired by Mary Warnock become clear; in both gametes are purchased either by doctors or through commercial agencies.

A traffic in human gametes and embryos clearly is a development of major social concern. I am not a philosopher so unlike Mary Warnock, I cannot argue the utilitarian ethics of such a traffic. What concerns me instead is why such traffic should have arisen recently. For just as the traffic in children in the 1920s had at its basis the social and economic conditions existing then, so today, I suggest, social and economic forces have created the conditions for a trade in human gametes and embryos.

Embryos are a unique source of information about human genetics, embryonic development and foetal growth which may provide clues about the causes of some of the most feared diseases of today, such as cancer and congenital abnormalities. As the Medical Research Council put it, 'Developmental biology is one of the most exciting areas of current research. The intellectual challenge it offers has attracted first-class investigators' (Medical Research Council, 1975–6, p. 43). But in today's political climate the Medical Research Council is reluctant to fund research whose sole aim is to expand the knowledge base of developmental biology for academic interest alone; it is interested in potential commercial applications. The Medical Research Council has established links with a company in the much-vaunted biotechnology industry. Here product innovation centres on moving around the genes of different biological materials (Yoxen, 1983, p. 19). There may be much to gain from the exploitation of gametes and embryos, a unique source of human genes. Like it or not, the infertile have been drawn into sustaining and participating in a market for human gametes and embryos.

The manipulation of human gametes and embryos has been attacked by those concerned not with the wider social implications but with the spiritual welfare of embryos. In effect, this vociferous campaign on behalf of the embryo may have obscured other issues.

Nevertheless, in the course of this latest controversy, the image of infertile men and women has been discredited in two separate ways. On the one hand, they stand accused of spiritual irresponsibility by agreeing to these so-called unethical techniques; on the other, they have become the sort of people who equate children with stair carpets and microwave ovens, that is items to be purchased in the market.

This mercenary image of the infertile, their alleged commodification of parenting, is reinforced by the ways in which the cash nexus has infiltrated the alleviation of infertility. Not only are there now commercial agencies arranging surrogacy and the adoption of orphans from developing countries but the medical solution for infertility has been commercialized. The cuts in funding in the NHS have led many District Health Authorities to cut back on services for the treatment of infertility which they see as an expensive luxury. Where in-vitro fertilization and embryo transfer are available in NHS hospitals, they are funded not by the NHS directly, but either by charging some patients for treatment or by a successful bid for research monies. In a number of hospitals, the patients themselves have clubbed together to raise funds to buy small items of equipment. The waiting-lists in the NHS hospitals that offer these treatments are very long. For many women, the private medical sector offers their only chance of receiving this treatment.[5] The letters columns of *NACK*, the quarterly journal of the National Association of the Childless, bear witness to the financial hardship this can entail. Although the private medical insurance schemes refuse to cover the cost of the investigation and treatment of infertility, the private medical sector has been very quick to respond to the challenge of in-vitro fertilization and embryo transfer. Clearly there is no dearth of custom. The infertile are seen to place a monetary value on an experience which, for many, ought to be a 'gift from providence'. Their very seeking after parenthood becomes the mark of their degradation.

The stigma of infertility is not irrevocable. A historical analysis demonstrates the ways in which social processes reconstitute it differently at different times. Nonetheless, to the infertile man and woman, the stigma is real; it exists as a quagmire to be negotiated usually alone. The real question about infertility remains unexplored; that is why personhood is equated universally with the capacity to reproduce.

Acknowledgements

I would like to thank the following people for their help in writing this chapter: Jocelyn Cornwell, Ludmilla Jordanova, Clare Moynahan, Michelle Stanworth and Anne Woollett.

5
'There is of course the distinction dictated by nature': Law and the Problem of Paternity

Carol Smart

Reproductive technology is not a new phenomenon. Apart from technologies designed to prevent conception, the technology of artificial insemination using donor semen (AID) has been available in Britain for over fifty years. Yet we are clearly experiencing an escalation in the speed of development of new technologies which necessarily raises vexed questions for feminists who are concerned to prevent the exploitation of the reproductive capacity of women. It is important to recognize that these 'new' technologies are being developed at a moment in history when there is a re-emphasis on fatherhood, growing demands from anti-feminist men's organizations for greater control over children and shifts in policy to decrease the legal status of mothers in the realm of child custody.

It is not my intention in this chapter to locate the development of 'new' technologies of reproduction in their economic and social context, albeit that that is a necessary task. Rather I wish to trace how the problem of paternity has been dealt with by the law in order to draw lessons to help us deal with the contemporary problems of fatherhood. It is perhaps important to define what I mean by the terms paternity and fatherhood. Although these terms are often used synonymously, I shall use paternity to refer to the legal status of men who are deemed to have fathered certain children. Paternity alone does not automatically bring rights of custody or control over children unless the father is married to the mother of the children. By fatherhood I shall mean the actual biological or genetic relationship between a man and his 'offspring'. When referring to men's role in parenting, which may occur independently of a biological link, I shall use the term social fatherhood.

These definitions may appear to be unnecessarily complex and confusing but they are unfortunately necessary. This is because, unlike motherhood, fatherhood has posed complicated problems for a legal system that has based the ownership and inheritance of property on descent through the male line – on that is, patrilineal and primogenital ordering. Paternity has been a continuing 'problem' for the patriarchal family in Western Europe (and undoubtedly elsewhere) and this is manifest in the tortuous complexity of the legal system designed to protect the descent of property and privilege. The following passage from the *Report of the Committee on the Law of Succession in Relation to Illegitimate Persons* (know as the Russell Report, 1966) gives some insight into the legal maze.

> There is of course the distinction dictated by nature between the association between a bastard and his mother and that between a bastard and his father; and this distinction has both an evidential and a familial aspect. Nature permits that a man may produce more bastards more secretly. Facts dictate that it must be generally far more difficult to establish the paternity of a bastard than the maternity: blood tests can sometimes deny an alleged paternity but at present cannot to any significant extent establish it: the facts of birth normally establish maternity. (Russell, 1966, p. 5).

This passage reveals the way in which apparent biological truths are used to give substance to a purely legal and social ordering of parenthood. It alleges that the paternity of illegitimate children is problematic and, by inference, that the paternity of legitimate children is not. I shall unravel this convoluted thinking below, but it is important in these introductory remarks to make plain the fact that the relationship between men and children in English law has been mediated by marriage. The biological relationship, although extremely important, has not been the primary factor. I shall therefore trace the way in which law has sought to 'attach' men to children (and in some instances has 'detached' them), in order to challenge the growing biologism of men's claim to children, engendered in part by reproductive technologies but also by the assertion of 'autonomous' motherhood. (By this latter concept I mean motherhood without the support of the 'traditional' nuclear family structure).

There is a danger that the moral panic arising from a fear of the disruption of the idealized nuclear family will only serve to increase the power of men in the family by the extension of the legal concept of paternity and the enhancement of paternal rights. Moreover the new technologies themselves extend the influence of the state, through law and medicine, to restrict 'autonomous' motherhood. In other words, the price to pay for the reward of children becomes conformity to the nuclear family ideal. A paradox therefore arises in which a quest to control biological reproduction engenders new forms of biological determination.

Although I shall concentrate on paternity and fatherhood, it is also the case that the new technologies present a challenge to ideas about, and the legal definition of, maternity. With the advent of egg donation it is possible for women to carry to term infants that are genetically unrelated to them. At the same time conception in the petri dish, as opposed to the uterus, not only allows subfertile couples to have their 'own' children, it allows men, for the first time in history, to be absolutely certain that they are the genetic fathers of their future children. In view of this it becomes increasingly important to understand the role of law in extending paternity or in protecting maternity.

It may seem ironic, however, to be expressing concern over the 'extension' of the legal status of paternity and the need to protect the position of mothers, at a time when it appears that fathers are extremely badly done by when it comes to legal battles over children. To judge by the mass media and men's groups like Families Need Fathers, it would seem that the law favours women and that there is now a need to 'redress the balance'. However I hope to show here that mothers do not have more 'rights' than fathers; for example, mothers tend to get legal custody of children only because they are the ones doing the caring when marriages break down. On the contrary I shall try to show that the law operates to reinforce the patriarchal family from which men benefit disproportionately. Attempts to extend men's rights over children and to assert legal paternity are not so much a claim for 'equal rights' as a reassertion of patriarchal authority in the family.

'There is of course a distinction dictated by nature'

The issue of paternity is most clearly articulated in the law on illegitimacy. For example the Russell Report presumed that the difference between legitimate and illegitimate children was self-evident. It assumed that paternity was a problem only in cases of illegitimacy because of the biological facts of conception and birth. It also assumed that it was the difficulty over ascertaining paternity that led fathers and not mothers to 'jettison' illegitimate children. To unravel the ideological content of these statements it is important to distinguish between so-called 'blood' ties and marriage ties.

Throughout the history of law in this area these ties have overlapped confusingly, at times being treated as synonymous and at other times being separated rigorously.

The 'blood' tie is of course the biological or genetic link between parents and children. This extends to ties with other 'blood' relatives such as uncles and aunts, grandparents and so on. In our culture the 'blood' tie is apparently given ideological primacy (blood is thicker than water etc.). However it is the paternity of a child, rather than the 'maternity', that provides the link with the kinship network. In English common law the illegitimate child was '*filius nullius*' which meant it was the child of no one. S/he had no legal relationship to her mother, father, grandparents or siblings. In the legal sense the illegitimate child did not exist. Biological links were therefore immaterial as far as the common law was concerned. (This was gradually changed in practice, however, and from 1841 the mothers of illegitimate children were entitled to the sole custody of their children. The position of fathers did not change). Hence the English legal tradition was prepared to ignore 'blood' ties under certain circumstances.

The marriage tie is a legal construct. It is a means of uniting biologically unrelated (or only distantly related) couples and their kinship networks. It is *marriage* and not the blood tie that confers automatic paternity on men and creates a legal relationship between children and their fathers. Marriage is the traditional means by which law recognizes the relationship between men and children. It is no longer the only means but it remains the most important one. As I shall discuss below, marriage could establish paternity in defiance of the 'true' biological relationship between men and children. Paternity was not dependent upon proof of fatherhood, only proof of marriage. Hence the law on paternity has never followed strictly the biological relationship between men and children. So whilst biology is important it has not been of overriding importance. This is significant where there is a growing presumption that law should follow biology and a belief that the biological relationship between 'fathers' and children is and always has been sacrosanct.

Constructing Paternity

The legal category of illegitimacy is crucial to an understanding of the construction of paternity because it is here that biological fatherhood and legal paternity most clearly come adrift. Whilst the legitimate child had an automatic relationship with its father, the illegitimate child has had to struggle over many centuries to establish a legal relationship with its biological father. This is because the legal relationship, once established, meant that the father was obliged to contribute in some way to the upkeep of the child. At various moments in history the state would help mothers to extract mainten-ance (through affiliation orders) from their former lovers; at other times the Poor Law Guardians were only interested in keeping the money to recompense the parish for the maintenance of the 'bastard'. At yet other times the state absolved men altogether of any financial responsibility for bastard children. At all times, however, the position of the mother and the child was a weak one and the father's obligations varied only according to the state's concern to protect public spending. Hence he was required to acknowledge his children and pay maintenance when their dependency began to cost the state (for example the parish) too much money. By the same token, men were absolved of this liability when it was felt that the dire financial consequences of having children outside marriage should be used to deter women from getting pregnant. (In fact such policies merely led to a dramatic rise in infanticide and concealed births.)

Even the recent history of affiliation orders is a dismal one. Not only have the courts traditionally been restricted in the amounts they could award to mothers for their illegitimate children, but the criminal nature of the proceedings, which until 1959 were heard in open court alongside criminal offences, was so stigmatizing that women were extremely reluctant to go to court. Marsden (1969) has documented how humiliating women found the proceedings and there is evidence that the magistrates' courts are still regarded as dispensers of inadequate and second-class justice in domestic matters (Smart, 1984).

One of the main problems of using the courts to secure financial provision for illegitimate children has been the difficulty of proving paternity. On one level there has been the problem of establishing a biological link at moments in history when the technology to achieve this was unavailable. Until the 1980s blood tests were only useful as a way of 'disproving' paternity. In other words they could only establish that a man was *not* the father of the child. They could not prove that a man *was* the biological father. On a rather different level, the mother's evidence as to paternity had to be 'corroborated in some material particular by other evidence'. (This wording dates from the earliest Poor Law legislation.) This requirement for corroboration, like the requirement in cases of rape, is based on a belief in the men-dacity of women. The Russell Report (1966) for example states that 'There are grounds for supposing that there are cases in which the mother successfully selects the man who is the best prospect.' The report does not clarify what these 'grounds' are, and it would seem that there is little evidence to substantiate this prejudice. In fact there is rather more evidence to substantiate women's reluctance to go to court at all. Marsden, for example, documents how the National Assistance Board (now the Department of Health and Social Security – DHSS) bullied unmarried mothers to try to extract the name of the putative father, and how its officers pressurized mothers into going to court. It is by no means certain that these practices have ended.

Nor was it difficult for alleged fathers to rebut 'accusations' of paternity. It was generally only necessary to allege promiscuity or to bring to court other witnesses who would claim to have had intercourse with the mother for the accusation to fail. The English courts did not have a system of making a number of men pay maintenance where any of them could be the biological father, so there was no deterrent to false allegations. Women therefore took a considerable risk in going to court. Not only would their circumstances become public knowledge but their damaged 'reputations' could be even more irreparably harmed.

Putative fathers therefore had little to fear from the laws of affiliation unless they provided support voluntarily or admitted paternity. In appearance the law sought to enforce the father's obligations to his biological child(ren), but in practice the law was organized to dissuade mothers from going to court, and ultimately offered them a pittance in the form of maintenance for the trouble of going.

Clearly the law had little real interest in attaching men to illegitimate children except to recoup public expenditure, but it showed even less interest in other important legal proceedings. An illegitimate child, for example, could not claim on its father's intestacy until 1969. Moreover, for the purposes of adoption the putative father is still not regarded in law as a parent with rights to consent or dissent unless he has a custody order or is the child's legal guardian. In spite of the rhetoric of the law little has been done yet to attach men to their illegitimate children. Indeed it is possible to argue that it has protected men from the obligations of paternity, while leaving the stigma and the punitive financial consequences of child-rearing to mothers. (As I shall point out below this situation may soon change to the greater detriment of the mothers of illegitimate children.)

The situation regarding legitimate children is rather different.

The 'Presumption of Legitimacy'

Common law gave the men who fathered legitimate children absolute 'father right' which meant that the 'paterfamilias' had absolute control over the lives of his children whilst, in legal terms, mothers had none. All the duties and obligations of parenthood rested with the father, as did all the rights and privileges (see Strachey, 1978). This absolute patriarchal power was gradually modified in the nineteenth century through the introduction of legislation on the guardianship of infants (Brophy and Smart, 1981).

Whilst the law gave considerable power over children to married men, at the same time it made it extremely difficult for men to rid themselves of their formal obligations to these children. These fathers were in exactly the opposite position to the fathers of illegitimate children. This was a result of what is known as the 'presumption of legitimacy'.

The common law presumed that all children born in wedlock were legitimate, but it went further than a mere presumption in practice. Until the introduction of the 1949 Law Reform (Miscellaneous Provisions) Act neither husband nor wife was allowed to give evidence of non-access (i.e., a lack of sexual intercourse) which would bastardize a child born during the marriage. In a case in 1777 the judge, Lord Mansfield stated:

> But it is a rule, founded in decency, morality, and polity, that [the spouses] shall not be permitted to say after marriage, that they have had no connection, and therefore that the offspring is spurious; more especially the mother, who is the offending party. (*Goodright ex Dim. Stevens* v. *Moss* et al., 1777, 2Cowp 591, p. 594)

The law in fact operated a dual standard as to the conditions under which children might be bastardized. On the one hand it appears that there was a reluctance to bastardize children if this meant that they would no longer be financially supported by the 'father'. For example in cases where wives were found 'guilty' of adultery this would not bastardize their children as it would be presumed that the husband could still be the biological father.

Yet there were cases where this strict application did not apply and these all tended to involve the inheritance of property rather than the issue of maintenance. So, where the husband was a man of property there was a tendency to bastardize children who were likely to have been fathered by another man. In more modest cases, for example those involving pauper children, the courts were less ready to absolve the man's responsibility.

Nonetheless, the point is that it was extremely difficult for a husband to divest himself of paternity until the law was changed by statute in 1949 (Law Reform [Miscellaneous Provisions] Act). If a child was to be bastardized the husband had the burden of proof, which had to be established 'beyond all reasonable doubt'. And the law tended to hold this rigid position even in the face of the growing use of reliable contraceptive methods or in the light of an 'admission' by the mother that the child was not her husband's.

Clearly the law in these cases was operating against the interest of individual men. It seems that it was serving a 'higher'goal, namely that of preserving the patriarchal family. Hoggett (1981) for example, has argued:

> The institution of marriage may well have been devised in early societies in order to establish a relationship between man and child. A man may derive spiritual, emotional and material advantages from having children, but whereas motherhood may easily be proved, fatherhood may not. A formal ceremony between man and woman, after which it is assumed that any children she may have are his, is the simplest method of establishing a link. It also enables him to limit his relationships to the offspring of a suitable selected mate. (Hoggett, 1981, p. 119)

This analysis is very persuasive, not least because throughout history the law has deliberately ignored evidence that husbands are unlikely to be the fathers of their wives' children. If marriage was the only method of attaching men to children, it was clearly meant to be an indelible method, impervious to indications of biological incompatibility.

The change of law in 1949 does not indicate that legislation had become more sensitive to a biological imperative however. Certainly with the growth of technology to ascertain paternity through blood tests and the reduction in the dire consequences of being found to be illegitimate, the law risked losing all credibility if it did not alter its doctrine on the presumption of legitimacy. But at the same time there was a growth in social fathering which also blurred the distinction between legitimate and illegitimate children, once thought to be so clear-cut and so desirable.

Undoubtedly law kept legitimate children firmly attached to their fathers in order to maintain a familial system of support of dependents. However with the increasing divorce rate in the 1970s and the creation of stepfamilies, and with the growth of cohabitation without marriage, other methods of ensuring that men assumed responsibility for dependent children developed. Without having to establish marital or biological ties, the concept of the 'child of the family' made all men responsible for the support of children whom they had treated as members of their family. As with the history of affiliation orders, this measure developed mainly to protect public expenditure and to prevent children, abandoned by their biological fathers, becoming dependent upon state benefits. This development was however wrapped in the rhetoric of the 'welfare of the child' and presented as a means of protecting children.

In large measure this development abolished the legal significance of paternity and legitimacy whilst enshrining men's responsibilities towards children. (The legislation also applies to women although women are less frequently in a position to provide maintenance or an inheritance). Nonetheless, as I shall argue below, the issue of paternity has reappeared in another form in contemporary family law, namely in relation to children conceived through artificial insemination by donor (AID).

The Unique Position of AID Children

The child conceived by AID is, legally speaking, illegitimate. As the law currently stands the donor is responsible for contributing towards the financial maintenance of the child and the child could claim provision from the estate of its genetic father. This legal 'right' is however, unenforceable in practice because of the anonymity of the donor.

The illegitimate status of the AID child is almost always obscured by the practice of the husband and wife, in collusion with the medical profession, of naming the husband as the father on the child's birth certificate. In so doing, however, the couple are committing an offence which has given rise to considerable concern (Law Commission, 1979). It has been argued that the law should be changed to make the AID child legitimate and that a child in this situation does not 'deserve' the status of illegitimacy. For example Mayo (1976) has argued:

> To call AID children illegitimate (as well as being unjust to them and a misnomer) is inconsistent with the policies behind the idea of legitimacy – monogamous marriage, family stability, aversion to illicit sexual relationships, property inheritance. These policies are promoted not infringed by the introduction of an AID child, born after thorough planning and careful thought, into a stable and hitherto childless home. (Mayo, 1976, p. 24)

This form of 'special pleading' for the AID child is a relatively new development. When the technology was first introduced the legal profession and the Established Church took an extremely dim view of the practice. For example the Archbishop of Canterbury's

Committee on Artificial Human Insemination (1948) took the view that it should be made a criminal offence. It was held to undermine the very foundation of marriage, and to be a means of foisting spurious children on an unsuspecting world. The Royal Commission on Marriage and Divorce (Morton, 1956) recommended that AID without a husband's consent should be a new, separate ground for divorce.

> In our view, if a wife accepts artificial insemination by a donor without the consent of her husband she is doing him a grave injury, an injury which, in its possible consequences, is as serious as that of adultery. The intention is, and the result may be, to father a child on the husband without his knowledge. (Morton, 1956, p. 31)

The Feversham Committee (1960), a government committee set up to report on AID, reflected the views of these earlier reports. It refused to recommend that the AID child accepted by the husband should be legitimate and continued to regard AID as a threat to the very basis of family life and society. The Committee did, however, acknowledge that the law should not totally disregard the welfare of the AID child. The doctrine of the 'best interests of the child' was gaining credibility in cases of divorce and was therefore, in theory at least, seen as relevant in all cases involving children. This doctrine, however, did not apply to illegitimate children until considerably later than 1960 and the Committee was not prepared to disregard the distinction between legitimate and illegitimate as a method of safeguarding the interests of 'innocent' AID children. Basically the interests of AID children were not regarded as sufficiently weighty to risk undermining the basis of marriage. Their status in law therefore remained unchanged.

By the 1970s this view of AID as a threat to marriage and society waned. The position typified by Mayo above became increasingly dominant. Instead of being a threat to the ideologically acceptable family, AID was seen as a way of enhancing family life for the childless. It was childlessness itself that was becoming the 'problem'. Childlessness was in fact the very antithesis of the nuclear family ideal.

According to this logic, the illegitimate child born outside wedlock or born of an extramarital affair was in quite a different position to the AID child who was 'wanted' by both husband and wife. (It was, and possibly still is, widely assumed that the illegitimate child was not 'wanted' by anyone, least of all its father.) The fact of being wanted, and consequently *acknowledged* by the husband has become the crucial element in the argument for legitimizing AID children. In other words, the fact that the husband wants to assume the legal status of paternity is the overriding factor.

A similar trend has occurred with illegitimacy. For example the 1926 Legitimacy Act allowed children born illegitimate to be legitimized if the child's biological parents married. Hence in choosing to marry, the father could assume the paternity of the child and, in addition, erase the stigma of illegitimacy. Of course, it is an over-simplification to argue that paternity as a legal status merely reflects the wishes or choices of men. As the cases involving the presumption of legitimacy reveal, men certainly could not divest themselves of the responsibilities of paternity at whim. Nonetheless, at different historical moments, certain elements of the law relating to paternity have come extremely close to this position. Basically however, family law appears to strive to preserve marriage as the basis of family life (Smart, 1984).

The Law Commission's (1979) proposals on AID are a good example of this focus on the patriarchal family. In their Working Paper they argued that AID children should be regarded as legitimate because the mother had had no personal relationship with the donor (so it was not really adulterous), because the husband had agreed to the procedure (this was assumed, as women need to have their husband's permission before AID is provided), and because the genetic father is unknown. The transformation of a marriage into a nuclear family by means of AID was therefore condoned. However, the Law Commission did not envisage that this presumption of legitimacy could be extended to the AID child born to an unmarried woman. In this case, not only is the 'accepting' husband missing, but a single parent would not constitute a 'proper' nuclear family. Undoubtedly the Law Commission, like the Warnock Committee some years later, presumed that AID would not in any case be available to single women.

Since the introduction of the technology of AID, views on its possible effect on family life have been transformed – even though the law has yet to be changed. This transformation has taken thirty years to reach the point at which it might produce legal changes. But its significance has now been overtaken by further and more dramatic advances in reproductive technology. For example, egg donation and in-vitro fertilization now so dominate the debates on infertility, that AID has been subsumed into a renewed panic over the preservation of family life. Ironically the old arguments over the dangers of AID are now being rehearsed in relation to other methods of infertility treatment. The legal issues may not be identical, but the Warnock Committee appears to be as preoccupied with questions of inheritance, primogeniture and the preservation of 'stable' nuclear family life as was its predecessors thirty or more years ago. Before discussing the limitations of Warnock, however, I wish to look at more general developments in family law which have affected the respective statuses of motherhood and fatherhood.

Recent Developments Concerning Children

Children are an increasingly important group as far as legislation on marriage and the family is concerned. Although legislators and lawyers expressed concern over children in earlier times, since the end of the Second World War there has been a marked trend towards giving greater priority to children's welfare as a principle to guide judicial decisions and law reform. This is particularly noticeable in the field of divorce. Although judges in the last century voiced the rhetoric of children's welfare, it is not until the second half of the twentieth century that the welfare of children began to take precedence over the legal 'rights' of parents.

It is of course important to recognize that the meaning of the 'welfare' of children is subject to interpretation, and, as Brophy (1985) has shown, this judicial interpretation is very ideological. Notwithstanding this, it is clear that during the latter half of the twentieth century judges increasingly regarded mothers as the most appropriate custodians of children on divorce. The common law doctrine of absolute father right was abandoned and judges increasingly voiced the benefits of mother love (as long as the mother was not 'promiscuous' or a lesbian). Hence, while children have become more of a focus, the relative statuses of motherhood and fatherhood have changed and developed. These developments are best outlined in the fields of illegitimacy and divorce.

Illegitimacy

Until the last quarter of the twentieth century the position of the unmarried mother was so undesirable that her parental obligations were seen as little more than part of her stigma and rejection. Having sole custody rights (in practice from 1841, although this was not put into legislation until the 1975 Children Act) was more a form of legal punishment than a concession. This has changed however. The growth of cohabitation leading to a situation in which illegitimate children are born into an unmarried but nonetheless two-parent household, and the rise in the illegitimate birth-rate have contributed to a number of social changes. The mother of an illegitimate child is no longer in a completely different position from other lone mothers (with the partial exception of widows). Although there may still be some stigma attached to being an unmarried mother, the state does not penalize her financially any more than it does divorced or separated mothers. So the disadvantages have diminished yet she is in a *stronger* position *vis-à-vis* her children than the divorced or separated mother because she is entitled to their sole custody.

The unmarried mother can exercise all parental rights herself, as long as the courts have made no order to the contrary. The married mother on the other hand, holds these parental 'rights' in common with her husband. She is entitled to sole custody only if a court has awarded her such an order. This difference can be extremely important when there is conflict over children, or when men attempt to exercise power over women through their children.

Shortly after the passage of the 1975 Children Act, the fathers of illegitimate children began to recognize that they could not exercise the same rights over children as married men. At the same time unmarried mothers began to recognize the advantages of their status which allowed them to have children without the disadvantages of marriage and beyond the control of men. Hence the traditional position of the 'putative' father wishing to deny paternity at all costs and, in the terms of the Russell Committee, jettisoning the child, began to give way to a situation in which fathers wanted not only the legal status of paternity but all the 'rights' of married fathers.

This transition, which is by no means complete or universal, is epitomized by the concerns of the Law Commission in its Working Paper on illegitimacy (1979). Their document, which is meant to consider the position of the illegitimate child, is in effect, a treatise on the wrongs of unmarried fathers and how they can best be modified. They state:

> From a strictly legal point of view, the father of an illegitimate child is today probably at a greater disadvantage than the child himself [sic]; and while many fathers may take little or no interest in their children born out of wedlock, other fathers who have lived with the mother for perhaps many years are clearly affected by the discrimination. (Law Commission, 1979, p. 14)

The Commission lists all the discriminations 'suffered' by the unmarried father and concludes that the best method of eradicating these wrongs and eliminating the problem of illegitimacy, was to give all biological fathers automatic parental rights on a par with the mother of an illegitimate child. Under this proposal the unmarried mother would have to go to court if she wanted sole custody or did not wish the father to exercise his rights. These rights include not only actual custody, but the right to decide whether the child should have medical treatment, which school the child should go to, where the child should live and what the child's name should be.

The Law Commission has since abandoned this proposal because of the strength of adverse reaction they received. Nonetheless, the Working Paper is an important document inasmuch as it points to, and legitimizes, a growing disquiet over the supposed power of mothers. For example, in the Working Paper the Law Commission acknowledged that there might be unmeritorious fathers (for example, rapists), who should not be able to exercise untrammelled authority over their biological offspring. They went on to state:

> But we think that the decision to exclude a father from all parental rights and duties is so important that it should not be the mother's alone; the final decision should lie with the courts, which are bound to regard the welfare of the child as paramount. (Ibid., p. 29).

This passage reveals the underlying concern that women should not be entitled to exercise parental rights exclusively without the prior permission of the courts. It reveals a concern that mothers will exclude fathers maliciously and without consideration for the interests of their children whilst, at the same time, it minimizes the possibility that fathers might harrass and unduly interfere with the lives of mothers attempting to bring up their children. Although the Law Commission acknowledged the possibility of unmeritorious fathers, it was clear that their crimes would have to be very serious to outweigh the 'justice' of giving unmarried fathers equal rights.

The Working Paper was particularly vexed at the situation in which an unmarried mother could refuse to have the name of the child's biological father on the birth certificate. This was a practice they wished to see ended, and in their later recommendations (1982) they did not rescind the proposal that all fathers should have the right to be named. (This of course excludes donors for AID whom the Commission view in a different light.) They state,

> It seems to us that if a man is obliged to accept the financial obligations of paternity it is reasonable that he should be entitled, if he wishes, to have the fact of his fatherhood recorded (on the birth certificate). (Law Commission, 1982, p. 115)

In other words the Law Commission recognized, and sought to legitimize, the economic power of men. There is little in this sentiment about the welfare of children, it simply reflects the power of money.

The Law Commission's first proposals on illegitimacy (1979) sought to abolish the status by enhancing paternity and attaching biological fathers automatically to all children. However the aim to improve the position of the unmarried father ran counter to their ideas on AID children. The last thing the Commission wished was inadvertently to give donors full parental rights. Hence with AID, the biological link immediately became unimportant, being overridden by the desirability of social fatherhood in a two-parent family household. It would seem that the biological father is expendable in some, but not all circumstances.

Divorce

There is a presumption that the courts favour mothers when it comes to decisions on the custody of children on divorce. This presumption is not altered by the weight of evidence which suggests that whilst judges subscribe to the ideology of motherhood, the courts in fact, in the vast majority of cases, only give legal recognition to custody arrangements previously decided by the parents themselves. It is also the case that the courts are more influenced by current arrangements which they are unlikely to wish to disrupt for fear of unsettling the children involved. This is known as the status quo effect (see Eekelaar and Clive, 1977; Brophy, 1985).

In spite of serious doubts that the courts do operate a system of maternal preference, it has become such a firm belief that there is now a growing reaction against it. This has taken the form of a demand that all custody decisions on divorce should award parental rights jointly to both parents. Actual care and control of the child would still tend to go to the mother under this arrangement, but the father would be able to make decisions about schooling etc. If the parents could not agree they would have to return to court to get a judicial decision.

This development (see the Booth Committee Report, 1985) is, like the developments on illegitimacy, linked to a disquiet about the power of mothers if they have sole custody. It is feared that the bitterness of a mother may deny a child the right to know and see its father. This disquiet is closely related to the development of a school of thought in psychology which now argues that a child must *know* and *interact* with its biological father to grow up to be a stable and well-adjusted (heterosexual) adult (Isaacs, 1948; Green, 1976; Wallerstein and Kelly, 1980).

To a large extent this idea is already enshrined in legislation. The 1975 Children Act gave adopted children the right to trace their genetic parents on the grounds that it is important that every person should be allowed to know his or her parentage. This legislation gives priority to the biological tie and is based on theories of psychological adjustment and development.

Not all theories of child development accept the thesis that a child must know its biological father to be a well-adjusted adult. Indeed some argue that even in cases of divorce where children know their fathers well, it may be harmful to the child's development for the courts to order access to the non-custodial parent. Goldstein, Freud and Solnit (1980) have argued the case that the custodial parent ought to be entitled to decide whether or not the other parent retains contact with the children in cases where there is conflict. This idea is the total antithesis to current developments in custody and access. Divorce courts in the United Kingdom and the United States are increasingly asserting that access to the non-custodial parent is a right of the child, a right that is necessary to ensure proper development. This means that unwilling children are forced to meet their fathers, or that children may be severely disturbed by access visits.

Thus, while the court appears to be protecting the interests of children in enforcing access and joint custody in cases of conflict, it is in fact reasserting paternal authority. The issue of a child's surname after the divorce of its parents is one small example of this process.

A Child's Name

There have been conflicting judgements on whether a child should adopt the surname of a 'reconstituted' family (i.e. the name of the mother's new husband or cohabitee) or whether it should retain its father's surname. A divorced mother does not have the right to change a child's name without the consent or agreement of her former husband, although in practice many probably do. The reasons for changing the name may be to save embarrassment at the child's school or to enable the child to feel a part of a new family. Nonetheless, some judges have taken severe exception to this and have argued that a child must retain this link with its biological father (Evans, 1978; Parry, 1978; Fortin, 1980). For example in one case cited by Evans the judge stated

> But to deprive the child of her father's surname, in my judgement, is not in the best interests of the child because, I think, it is injurious to the link between the father and the child to suggest to the child that there is some reason why it is desirable that she should be called by some name other than her father's name. (Evans, 1978, p. 113)

Although the courts no longer operate a straightforward paternal preference in this matter, the courts will insist on a child retaining its father's name if the judge decides that this is in the child's interests. As the quotation above reveals, some judges may perceive the welfare of children in very narrow ways.

W(h)ither Paternity?

The law appears to be moving in two conflicting directions at the same time. In the cases of divorce and illegitimacy there is a growing emphasis on the importance of biological fatherhood and paternity. In the case of AID, however, the opposite is occurring, and the legal concept of the 'child of the family' seems to ignore the importance of legal paternity altogether. Underlying both of these developments, however, is the legal antipathy shown towards women mothering children alone and the goal of properly attaching men to children to prevent women exercising too much independence. It would seem that the law is agnostic on the issue of whether women do all the caring for children, but it takes a strong view if women try to detach children from men, and by implication, from the nuclear family.

If these apparent contradictory trends are examined more closely it is possible to see that they in fact lend support to a particular family structure, namely one in which there is 'a heterosexual couple living together in a stable relationship, whether married or not' (Warnock, 1985, p. 10). In other words, the primary aim of law is to link biological fathers to children where it is the biological father who is most likely to reproduce the ideal nuclear family structure. Where the biological father is not available, or is unsuitable (for example, the Law Commission's unmeritorious father), the social father will suffice. Where there is a biological father and a social (step)father (as in the case of divorce and remarriage) the law preserves the rights of the biological father in the 'best interests of the children'. In other cases where there is both a biological and a social father (as with AID) the tendency is to ignore the biological father and to invest all the rights of paternity in the social father who will be the head of a two-parent family.

The advent of the new reproductive technologies has, in itself, neither strengthened nor weakened the law's ability to attach men to children. Rather I hope I have shown that the methods have altered, and the emphasis on biological links has undergone transformations, whilst remaining highly salient. However the development of the new technology does have implications for 'maternity'. For the first time the law must contemplate the idea that a woman may bring to term offspring derived from the ovum of another woman. In this case the 'fact of birth' is no proof of genetic connection.

Whilst AID, adultery and other practices that cast doubt on the paternity of children have posed considerable problems for the legal system, it is unlikely that egg or embryo transplants will pose similar problems unless the procedure interferes with patrilineal inheritance rights. Basically the law has not been interested in maternity as a vehicle of 'rights' for women in the way that paternity has always implied 'rights' for men. To a large extent the law has seen women solely in terms of whether they produce legitimate children and then whether they care for children adequately. The fact of mothering children has never involved a question of rights except, as I have outlined above, in relation to the punitive consequences of illegitimacy. Once mothers began to demand certain rights from the law, the parameters of debate changed; the law became interested only in the welfare of children and asserted that parental rights were an inadequate concept when dealing with minors.

So it is for the first time that the law must look at this issue in terms of deciding which woman in a surrogacy arrangement should be the legal 'mother'. *The Warnock Report on Human Fertilisation and Embryology* (1985) has recommended that a woman who gives birth following egg or embryo donation should be regarded in law as the mother of the child. In this respect their recommendations follow closely the long-standing recommendations on AID, namely that the mother's husband should be regarded in law as the father of the child. However the different legal statuses of paternity and maternity become apparent when the Committee turns its attention to inheritance and succession. The Committee states 'The use by a widow of her dead husband's semen for AIH is a practice which we feel should be actively discouraged' (Warnock, 1985, p. 55). It goes on to recommend that

> legislation be introduced to provide that any child born by AIH who was not *in utero* at the date of the death of its father shall be disregarded for the purposes of succession to and inheritance from the latter. (Ibid., p. 55)

The Committee makes the same recommendation in respect of children born following IVF, using a frozen embryo where the husband is dead before the embryo is *in utero*.

There are no recommendations restricting the inheritance rights of children born of these same methods where the husband is alive but where the biological mother is dead. Should a widower elect to implant the egg or embryo of his dead wife into an infertile second wife, the child born as a consequence will not be disinherited or ignored for purposes of succession.

In effect the Warnock Report attempts to create a new form of illegitimacy, but one in which the child has fewer rights than illegitimate children born today without the help of new technology. At least these children can claim from the estate of their biological fathers.

The case of posthumous embryo, egg or sperm donation may be relatively rare although it has clearly worried the Warnock Committee because it attaches such importance to the legal consequences affecting inheritance through the male line. But whilst making recommendations on this subject, the Committee did not even consider the legal position of the child born, with the assistance of reproductive technology, to the mother without a male partner, or to the lesbian. This was because the Report recommends that only *stable heterosexual couples* will be able to benefit from this form of infertility treatment.

In this respect, the Warnock Report is no more progressive than was the Russell Report of 1966. Its aim is to preserve the narrow ideal of patriarchal family life. What is more it is far more limited than existing legislation on adoption which allows single women and men to adopt children. Presumably the Committee's logic would argue that it is more in the interests of children to be adopted into 'unconventional' households than to remain in care, but that 'as a general rule it is better for children to be *born* into a two-parent family' (Warnock, 1985, p. 11, emphasis added).

Concluding Remarks

Discussions on reproductive technologies in feminist literature have mainly focused on the issue of male/medical control over the technology and the exploitation of women's reproductive capacity. There has been little on how it affects the issue of fatherhood and paternity and the meaning of these concepts in terms of control over women and children. There is a growing awareness of the centrality of children to an understanding of the position of women. In recent years this has been linked to the problem of custody of children on divorce (Brophy, 1985; Sevenhuijsen and de Vries, 1984) as well as to the issue of illegitimacy (Rights of Women Family Law Subgroup, 1985). It is vital that the women's movement does not ignore these crucial issues. The fact that the Warnock Report proposes that 'single' women should be excluded from new forms of medical help for infertility is extremely important; and it should not be overlooked that there are proposals to recognize new forms of paternity whilst continuing to deny certain rights to children who inconveniently upset the rules of inheritance. What is more, whilst women still want children we should not ignore the abysmal status of maternity in law. It may be that a demand for total and automatic rights over children is misplaced whether the demand comes from men or women. It is important however, that as law is created in this area that the position of mothers is not relegated to third place behind fathers' rights and the welfare of children.

In spite of the fact that reproductive technologies contain the possibility of rendering biological or 'blood' ties immaterial, it remains the case that the legal parameters outlined for its development still give priority to paternity. It is more than an irony that maternity is legally insignificant whilst motherhood is so important for the actual physical and emotional care of children. The importance of paternity seems to be in an *inverse relationship* to the amount of physical and emotional care provided by fathers. As long as this remains unchanged women will be powerless in the face of the reassertion, by men, of their claim to children. Reproductive technologies increase the opportunities for relatively privileged men and women to have children, but as long as the technology is contained within legal parameters that prioritize the patriarchal family, it does nothing to challenge existing notions of fatherhood and motherhood. In fact, in ideological terms, it adds to the celebration of the biological, nuclear family that affects us all. In this respect the development of the legal concept of paternity outlined here, and the recommendations of the Warnock Committee should give rise to concern. This is not so much for the vision of a brave new world peopled only by men and 'mother-machines', but for the way in which these developments will bind women more securely to the confines of the patriarchal, nuclear family – not through marriage as in the past, but for the sake of children.

6
Surrogacy: Feminist Notions of Motherhood Reconsidered
Juliette Zipper and Selma Sevenhuijsen

Is Surrogacy a Feminist Issue?

Ten years ago a friend of ours was pregnant for somebody else. In this case the somebody else was her boy-friend, who was also the begetter of the child. They were not sharing a home. People around her reacted in different ways, some were disapproving, others were surprised but had nothing to say against it. Neither of them being married, there were no legal problems. She gave him permission to make legal recognition of the child. (In the Netherlands the written permission of an unmarried mother for legal recognition is required by law.) Later he acquired sole custody of the child. It all went rather smoothly; the child now lives with her father in a communal household and so far everyone involved is quite content. Our friend enjoyed this (her second) pregnancy. The child has known ever since she was four years old where she came from, and about once a month she enjoys a weekend with our friend.

Although we got acquainted with our friend through the women's movement, we never considered her arrangement concerning parenthood a relevant issue for feminism. After all there are nowadays all kinds of arrangements to do with child-bearing and rearing, so what should it have to do with feminism or politics at all? – and if unwed motherhood is considered normal, why should you bother when a man wanted to be a single father?

It is precisely the definition of what is political in the area of parenting that has undergone an amazingly sudden change during the last four or five years. Our friend's reproductive behaviour has got a label now: 'surrogate motherhood' or 'surrogacy' (in Dutch: '*draagmoederschap*' which literally means 'carrymotherhood' or 'bearmotherhood'). Although there are only a few known surrogate mothers in the Netherlands (the issue is clearly imported from the Anglo-Saxon world by horror stories about commercial practices and cases like that of Baby Cotton) these few women have become national personalities, regularly appearing in the media. All kinds of experts and policy-makers have been investigating this rare 'species' ever since, so whether we like it or not, surrogate motherhood *has* become a political issue. Public debate focuses now on the question of whether the state has to intervene to regulate or even prohibit the practice of surrogacy.

Most authors agree that surrogate motherhood has existed in history in a range of forms. Some of them even interpret the Bible literally, citing the story of Sara and Hagar in order to prove the normality of surrogacy. Public anxiety does not arise, then, because surrogacy is in any sense a new phenomenon, but because it is seen in the context of the introduction of reproductive technology, especially in-vitro fertilization.

On the one hand, this link is justified. In-vitro fertilization indeed introduces new possibilities for surrogacy. While in-vitro fertilization has been introduced in the context of involuntary infertility, surrogacy acquires the status of a solution for involuntarily childless *couples* where the woman is infertile. A 'surrogate mother' gets pregnant, bears and gives birth to the child and hands it over to the intended parents. Beyond this, medical techniques like egg donation and lavage introduce the possibility of pregnancy even when the child is not composed of the pregnant woman's genetic material. The story of our friend, in which the bearing of the child was a 'service' to a man who wished to be a single father, does not correspond to either of these practices.

On the other hand the introduction of technology does not tell the whole story. The invention of reproductive technology seems to shake up all 'normal' arrangements and belief-systems about human reproduction. It is striking that surrogacy often arouses more attention, anger and calls for prohibition than developments in fertilization itself. The Warnock Committee approves of in-vitro fertilization and artificial insemination as techniques for treating involuntary infertility, provided they are only used by stable, heterosexual couples. The same committee disapproves of surrogacy. This seems to be the trend in official reports in other countries as well (Benda-bericht, 1985; Gezondheidsraad, 1984). Commercialization is usually posed as *the* problem that has to be solved in the context of surrogacy. But underneath this critique of commercialization lingers a condemnation of the woman who gives away her child, or worse still, consciously and rationally decides to get pregnant and to 'abandon' her child. The discourses around surrogacy reveal that stories of a brave new world are inspired not just by anxieties about the development of technology, but also by fears about the fate of a world where the mother–child bond is more transient and more fragile.

It is in the context of reproductive technology that surrogacy has become defined as a feminist issue as well. Test-tube babies are not new in feminist discourse. In the beginning of the seventies, Shulamith Firestone elaborated the view that the development of birth-technology is potentially liberating for women, because it could free them from the burden of biological motherhood (Firestone, 1970). Recent feminist analysis, at least the strand that voices itself loudest as for example in the work of Maria Mies and Gena Corea, has a different point of view. Just as the development of in-vitro fertilization is seen as a form of patriarchal exploitation of woman's body, and the women who undergo this medical treatment are portrayed as victims of medical power and the false ideology of motherhood, the surrogate mother is seen as a *victim* of commercialization and its seemingly unavoidable counterpart, exploitation. Some even call surrogate motherhood a new form of prostitution, and cite the existence of these 'new prostitutes' as the proof that we have reached the highest stage of patriarchal domination (Cortese and Feldmann, 1984; Dworkin, 1983, pp. 181–88). Women are invited to reproduce themselves in the 'normal' or 'natural' way or not at all; they are encouraged to accept their infertility and adopt a 'poor' handicapped child. The state is invoked by, for example, both the prominent West German social democratic politician Däubler-Gmelin and the Feminist International Network of Resistance to Reproductive and Genetic Engineering (Finrrage) to prohibit surrogacy in the name of Woman (Däubler-Gmelin, 1986; Brockskothen, 1986, pp. 16–19).

Nowadays feminists seem to stress oppression, whereas Firestone saw the issue of reproductive technology in terms of liberation. In this article we do not want to take sides in a potential debate between liberation and oppression. Both perspectives have a degree of plausibility, but it is doubtful whether feminist analysis will develop any further when it remains caught in an opposition between liberation and oppression. It is not technology itself that complicates theory and strategy. What makes it complicated are the *terms* in which technology and its social consequences are spoken about, as well as the power relations surrounding it. The issue of surrogacy raises questions about the naturalness of the mother–child bond, more clearly than other issues in the field of reproductive technology. Connected to this is the question: What constitutes motherhood? Why are women who bear a child and give birth to it called 'mothers'? – and why are surrogate mothers called mothers? Is a mother a woman who produces an egg, or a woman who bears a child or a woman who raises a child? The development of reproductive technology in combination with surrogacy introduces for the first time in the history of humankind the possibility of even asking these questions.

In the first part of this chapter we will comment upon the historical roots of the interconnections between motherly and sexual images within the women's movement. Our thesis is that negative attitudes to surrogacy from within the women's movement are related to developments within feminism itself. We conclude the discussion with some principles which we judge to be important for a feminist political strategy with respect to surrogacy.

In the second half of the chapter we deal in more detail with the question of commercialization, and examine problems that are covered up or forgotten when commercialization is seen as the central issue. In our concluding discussion we will try to evaluate the meaning and effects of policy proposals that have been made recently in some European countries.

The Mother-child Bond

Surrogacy has not been a feminist issue before, but unwed motherhood has a long tradition within feminist politics, at least in the Netherlands. It is in this context that the issues of the mother-child bond and of the possibility of giving away children were given a feminist conceptualization.

In the 1890's feminists started a political campaign to attribute a maintenance-duty to the begetters of illegitimate children. In this project they tried to change legal concepts around filiation and rights and duties based upon filiation. Whereas Dutch law had a clearly patriarchal definition of filiation, in which marriage was the only legitimate place for fatherhood and for the transmission of property and social identities, feminists used the language of nature and blood-relationships to advance the claim that 'everybody is responsible for their own offspring.' This emphasis on biological bonds between fathers and children should be seen in the light of the feminist indignation about a 'dual standard of morality', a concept that was a leading image in feminist politics in sexual matters (Sevenhuijsen, 1986a).

The language of the dual standard was developed primarily in the prostitution campaigns, in the *legal* context of the issue of regulation of brothels. The campaigns around both unwed motherhood and prostitution had a wider meaning than a political struggle on behalf of the 'fallen woman'. They produced political images around sexuality and sexual identities as well. As a 'mirror image' of the fallen woman, a concept of decent legitimate sexuality and permissible reproductive behaviour was formulated, often implicitly and sometimes openly (DuBois and Gordon, 1984). Sex, love, steady relationships and motherhood were supposed to belong together, whereas passion and commercial sex were banned to the 'dark' and forbidden side of the border. Feminist legislative campaigns in the twentieth century show the complexities of these attitudes in the field of motherhood and sexuality in a concise way, a reflection of the fact that law and legal rules are an important source of power resources in this field. The unassailability of the mother–child bond was part of a dogmatic system and a political strategy that tried to tackle the sexual vulnerability of women. Two legal issues are especially important here.

First there is the issue of adoption. In the daily practice of social work of feminist organizations until the 1950s, unwed mothers were discouraged from giving away their children, in order to save them from a second 'fall'. The mother had wronged the child by withholding from it a father and a 'normal' family life and she was supposed to 'repair' this injury by being a good, loving mother. The same motive was the reason for long-standing political opposition by feminists against the introduction of legal adoption in Dutch family law, a struggle that was lost with the introduction of adoption in 1957. Thus, motherhood served as a 'protection-racket' against the dangers of sexuality. In its insistence that a motherly image of Woman could not be combined with a sexual image, feminism clearly reflected the general culture of the time.

Secondly there is the issue of the legal tie between the unwed mother and her child. Since 1837 an unwed mother has had to make a legal acknowledgement of her child before they had any family ties in Dutch law. Feminists have opposed this rule since 1900. The motives for their opposition were stamped by a mixture of protective and moralizing attitudes. On the one hand, they involved a protest against a facile appropriate of children 'without a legal existence' by children's welfare agencies. On the other hand, they were intended to discourage the unwed mother from giving up her child. This last motive was adopted by the legislative bodies: the rule requiring acknowledgement was abolished in 1947. Since then an unmarried mother has automatic family ties with her child: the old rule '*mater semper certa est*' was reintroduced in family law. From the day she reaches the age of consent, the unmarried mother also has automatic custody of her child(ren).

Thus the dogma of the mother–child tie remained unquestioned in dominant feminist politics in this field. Feminist politics could 'handle' the unwed mother if she was a victim of male sexual lust and if she was prepared to be a 'good' mother. Although this attitude clearly had moralizing roots, it was often voiced in the language of biology in which women are seen as better carers by definition and in which the relation between mother and child is seen as necessary and inescapable.

Sometimes expression of diverging views can be perceived at the margins of feminist discourse. Fiction is one of the places where less unambiguous images could be voiced. Novels about lesbianism, emotional bonds between women, free love and sexually unconventional behaviour are recently being 'discovered' in women's history as an important source of women's voices which did not effectively penetrate feminist political discourse and are thus absent in feminist historiography. In the Netherlands, informal arrangements of 'surrogacy' join this list of hidden voices.

In a novel by Emmy van Lokhorst, which appeared in 1929, the two heroines, a lawyer and a young office-worker, are depicted as independent free women, with sexual identities and career ambitions (Lokhorst, 1929). The office-worker gets pregnant as the result of a short affair with her married boss. In her distress a close emotional bond develops between her and the lawyer, whose husband has just died. The lawyer consoles the office-girl and takes her away to Italy to give birth to the child. During the journey the two women decide that the biological mother shall give the child to her friend, who longs for a child because she misses the beauty of motherhood in her life. As a lawyer she is acquainted with the legal loopholes in family law. When the child is born, the friend registers as the biological (and thus the legal) mother while her deceased husband is counted as the father. Within two months she is the one with the motherly feelings and a bond with the child, while the biological mother feels nothing but alienation and frustration in contact with the child. The office-worker leaves for New York for a brilliant career and everybody lives happily ever after. The novel can be interpreted as the voice of a woman writer who tries to distance herself from the older feminist images of female identities in the sexual sphere (Romein-Verschoor, 1935, 1977). Besides this it shakes up all the common feminist presuppositions about motherhood and female life-styles and it depicts an informal and sunny arrangement around social motherhood, which now would be labelled surrogacy. No negative connotation whatsoever can be read in the book. Of course one can speculate on the question whether the novel reflects a surrogacy practice *avant la lettre*. This question seems unanswerable to us: the fact of the positive images is remarkable enough in itself.

From Radical to Cultural Feminism

Feminism since the 1960s has, at least in its first period, lessened the ties with biological thinking. In the initial phase of the feminist movement mothering capacities were defined as a product of gender-socialization or as political constructions rather than innate capacities. A distinction was made between the biological capacity of mothering and the social institution of motherhood. This idea was intrinsically linked to a strategy of radical change of the sexual division of labour in the direction of equality. In later years however, motherly images and metaphors became a more complex area of feminist discourse. In fields that are not connected primarily to the division of labour, women claimed a *political* identity as mothers. For example, in the women's peace movement and in the eco-feminist movement women speak in the name of motherhood, which is supposed to give a special wish and capacity for protecting life and nature, which are said to be threatened by patriarchal and/or male principles. In the wake of these activities the connection between Woman–Mother and Nature is restored.

Cultural feminism is a current that originated in the United States and which evolved a way of theorizing that furnishes a powerful and closed conceptual system. Cultural feminism increasingly dominates feminist discourse on issues of sexuality and motherhood in a mood strikingly different from the radical feminism that marked the beginning of the seventies (Echols, 1984). Sexual violence is seen as the paradigm of women's oppression, in terms that equate sexuality, heterosexuality and sexual violence (MacKinnon, 1983). Women's oppression is defined as the appropriation of women's bodies by men and male principles. The fact that many women consent to or even enjoy sexual relationships with men is interpreted as a proof that male ideology defines the female.

It is this kind of theorizing that has until recently dominated the issue of reproductive technology and surrogacy. According to Andrea Dworkin, motherhood is becoming a new branch of female prostitution (Dworkin, 1983, pp. 181–88). Because the traditional 'model' of mothering (labelled by Dworkin 'the farming model') does not work any more for the system of male domination, patriarchy extends 'the brothel model' to biological reproduction. In this model, parts of the body (for example, eggs) can be sold and women can be used, tortured and thrown away; the impulse to use women in this way is presented as the essence of maleness. Applying the brothel model to biological reproduction brings advantages for patriarchy, because it disposes of women as women, who as a result of feminism have become a threat to the stable continuation of male supremacy. The invention of the artificial womb will make women redundant as mothers and lead to general femicide, or in Dworkin's terms to 'holocaust' (ibid., p. 188). The problem of women 'co-operating' in this project is done away with by posing a feminist 'truth' that tells us that the will is constructed outside the individual: 'Individual woman is a fiction, as is her will' (ibid.; Corea, 1985a, p. 228). Surrogates are the kin to prostitutes, the scientists and the doctors are the new pimps. Women who do not reproach them and their doings are nothing else but 'the handmaidens of patriarchy'. The 'soft rhetoric' of feminists who are 'not opposed to co-operation with the proposed regulatory bodies', is said to be 'detrimental to infertile as well as fertile women in all parts of the world, because by accepting to "live with" the nRTs [new Reproductive Technologies] rather than "fight" them, they become handmaidens of mechanical science and vested industrial interests' (Duelli Klein, 1986).

In the conceptual combination of the surrogate mother, the prostitute and the supposed innate male longing for power and death, a feminist paranoia about men is voiced. A moral panic is created and spread. Whereas in the beginning of this century the metaphor of the prostitute was a way of delineating decent heterosexual behaviour, cultural feminism now tends to use it as a way to create an overall feminist identity that denounces heterosexuality itself (Echols, 1984). Those who use the metaphor of prostitution seem to be unaware of the debates surrounding the 'mistakes' that feminists made in their moralistic evaluations of the women involved, as Silvia Kontos points out (Kontos, 1986).

In this process the definition of oppression itself is becoming more and more shadowy. By denying the existence of any free will or the legitimacy of passions (for heterosexual love, for lesbian lust, for motherhood or for anything else) the question *what* is being oppressed in women's oppression can only be answered by referring to a hypothetical Woman or Femaleness. Nurturance, naturalness and love are assuming the status of oppressed entities: the problem seems to be that patriarchy denies us our femininity. This is a striking point when we remember that in the first stage of feminism it was that same patriarchy that imposed femininity upon us. In this way, surrogacy is the 'ideal' issue for stating both the legitimacy and the 'truth' of cultural feminism. Natural motherhood and natural procreation can become the real values of feminism, and surrogacy is the ideal negative mirror image. The contradiction in cultural feminism that women are supposed to be socialized as women while men are born as men, is increasingly solved by positing an inborn femininity as well. Feminism is not any longer that vivid and colourful process of changing gender; instead it becomes a struggle of life and death between fixed males and females. Maria Mies calles reproductive technology a new stage in the patriarchal war against women (Mies, 1986; see also Nilsson, 1985). In the battle against patriarchy, she suggests, our last hope is to halt the commercialization of motherhood; and because commercialization assumes this importance, we are prevented from asking whether commercialization really is the most urgent problem.

When feminist analysis wants to shake free from the ideological inheritance of cultural feminism, several presuppositions should be kept in mind:

1   The mother–child bond is not sacrosanct. This implies that children can grow up happily with parents who are not their biological parents. It also means that women who give birth to a child and give it away can have sound motives: we should respect their choice. It does not mean that these arrangements are always unproblematic, but we should be careful not to generalize.

2   In concrete events of life we have to accept will and longings as given. There is a difference between individual choices of women and political strategies of feminism. In our opinion it is a mistaken interpretation of the slogan 'the personal is political' to deny women these choices and decisions and to develop a feminist morality about the rights and wrongs of life-styles. We have to develop concepts that do not subsume individual women under a supposed collectivity of women.

3   The fact that people want to use technology is not reprehensible, nor is the fact that doctors want to develop technology to 'treat' people's medical problems. We should, however, be critical about uncontrolled power of the medical–pharmaceutical complex in developing new techniques and in defining norms of acceptable reproductive behaviour.

4   There are many aspects of surrogacy and reproductive technology which are important for collective choices in this field and for the women concerned. These issues cannot always be called feminist. Pregnancy and motherhood are important for the women concerned. But it is another thing to declare the protection of the ethics of life as a collective issue for women or even for feminism.

5   The problems around commercialization need to be discussed seriously, without letting emotional reactions foreclose analysis. What about the role of commercial agencies, should they be forbidden or regulated to prevent possible exploitation of both surrogate mothers and would-be-parent(s)? What about the problems

that could arise when a surrogate mother delivers a child with a handicap? (Hollinger, 1985)

Commercialization, Money and Payment

In some countries a market has been organized for commercial surrogacy. The usual model is that a surrogate mother carries a child for a married couple, of whom the woman is infertile. The fertilization can take place in several ways. The easiest way seems the traditional coital model. In commercial and other arrangements artificial insemination is preferred: the surrogate mother is inseminated with the sperm of the husband. This is the 'classical' model of surrogacy. Where a surrogate mother becomes pregnant after egg donation, the term 'full surrogacy' is used, to contrast it to the classical model. It means that the surrogate mother gives birth to a child who will be raised by someone else, but the surrogate mother does not donate any of her own genetic material. In other words: the criterion for surrogacy is whether the child is born and raised by the same woman or not. Egg donation and implantation by in-vitro fertilization in our view should not be labelled surrogacy if the child remains with the woman who gave birth to it. (This procedure is sometimes likened to adoption or even seen as adoption before birth.) For example: if a fertilized egg of woman A is carried to term by woman B and the child is then given/returned to woman A, then we could speak of surrogacy.

In the United States the commercial market for surrogacy is by far the most developed (Hollinger, 1985). There have been debates about the legality of surrogacy contracts. Contract law has a different and far more developed status in the United States than in most European countries. In some American states surrogacy contracts are illegal. In other states, surrogate agencies seem to flourish; family law and adoption rules can be interpreted to allow surrogacy. Lawyers and commercial agencies act as brokers between potential surrogate mothers, eventual parents and doctors. (As usual the brokers make the greatest amount of money on the transaction.) Contracts are drawn to guarantee all parties concerned almost everything. Guarantees are demanded that the child, once born, shall be given to the intended parents and guarantees that the intended parents will take the child. The contracts include clauses about responsibilities for the child in case of a handicap. As is the case with any other form of commercial production, people demand 'quality' for their money. To stimulate the birth of a 'healthy' baby, there is an overwhelming amount of control over the daily life of the surrogate mother. In most cases the contract stipulates that she is forbidden to do anything that could possibly harm the unborn child (Brophy, 1981; Singer and Wells, 1984; Ince, 1984).

In the Netherlands, as in most European countries, such contracts are not enforceable. Traffic in children is explicitly forbidden by law, and therefore the legal basis for enforceability is absent. Although there have been some advertisements in the newspapers for surrogacy, the incidence of a marketing network seems to be minimal (Kilian, 1985). Other, more informal forms of surrogacy are however possible. One case that has become well known concerned a woman who gave birth to a child for her involuntarily childless twin sister. The child was begotten by artificial insemination with the sperm of the brother-in-law and after its birth it was adopted by the couple. All this occurred in co-operation with the state child welfare board.

The fact that commercial surrogacy is not (legally) possible in the Netherlands determines the terms of the public discussion. The trend in public opinion, at least as voiced in the media, is to consider surrogacy a respectable thing to do for a close friend or a relative, who for medical reasons cannot bear a child. The previously mentioned case of the two sisters was not only approved by the child welfare board but by public opinion as well. Mediation through commercial agencies is almost unanimously rejected among all authors writing on the subject and in official reports (Holtrust and De Hondt, 1986). The dominant opinion is that money should not enter into surrogacy arrangements except in the form of a restitution for maternity wear and medical costs. This implies that not paying women for the 'work' of the pregnancy is seen as the most effective remedy against commercialization, an attitude which attributes the problems to the motivations of the women involved. It is an example of the one-sided and moralistic interpretation of the role of money in the whole process (Struck, 1986). This strategy overlooks an important aspect of commercialization: the fact that commercial agents make large profits by their 'mediation'; and the physicians who co-operate are not doing their job for free either.

The denial of payment for the women can indeed be a defence mechanism against a system in which poor women might earn their living by bearing babies for the rich. For that reason caution seems to be justified in calling pregnancy 'work' like any other work. The producing of babies in one's body is essentially a different kind of activity from labour in the labour-market. On the other hand, it seems reasonable that women who do bear a child for someone else and have thereby no opportunity to earn their living in another way, receive a payment for this 'service': this could be done in the form of a refund for loss of income. It stands to reason that women who are not employed at the time of their surrogacy, should also receive payment.

Some Legal Aspects of Surrogacy

The enforceability of contracts is definitely not the most important legal aspect of surrogacy. Just as the introduction of artificial insemination had the potential to overturn legal rules concerning paternity, surrogacy questions legal rules about who counts as a mother. The legal rule *'mater semper certa est'* ('it is always certain who the mother is'), cannot be held for an eternal truth anymore.

When news about surrogacy in the United States reached the Netherlands, a leading Dutch professor of family law Rood-De Boer proposed to abolish this rule altogether. By extending the judicial competition she expected to conjure a potential conflict of interests between egg-donating women, child-carrying women and childcaring women. This was defended in the name of the interests of the child. Her proposal is part of a long-term political strategy of juridification and state adjudication of everything that could be considered 'the interests of the child'.

The most important argument against the proposal from a feminist point of view is that it eradicates the protective elements of family law for women. *'Mater semper certa est'* is a legal confirmation of the 'right' of a woman to keep a child that she bore for nine months and with which, after its birth, she usually builds up a caring relationship. The rule can give protection against men claiming a child as theirs against the will of the mother. This protection counts in situations where mothers have no relationships with the begetter of the child, or where women have been inseminated under an agreement that the donor shall be anonymous. It can also give protection in cases of surrogacy, when a woman changes her mind and wishes to keep the child. If *'mater semper certa est'* were to be abolished, women could be brought before court about their legal and real relationship to their child. It opens the door to a further state supervision of motherhood. This trend can also be perceived at the moment in proposals to abolish the permission of the mother for legal recognition by the begetter of a child. In our opinion it is important to maintain the protective elements of family law for women, and not to surrender them with arguments about situations that will be rare, or in which the power of men as sole begetters will be reaffirmed. When the protective element is maintained, the onus of proof is placed with the exceptions, instead of turning this around. This is especially important, since we live in a situation where women have no established position of power in the legal apparatus.

If surrogacy contracts were made legally enforceable, this would generate the question whether men can claim the products of their sperm, a question that has important consequences beyond the issue of surrogacy. This question is connected to matters such as abortion, visitation rights and custody rights as well. At the moment there is a trend in jurisprudence towards basing family claims on blood-relationships in an extreme way, irrespective of the social relations of parenting. In the Netherlands the fathers' rights movement invokes Article 8 of the European Convention of Human Rights (which deals with the protection of family life) to claim right of access even for begetters who have had no social relationship with the child. The same article is invoked as a fundament for joint custody (Hondt and Holtrust, 1986). Women and children are almost defenceless against this legal development, in which their family life and their will is potentially made subsidiary to male outsiders. (For example, in the United States a donor who did not want to be anonymous any longer and decided that his child should have a father, has been able to get visiting rights, against the wishes of the mother – Kern and Ridolfi, 1982; Smith, 1978.)

Thus, there are many reasons to maintain the '*mater semper certa est*' rule. Maintaining this rule creates a situation in which there will be legal problems only in the case where a surrogate mother wants to give the child away, but the intended parent(s) will not accept it. It would be hard to give general rules for this case, but there seems no reason why the existing rules for giving up children and adoption cannot be applied.

If there is agreement that the spread of commercial surrogacy is not desirable, but that non-anonymous 'informal' forms of surrogacy are admissable, then changes to the law – and in particular to the rules governing adoption and custody – would still be necessary. For example the possibility of adoption by a single person would have to be introduced, something which is impossible in Dutch law at the moment, and adoption procedure would have to be revised, so that the wishes of all parties concerned could be respected without extensive screening and controls. In addition to this an extension of affiliation rules could be considered. In current Dutch filiation law a married man can make no legal recognition of a child born to a woman other than his wife. To facilitate informal surrogacy, husbands could be enabled to recognize the child of a surrogate mother as their legal off-spring, and to request a change of custody. But again in this situation there should be guarantees against forcing women to give up children to whom they have given birth. This would be possible by maintaining the condition that the mother must consent in the legal recognition (a condition that still is the rule in Dutch law, although this rule is threatened at the moment by the invocation of Article 8) as well as in the custody change.

The Wish for a Child

The consequence of the fact that the issue of commercialization is stressed in the formation of political strategies is that other important issues tend to be overshadowed.

For example there is the discussion about the legitimacy of the wish for a child. The introduction of in-vitro fertilization and surrogacy opens up new possibilities for extended debates about this issue, in a way that strongly resembles debates about artificial insemination in the 1950s and 1960s (Zipper, 1986b). There is a double edge in most discussions about the child-wish: as Macintyre showed in her research a woman is considered egoistic either when she wants a child or when she does not want a child, depending on her marital state (Macintyre, 1976). An implicit scale appears in which the legitimacy of women's wishes are evaluated according to their marital state. Single women are not supposed to want children. Married women who explicitly state that they have no wish to reproduce themselves are condemned for not being 'real women'. Women who want children and get pregnant more or less easily are 'normal' and have nothing to worry about. Woman who want children but have problems getting pregnant are judged to be too fanatical in their wishes if they try other methods. According to the medical experts, if she tries too little she is not motivated and if she tries too hard she is judged neurotic and therefore unfit for motherhood: 'You're damned if you do and you're damned if you don't.'

In most reports from national committees on reproductive technologies the importance of heterosexual relationships is taken for granted. In-vitro fertilization and artificial insemination are considered beneficial because they can give people a 'normal' marriage and family life. The quality of the marital relationship is judged by its potentiality to be fertile. Marriage can be 'saved' by the presence of children. On the other hand, the wish for children is considered potentially dangerous as well, because too strong a wish is seen as a sign of neurotic character-structure. The consequence, at least in the eyes of ethical experts, is that couples wishing to have a baby by surrogacy have to be examined (or offered 'help') about the origins of their wish for a child and about their ability to handle the tensions of non-biological parenthood. To be approved for the procedure you have to have a strong wish for children, but you must also be able to abandon this wish. In addition to this, the surrogate mother-to-be has to be screened about her motives for getting pregnant and her ability to give up the child (Christiaens et al., 1985). We can conclude that the introduction of reproductive technology and the practice of surrogacy open up a new range of power mechanisms in which strategies of knowledge and control are closely related.

The other side of the coin of the heterosexual norm is that only married couples are considered fit for parenthood. A precondition for any form of reproductive technology is that it is only available for stable heterosexual couples, or at best stable female couples (Council of Europe, 1986). Single persons are excluded altogether. Different rationales are given for this precondition, mostly formulated under the umbrella of 'the interests of the child'.

The 'interests of the child' is a catch-all formula, which can contain the opinions of dominant political actors (usually not children, but adults with all kinds of opinions, feelings and images about childhood). The formula is defined differently according to the issue at stake. In the recent political struggle around the rights of access after divorce, the 'interests of the child' have been defined by the father's rights movement as having access to fathers. In the context of the legal proposals, it became a *duty* of children to see their fathers rather than a right, though no corresponding duty to be loving fathers was imposed (Verbraken, 1981; Holtrust and Sevenhuijsen, 1986). In the context of reproductive technologies, 'the interests of the child' are defined predominantly in terms of growing up in a two-parent, heterosexual family setting; a family with a mother and a father, two parents with different roles of different sexes. Through the formula of 'the interests of the child' the issue of technology seems to be used to exorcize the spectre of a fatherless and genderless society, a spectre evoked by the growing number of single mothers and by 'stories' about lesbian women using artificial insemination.

In the context of surrogacy some ethical experts define the child's interests in terms of knowing itself to be the product of a loving relationship between a man and a woman: a child has to be a 'child of love'. A person cannot grow up happily when it is not begotten in the mysterious love-act between husband and wife (Christiaens et al., 1985). Another proposed 'interest of the child' is 'to know where it comes from'. This interest is immediately translated into the 'right' of the child to know its male ancestor, which has to be enforced as a legal right. This 'need' and 'right' of the child is often illustrated by stories of adopted children who want to meet their 'real' mother and/or father. The striking point is that this phenomenon is not so much cited as a problem of which the dimensions should be known or for which solutions have to be found in concrete cases, but as an argument for a prohibition of 'unnatural' forms of reproduction. More particularly, the 'right' of a child to know where it comes from is used to challenge forms of family life that are not based on the blood tie between a woman, a man and a child (see for example Däubler-Gmelin, 1986). On this issue there is an amazingly quick and unchallenged translation from 'longing' to 'interest' to 'right' in the moral sense, to 'right' in the legal sense. We think it is an urgent matter to question this chain of reasoning, without denying the authenticity of these feelings about 'roots'. Besides this we should realize that the whole issue is a clear case of 'selective indignation': being deprived of a father is defined as a problem in situations where a mother chooses for 'autonomous motherhood', much more than in cases of orphans or children of widows, or in cases of child abuse.

The discourses around the 'wish for a child' speak – usually in negative and critical terms – about a 'right to have children'. Opponents of reproductive technology often prefer that we should consider children as a gift (of God, or of happiness). This reflects an attitude that refuses any rational consideration of the fertilization process and wants merely to preserve the mysticism. Some feminists equate the concept of a 'right to a child' with submission to the ideology of motherhood, which dictates that every woman should be a mother (Arnold and Vogt, 1986).

However, the most important implication of the concept of 'rights' in this respect lies in the political struggle about the payment for medical treatment for assistance with reproduction. The issue at stake in the Netherlands is whether the National Health Service (which is a compulsory form of insurance for lower-income groups) pays the costs. Private insurance companies give a refund at present, but the national insurance system still denies this refund with the argument that there is no such thing as a 'right to children' (though it pays for numerous operations such as refertilizing sterilized people and operations on the oviducts). This debate on the spending of public money has tended to strengthen further the heterosexual norm: for example the costs of artificial insemination were until recently tax-deductible for married couples, but not for single women (Zipper, 1986a).

In the debate about whether or not there exists a 'right to children', adoption is often mentioned as an alternative to surrogacy or to the use of reproductive technologies. The existence of impoverished children in other countries is often pointed out as if infertile women who chose surrogacy or who had recourse to reproductive technology were selfish for overlooking their needs (Mies, 1985,

1986; Brockskothen, 1986). The invoking of adoption, and of the needs of children in poorer countries, is misleading on two grounds. First, it ignores the many difficulties surrounding adoption: in the Netherlands, for example, a couple has to be married for at least five years, and they have to be affluent; single-parent adoption is forbidden; if a couple is judged fit to be adoptive parents by the State Board of Adoption, they face a long period of time on a waiting-list. The only possibility for relatively swift adoption concerns children from poorer countries, but – assuming the children there are available for adoption – there are still formidable administrative, financial and ethical barriers. The second problem with the recommendation that infertile women should adopt concerns the selectivity of the argument – it is only women who need medical intervention in order to have a child who are expected to justify their choice to bear a child, to shoulder personal responsibility for poverty in other countries, to feel guilty about the 'selfishness' of their desires. If these considerations are important enough political principles to be pressed upon all people, men or women, with children or childfree, then so be it. What is unacceptable is that the legitimacy of the wish to bear and raise a child is questioned only in the case of women whose reproductive organs do not work in the 'normal' way.

Regulation and Control

Almost every European government appointed an official commission to study the consequences of reproductive technologies and to recommend policy measures: in Britain the Warnock Committee; in West Germany the Benda Committee; in the Netherlands the Gezondheidsraad Committee. Surrogacy appeared on the agenda of every commission. The committees not only have to discuss policy, but have another function as well. They serve to rechannel the moral panic: the public can ease its mind because the experts are working on it. Governments can claim to have a firm grip on new developments. The issue of surrogacy plays a role in the canalizing of the moral panic.

Different national committees have broadly come to the same conclusions. Although most attention was given to medical–technical innovations like in-vitro fertilization and gene therapy, subjects less strictly medical such as artificial insemination and surrogacy were also discussed. Similarities between conclusions and recommendations are particularly to be found in the importance that is given to legal marriage. There is a consensus about surrogacy and notably about the reprehensibility of commercialization: there should be a prohibitive law against it. But only when it means that *women* could make some money. Not a word about the commercial practices of the pharmaceutical industry where, for example, ovulation-inducing medicines are produced, or about the doctors who do quite well financially out of treatments for infertility. Commercial agencies are explicitly prohibited in the proposals.

Proponents of restrictive laws do not always realize that surrogacy can already be legally complicated. So-called surrogacy contracts are not valid in most legal systems because they are either forbidden by criminal law as traffic in children, or because they are contrary to the legal definition of public morality (Däubler-Gmelin, 1986). Some committees mention that exceptions can be made in cases where family or friends are concerned, provided they are controlled by the proper authorities. Thus norms have to be developed to specify which couples in which circumstances can apply for surrogacy. A whole series of officials have to be installed in special clinics to evaluate the physical state, but above all the psychological make-up, of the candidate surrogate mother (Parker, 1982). Procedures, analogous to those applied by the Adoption Boards, are being proposed. There are also committees which state that permission of exceptions sets the door ajar: the slippery slope argument.

How should we evaluate the proposals for regulation? Often a clear division surfaces between the principled and the pragmatic. The first group feels that 'It Won't Do' and 'It Should be Abolished'. Whether this option is realistic, whether surrogacy can be prohibited and whether such a prohibition can be executed is not open to discussion. A policy to prohibit all forms of surrogacy is motivated from left to right wing, with first the vague formula of 'the interests of the child'. Secondly a fear (whether or not sincere) for the exploitation of women is voiced. (Quite a remarkable argument. Since when is the exploitation of women so high on the agenda? This is an example of the selective way in which some feminist points of view are translated into public policy.)

The official proposals to prohibit surrogacy correspond to those of the feminist opponents of surrogacy (Corea, 1985a; Brockskothen, 1986). In their endeavours to halt surrogacy (amongst other technology) they cry for governmental control.

The question is whether feminists should go along with this judicial discourse. In practice it can lead to amazing and dangerous alliances. The opponents of surrogacy in the Social Democratic Party in West Germany have a point of view which the Right will applaud: the ties between marriage, love, sexuality and reproduction may not be loosened; surrogacy must be prohibited and reproductive technology may not be applied outside of marriage. In some countries the 'pro-life' movement is taking over the issue of reproductive technology; feminist opponents acquire strange bedfellows in a conservative politics where contraception, abortion, divorce and surrogacy are prohibited. The result of such actions and alliances can be seen in the debates and actions around the issue of pornography in the United States (Sevenhuijsen, 1986b). MacKinnon tried to get pornography into civil law, which would give individual women the opportunity to sue on the grounds of 'damage'. The definition of this 'damage' poses a problem, and even more so because it was supposed to be collective damage. Opponents of reproductive technology acclaim the inspiring actions of Andrea Dworkin and Catherine MacKinnon, and they propose the same political strategy. During a hearing of the Green Fraction in the European Parliament in March 1986 in Brussels, Finrrage spokeswoman Duelli Klein envisaged the same route: individual women should file complaints against doctors on the grounds of 'malpractice' as reproductive technology is a 'violation against the human rights of women'.

The second (pragmatic) group holds the view that some of the consequences are indeed questionable, but expects that surrogacy cannot be forbidden. Their proposals to regulate and control surrogacy are mainly inspired by the idea that although application of medical-technical developments cannot be forbidden, at least they can be kept within boundaries. This group is opposed to harsh legal measures. Instead it proposes to follow developments resulting from directives from the experts and regulation that follows jurisprudence, which Parliament then only has to confirm. Thus the whole area escapes control of the legislative and controlling powers of Parliament, which Rood-De Boer sees as an advantage (Rood-De Boer, 1986). This strategy, however, poses the problem that public debate is avoided.

This can also happen as the result of a *laissez-faire* policy. In that case the physicians decide who is or is not a candidate for treatment, simply by practising. Doctors do not object to this policy, they see themselves as responsible types of high moral standing. Furthermore, the second group stresses that there is already a controlling body in existence, the Medical Disciplinary Boards (Medische Tuchtraad). Unfortunately for them, this opinion is not shared by everyone. When one takes into account the ways in which doctors and particularly gynaecologists behave in respect to the reproductive abilities of women, this trust in the medical profession is clearly misplaced. One only has to think of forced sterilization or the refusal of contraceptives; the prescription of dangerous contraceptives like the Dalkon Shield, Depo-Provera, Norplant; the prescription of diethylstilboestrol (DES), a drug that was known for years to be unsound and dangerous, to name but a few, to realize that to put confidence in the integrity of doctors would be naïve (Ehrenreich and English, 1979; Dreifus, 1978).

The Myth of Control

Proposals for the control of surrogacy depend upon medical and state intervention to limit the circumstances in which surrogacy is available. In the case of so-called 'full surrogacy', where the surrogate mother brings to term a foetus conceived outside her body, medical assistance is required for the process of in-vitro fertilization and embryo transfer. Women have to be admitted to programmes, to have their moral and maternal 'fitness' evaluated; proposals for regulation entail that the entire procedure should be controlled by doctors and psychologists and state boards and ethical committees and social workers. But in spite of the obvious potential for intervention in some women's lives, the claim that surrogacy itself can be controlled is a myth.

The discussion of surrogacy in the context of reproductive technology has obscured the fact that surrogacy does occur and could occur with even greater frequency in the future, without medical or other regulatory intervention. Surrogacy without egg donation is easy. Ever since the public appearance of 'BOM'-mothers (consciously unmarried mothers) in the 1970s, private arrangements of women who bear children for other women (and men) have been known to exist in the Netherlands. It may very well be the case that women 'help' each other in this way more frequently than is known. In practice, 'surrogacy' – without the label – may be common. As in the case of self-insemination, there is no need for a doctor, and the experts who might pronounce on a women's fitness for motherhood need never be consulted. Like self-insemination, surrogacy is a form of self-help for women who would otherwise be barred from raising a child of their own. Informal surrogacy arrangements are not merely one reproductive practice among many; surrogacy could become an alternative, more widespread than it is at present, to medical treatments such as in-vitro fertilization, for people who want a child but are unable to have one without help. The advantage of surrogacy over other forms of reproductive technology is that it does not depend on either medical approval or medical technique.

One of the most endearing characteristics of self-help is precisely that it is not readily controllable or susceptible to regulation. Indeed, this may be one of the reasons why the national commissions on reproductive technology tended to pretend that all surrogacy depends upon medical intervention. A few of the government commissions, to be sure, do recommend that self-help techniques, such as self-insemination, should be prohibited; but in so far as 'in vivo' insemination or self-insemination cannot effectively be prevented, such proposals are quixotic to say the least. The Surrogate Mother has become, in these proposals, the personification of anxieties about unpredictable technological and social developments. Opponents of surrogacy like to believe that if The Surrogate Mother cannot be eliminated, at least her motives and personality can be put under the looking-glass of politics.

Acknowledgements

We would like to thank Nora Holtrust, Joyce Outshoorn and Michelle Stanworth for their advice and comments.

7
Eggs, Embryos and Foetuses: Anxiety and the Law
Janet Gallagher

The story broke in the American press in June 1984: Mario and Elsa Rios, a wealthy Los Angeles couple killed in a plane crash, had left behind two frozen embryos at a fertility clinic in Australia. The 'orphan embryos' – immersed in a tank of liquid nitrogen at the Queen Victoria Medical Centre in Melbourne – became objects of fascinated attention and speculation, tokens in a symbolic battle over the limits of human decision-making in reproduction and over the rights of the unborn. Did anyone own the embryos? Did the embryos have a claim to the fortune? Did they have a right to life, a right to be implanted? In whom? Could they be donated to another infertile couple? Could they be thawed and allowed to die, or must they be maintained indefinitely in their limbo-like state? Who should decide?[1]

The drama of the Rios embryos reawakened the public interest and anxiety over new reproductive technologies that had been sparked by the birth of the first 'test-tube' baby in England in 1978. Commissions of experts were besieged by opponents of the new techniques. Critics were especially horrified by *in-vitro* fertilization (IVF), the process in which the human egg and sperm are united in the culture dish and then, after developing to a multi-cell stage over several days, introduced into a woman's uterus for implantation.

Objections to IVF

IVF was denounced as 'unnatural', a usurpation of God's prerogatives, a step down a slippery slope toward a terrible 'brave new world' of made-to-order people and callous disregard for human life. The Roman Catholic Bishops of Victoria, Australia rejected it as a violation of the natural law: 'In pursuit of the admirable end of helping an infertile couple to conceive and have their baby, I.V.F. intervenes in their supreme expression of mutual love. It separates "baby-making" from "love-making" ' (McCormick, 1985, p. 399).

Such separation of what the Church labels the 'unitive' and 'pro-creative' aspects of sexual intercourse remained absolutely unacceptable to the Bishops. The inseparability of the two had been, after all, a central argument put forward when Pope Paul VI confounded all expectations and overrode his own Commission in 1968 to reassert the Church's condemnation of 'artificial' contraception (ibid.).[2] IVF also suffered from another moral flaw: like artificial insemination (roundly rejected by Pope Pius XII in 1949), IVF requires masturbation, an act condemned by the Church as 'intrinsically and seriously disordered' (Singer and Wells, 1984, p. 56). Some Australian priests carried their objections to IVF so far as to launch a protest hunger-strike in the lobby of one hospital-based clinic (Andrews, 1984, p. 142).[3]

Other concerns arose about the possibility that scientists would attempt to create animal–human hybrids for specific purposes (ibid., p. 144). To some, IVF seemed bound to lead to ever more disturbing developments like ectogenesis, in which prenatal life would be sustained in an artificial womb throughout gestation. Ethicist Leon Kass gave voice to widespread misgivings about setting foot on such a slippery slope. Testifying before a United States Ethics Advisory Board, Kass declared, 'Once the genies let the babies into the bottle, it may be impossible to get them out again' (Singer and Wells, 1984, p. 45).

The Embryo Focus

Most of the ethical and legal discussion, however, has been centered on the more immediate realities of research and treatment. Alexander Morgan Capron suggests that issues raised by the new reproductive technologies fall into two main categories: 1) those posed by the handling and control of human germinal material outside the body; and 2) questions about the new multiplicity of parenthoods – genetic, gestational and social – now possible through infertility treatments (Capron, 1984, p. 195). The most intense, continuing public debate has focused on the moral and legal status of embryos outside the human body.

Issues involving the status and treatment of the extra-corporeal embryo arise out of the very technology of IVF itself. Women undergoing IVF are subjected to hormonal stimulation to bring about 'superovulation' so that the laparoscopic surgery used to remove the ripened eggs can retrieve a number of eggs suitable for fertilization.[4] Hormonal stimulation thus enhances the possibility of obtaining several 'good' embryos for implantation and the consequent likelihood of a successful pregnancy. (It also lessens the need for additional laparoscopies, invasive procedures usually carried out under general anaesthesia). But because implanting more than three embryos significantly heightens the risk of multiple gestation, thereby posing risks to the success of the pregnancy and the health of the woman herself, the extra fertilized eggs may be frozen. This cryopreservation, or freezing, of the fertilized eggs allows future attempts at implantation if the first proves unsuccessful (as happened, in fact, in Elsa Rios's case) or if the woman wants to bear an additional child later. But the existence of these 'excess' frozen embryos raises a number of troublesome questions.

Can there be 'ownership' of such entities? Can, for example, they be bought and sold? Should courts and legislators regulate private transactions involving embryos? Who controls the disposition of such germinal material in case of the death or incompetence of the progenitors? What happens if a couple divorces, or disagrees about the future of the frozen embryo? Can embryos be the subject of research and experimentation? Should scientists be allowed to produce embryos specifically for research? Does the embryo's status change as it develops? Why and how? What does all this mean for pregnant women's rights?

The Legal Status of the Embryo

Britain's Warnock Commission, appointed to consider issues arising out of the new technologies, found that the embryo had no legal status *per se* (Warnock, 1985, §.11.16). Some levels of protection are provided under various statutes. Abortion, for example, is criminalized under certain circumstances; foetuses or embryos might be said to be 'accorded a kind of retrospective status' if they are ultimately born injured as the result of the negligence of a third party while they had been *in utero* (ibid. §.11.16). But, generally speaking, the Commission declared that the human embryo 'is not under the present law in the UK accorded the same status as a living child or adult, nor do we necessarily wish it to be accorded that same status' (ibid., §.11.17).

The legal picture in the United States is somewhat more complicated. Embryos, like foetuses, are not treated as legal persons (*Roe v. Wade*, 1973). The legal status of the unborn varies from jurisdiction to jurisdiction and according to the issues involved. Thus, while the inheritance rights of foetuses are protected, foetuses have no mandatory constitutional claim to benefits under Aid to Families with Dependent Children, are not counted under the census, or regarded as children for income-tax exemption purposes (*Burns* v. *Alcala*, 1975; *Roe* v. *Wade*, 1973).

Before the mid-nineteenth century, the idea of the foetus as a human person prior to 'quickening' or of abortion as 'murder' was practically unheard of in the United States. Even the harshest anti-abortion laws allowed exceptions and the penalties for criminal abortion were always considerably less than those for homicide (Mohr, 1978). The common-law rule has been that the criminally caused death of a foetus is not homicide unless there has been a live birth – an existence, however momentary, independent of the mother (see, for example, *Hollis* v. *Commonwealth*, 1983).

American states are divided on allowing for recovery of damages for the wrongful death of the unborn. Many of the states permitting such lawsuits require that there should have been a live birth or that the foetus would have been 'viable', or able to survive outside the womb, at the time of the injury. Furthermore, the court rulings allowing recovery in such cases have more to do with compensating the prospective parents than with any attribution of personhood to the foetus (*Dunn* v. *Roseway*, 1983).

In recent legal cases, children have been allowed to sue third parties for injuries caused by prenatal events, such as exposure to toxic chemicals. Some lawsuits, like the one charging that a negligent blood transfusion given to a young woman caused Rh-factor blood problems to the child she ultimately bore, have even involved preconception injuries (*Renslow* v. *Mennonite Hospital*, 1976). Anti-abortion theorists have attempted to exploit these cases, arguing that it is inconsistent to acknowledge a right to sue while denying a 'right to life.' But such cases do not really rest on claims of foetal personhood. The compensation is paid to an individual, born alive, who suffers from injuries attributable to pre-birth causes.

Even in contexts such as inheritance and trust matters where legal protection is accorded to the unborn, the rationale for such treatment is respect for the intent of the person disposing of the property, not a view of the foetus as a separate legal personality (Shaw and Damme, 1980).[5]

Recent cases in the United States, however, represent an alarming new drive to attribute legal personhood to the foetus in order to assert government control over pregnant womens' life-styles and birthing choices. A California woman was jailed in 1986 on charges that her 'deliberate disregard of a doctors' orders' contributed to the subsequent brain-death of her baby. The woman was accused of drug use, having had sex with her husband despite doctors' warnings that it would pose a danger to the fetus, and of having delayed reporting to the hospital after she began losing blood (*New York Times,* 1986b).

A number of American women have been forced to undergo caesarian delivery despite their refusal to consent after doctors convinced judges that surgery was necessary for the health of the foetus (Gallagher, 1984; 1987). In 1981 a Los Angeles juvenile court confined one woman to a hospital for the final two months of her pregnancy by 'taking jurisdiction' of her foetus; a local welfare agency had charged that she was unable to care for herself. The woman had, in fact, been examined by psychiatrists who had found no basis for committing her under California's mental health law. A higher court later overturned the ruling, but by then the pregnancy and the detention were over.

The Warnock Committee Report

The Warnock Committee, reporting to the British Parliament in 1984, attempted to answer at least some of the questions raised by IVF. The Committee flatly refused to tackle the explosive issue of when life or personhood begins, saying, '[T]he answers to such questions in fact are complex amalgams of factual and moral judgements. Instead of trying to answer these questions directly we have therefore gone straight to the question of *how it is right to treat the human embryo*' (Warnock, 1985, §.11.9). It recommended legislation declaring that there was no right of ownership in a human embryo (ibid., §.10.11). The Committee also proposed that couples[6] be required to make decisions beforehand as to the disposition of frozen embryos and to review them every five years, and that embryos not be stored for more than ten years (ibid., §.10.10).[7]

The Warnock Committee adopted a self-consciously moderate stance on the question of research on embryos, declaring '[T]he embryo of the human species ought to have a special status and that no one should undertake research on human embryos the purposes of which could be achieved by the use of other animals or in some other way' (ibid., §.11.17). It proposed strict limits – under a national system of licensing and monitoring – on all research involving *in-vitro* embryos, and recommended criminal penalties for anyone making unauthorized use of them (ibid., §.11.18). Research should be undertaken only with the informed consent of the progenitors (ibid., §.11.24).[8] While there was considerable disagreement among members on the issue, the Committee did not suggest a ban on the production of embryos specifically for research (ibid., §.11.30).

The Committee recommended that no research at all be allowed on *in-vitro* embryos later than fourteen days after fertilization (excluding any period during which the embryo was frozen), and indeed proposed that no embryo be kept alive beyond that point (ibid., §.11.22). The fourteen-day limit was based on a rationale that 'One reference point in the development of the human individual is the formation of the primitive streak' within the blastocyst or embryo, 'the latest stage at which identical twins can occur' (ibid., §.11.5). The Committee conceded that its choice of the emergence of the primitive streak as a point of ethical and legal demarcation was somewhat arbitrary, but observed that 'this was an area in which some precise definition must be taken, in order to allay public anxiety' (ibid., §.11.19). The fourteen-day limit had the effect of precluding research and experimentation beyond the point at which – in even the most conservative view – there could be even a remote possibility of embryonic pain, since the neural groove, the most rudimentary beginning of neural development, does not appear until the seventeenth day after fertilization (ibid., §.11.20).[9]

Even so, the majority's conclusions proved unsatisfactory to several Committee members and to those who had argued for recognition of full personhood of the embryo and for a ban on research. The Report summarized the dissenters' position:

> The human embryo is seen as having the same status as a child or an adult, by virtue of its potential for human life. The right to life is held to be a fundamental human right, and the taking of human life on this view is always abhorrent. To take the life of the innocent is an especial moral outrage . . . [S]ince an embryo used as a research subject would have no prospect of fulfilling its potential for life, such research should not be permitted. (ibid., §.11.10)

Embryo Research in the United States

No governmental standards for embryo research have yet been developed in the United States, although the American Fertility Society adopted a set of ethical guide-lines for doctors and researchers in September 1986 (*New York Times*, 9 September 1986). A national Ethics Advisory Board held hearings on IVF in 1978 and 1979 and found no ethical bar to funding research, but there has been a *de facto* moratorium on federal funding (Andrews, 1986).

Political hostility to the 1973 Supreme Court decision recognizing the legality of many abortions provoked a burst of state legislation, including many statutes that restricted research on foetuses or embryos. While adopted specifically in response to the abortion ruling, such laws have the effect of inhibiting infertility research and treatment. Attorney Lori Andrews (1986) notes, for example, that state laws prohibiting research involving pre-implantation embryos might preclude the use of still-emerging techniques like cryopreservation or embryo donation. A recently proposed statute in Louisiana that would grant the IVF embryo status as a legal person until it was implanted could result in women who choose not to risk multiple gestation by undergoing implantation of all the fertilized eggs resulting from IVF being compelled to 'donate' their embryos to another woman (ibid.).

Feminist Concerns

Feminist commentaries on the new reproductive technologies have tended to focus on a set of issues very different from those that have preoccupied official commissions, legislatures and the media. In regard to IVF, for example, there has been considerably less attention devoted to the status and treatment of the embryo than to the technology's impact upon prospective parents, especially women. Gena Corea, for example, raises disturbing questions about whether IVF programmes have subjected women to invasive and risky procedures more suitably labelled experimentation than therapy (Corea, 1985a, p. 111–21). There are real grounds to doubt that patients fully understand the low success rate for IVF generally or realize that among the many new clinics now springing up, a good number have *never* achieved a successful pregnancy. Lori Andrews proposes that clinics and practitioners be required to make available annual reports disclosing, among other things, the number of their attempts at using particular reproductive technologies, their success rates, and any risks that materialized affecting the participants and the resulting children (Andrews, 1986).

Another area of concern has been doctors' or researchers' removal of the ova of women surgical patients, or even their fertilized eggs, for experimental or research use, without informing the women or obtaining consent (Corea, 1985a, pp. 100–7). American commentators have proposed, as did the Warnock Commission, that research on gametes or embryos be conducted only with the informed consent of the progenitors (Andrews, 1986; Annas, 1984).

No unified feminist stance towards the reproductive technologies has emerged as yet. Some feminist commentaries, notably Gena Corea's *Mother Machine* (1985a) and Arditti, Klein and Minden's *Test-Tube Women* (1984) seem to reflect a generalized hostility towards them. They have suggested, for example, that women's choice to participate in infertility treatments is so conditioned by the socially constructed stigma of infertility and a societally imposed norm of maternity as to be no real 'choice' at all (Corea, 1985a, pp. 166–85; Rothman, 1984, pp. 23–34).

A number of other feminists take issue with this view, arguing that it defines women as victims and demeans our capacity to make decisions even within the acknowledged limits of the social context (Lindsay, 1985; Paltrow, 1986). Rosalind Petchesky (1985), examining the 'no real choice' criticism levelled at another technology (amniocentesis), declares:

> I do not subscribe to the view that the existence of a technique limits choice because it compels its use. This is an antitechnological form of technological determinism, attributing to the technique magical power over people's relation to it . . . . The very real potential for *abuse*, on the other hand (e.g., pressure on women to undergo the procedure when it may be unnecessary or risky), is a function not of the technique but of the organization and politics of existing medical care. (ibid., p. 362)

In the context of IVF, the views that technology will victimize women finds expression in anxiety over the threat of male appropriation of female power over reproduction. Robyn Rowland, an Australian social psychologist, worries that

> [W]e may find ourselves without a product of any kind with which to bargain. For the history of 'mankind' women have been seen in terms of their value as child-bearers. We have to ask, if that last power is taken and controlled by men, what role is envisaged for women in the new world? Will women become obsolete? Will we be fighting to retain or reclaim the right to bear children – has patriarchy conned us once again? (Rowland, 1984, p. 368).

It is true that the technologizing of pregnancy and childbirth has often had a disempowering, dangerous, impact on women (Arms, 1975; Corea, 1977; Hubbard, 1982; Rothman, 1982). Recent American legal trends awarding joint or even sole custody to fathers after divorce have created a widespread uneasiness among women, reflected not only in the legal literature (Polikoff, 1982) but in the popular culture as a recurring motif in television soap operas and as the theme of best-selling novels like Susan Miller's *The Good Mother* (1986). Nonetheless, this anxiety over the possible snatching away of the role of motherhood sometimes manifests itself as a self-conciously feminist variant of the same insistence on a specifically female sphere of nurturance, a strict emotional and social division of labour along gender lines, that Kristin Luker (1984, pp. 158–63) found in her study of 'pro-life' activists and that Beverly Harrison (1983, pp. 79–84) discerns among otherwise liberal opponents of abortion.

Ironically enough, this fear of the loss of *motherhood* emerges contemporaneously with an obsessive male fear about the loss of *mother*, a belief that women's demand to use technology (abortion) to choose whether and when we will bear children presages the very end of nurturance (Willis, 1983). These oddly complementary fears rest upon and reinforce a static, polarized vision of gender roles and may spring from anxiety generated by changes in gender relations and expectations.[10]

In fact, it is anxiety – sometimes with wildly inconsistent causes – that seems the predominant force shaping public response to the new reproductive technologies. The Warnock Committee Report refers over and over again to the necessity of allaying public fears (Warnock, 1985, 'Foreword', §.1.1., 1.3, 1.8, 4.13, 4.14, 5.6, 6.4, 12.1, 12.8, 12.16, 13.1). At times, the Committee's recommendations seem pegged to nothing so much as the need for reassuring the public that limits of some sort are being imposed to contain and slow the pace of change (ibid., 'Foreword', point 5).

The impassioned, absolutist opposition to embryo research and the insistence that all fertilized eggs must be implanted – at whatever physical or psychic cost to the women involved – echo the claims of 'foetal rights' now being asserted by some conservative American doctors and legal commentators. The demands put forward sweep far beyond mere limitations or bans on abortion; they would impose unprecedented restrictions on all pregnant women and enforce them through criminal and civil penalties. Under the 'foetal rights' regime, women could be prosecuted for 'foetal abuse' for unhealthy behaviour during pregnancy, subjected to forced treatments – even major surgery – for the sake of the foetus, and confined to hospitals if doctors regarded them as risks to their unborn children. Home births could be criminally prosecuted, drinking during pregnancy criminalized and mothers could be sued by their children for 'prenatal negligence' (Gallagher, 1985 and 1987).

The protective, almost cult-like attitudes toward embryos and foetuses reflect a fierce, frightened sort of identification with them (Gallagher, 1979, p. 79; Petchesky, 1985, p. 335), an identification cultivated and exploited in the service of a conservative agenda on sexuality and woman's role.

One 'foetal rights' advocate writes that legal provisions for foetal protection can be justified at least in part by the expectation that they will provide people with 'the gratification at the thought that their wishes were significant even before they were born. They can thereby escape whatever insecurity may be aroused by the notion that at one time in their prenatal existences they were deemed wholly undeserving of legal respect' (King, 1979, p. 1672). The terror underlying some responses to abortion or to the prospect of scientists tampering with embryos is not just retrospective anxiety about prenatal security; but rather it is the product of anxiety about safety now in a hostile and selfish world. Kristin Luker's study (1984, p. 145) of American 'pro-life' activists notes their shock that the personhood they believed had actually belonged to embryos and foetuses was being stripped away from that vulnerable group and their fear that other 'imperfect' or not 'socially useful' or 'inconvenient' people will be next, so that they themselves are at risk.

The Need for New Feminist Responses

As feminists we have to refuse to allow amorphous anxieties – even our own – about the pace of social and technological change to distort law and public policy about human reproduction. But we must, at the same time, move to address and calm those anxieties. Not just because it will make it easier for us to protect reproductive rights, but because societies permeated by fear are no more acceptable than societies that respond to that fear through state coercion.

Creating a less fear-ridden public climate requires not only that we expose and battle those who would whip up public anxiety and ride it to power, but that we take affirmative steps – concrete and symbolic, individual and communal – to reassure. Those of us who support a right of reproductive choice have to make it clear, for example, that we'll help build a set of social supports and attitudes that make it possible for a woman to choose to go through with a pregnancy when she gets a 'bad' amniocentesis report; that we won't tolerate a situation in which the lives of the disabled are so distorted by denial of opportunity and support that women feel obliged to abort. There are, in almost every area of concern, affirmative policy and legal steps that we can take to address people's real and legitimate worries.

Our scepticism about the way medical technologies have been developed and used is warranted. We are right to be wary of the idolatry towards prenatal life, to regard it with ideological suspicion. The exaggerated solicitude towards unimplanted IVF embryos appears bizarre when one remembers that less than a third of the eggs fertilized within a woman's body will ever survive to live birth (Biggers, 1981, p. 339). The foetal rights drive – objectionable enough on its own political and legal terms – is all the more outrageous when seen played out against a backdrop of scandalously high infant mortality rates, of news stories revealing that there are entire American counties in which poor pregnant women can find no doctor willing to treat them under Medicaid, the federally funded programme for medical care.

Nonetheless, feminists have too often allowed ourselves to be driven into narrowly defensive, ultimately unsustainable public positions in which we seem to belittle both the pain of infertility and the satisfactions of motherhood. We have to learn better to avoid the media caricature of feminism that ignores our carefully wrought and balanced agendas. We need to project a vision that addresses the whole range of women's reproductive experiences, to publicly associate ourselves with affirmative proposals and demands supportive of a woman's choice to become a mother.

Kristin Luker (1984, pp. 151–7) found that one-third of the 'pro-life' activists she interviewed had been galvanized into anti-abortion work by a personal experience of loss: an inability to conceive, a miscarriage, the loss of a newborn. Their mobilization around this issue came in part because they interpreted feminist support for the right to choose abortion as somehow trivializing their own loss. They heard it as a rejection of the value and the humanness of their 'imperfect', lost babies. We have to learn to speak in terms that do not lend themselves to that misinterpretation.

The widespread anxiety about the commodification or abuse of human embryos is being exploited by conservative forces, but it is not without foundation. Feminists must not allow our legitimate concern that attribution of legal personhood to embryos and foetuses might threaten women's rights, to lead us to ignore our own gut instincts that embryos ought not be bought and sold or subjected to totally unrestricted experimentation.[11]

The focus on prenatal life isn't confined to fanatics. Birth and children are traditional symbols of promise and continuity and renewal. The new visual access to the embryo and to the womb, the increased experience of fertility problems, even the fact that the legal availability of birth-control and abortion has transformed so many people's experience of pregnancy into a chosen and joyfully celebrated undertaking, makes us all responsive. People approaching parenthood often develop a particularly intense awareness and concern about the coming child. Respect for the right to choose when and whether to undertake motherhood does not require that we dismiss the ethical or emotional reality of the embryo or the foetus.

Cases

Burns v. *Alcala*, 420 U.S. 575 (1975).
Dunn v. *Roseway, Inc.*, 333 N.W. 2d 830 (Iowa, 1983).
Hollis v. *Commonwealth of Kentucky*, 652 S.W. 2d 61 (1983).
Renslow v. *Mennonite Hospital*, 40 Ill. App. 3d 234, 351 N.W. 2d 870 (1976).
Roe v. *Wade*, 410 U.S. 113 (1973).

8
Victorian Values in the Test-tube: the Politics of Reproductive Science and Technology
Hilary Rose

Sometime back in the early seventies I was spending a good deal of time with a friend who was going through a difficult time with her male lover. The problem turned on the issue of children, to have or not to have. Late one evening – we had been talking about books we had been reading – she explained to me that she thought Shulamith Firestone (1971) was absolutely right about the liberation of women. Through that discussion, Firestone became, for me, more than an exhilarating read, more than a wonderful turning of the brave new world onto its sexist head; I realized that Firestone's unrealistic Utopian hopes and the theoretical naïvety of her analysis had made it more difficult for women to see the political threat flowing from some of the fast-developing techniques of reproduction – not least the test-tube baby. It became important to try to convince my friend that the kinds of science and technology that were presently around were profoundly unlikely to supply a technological fix to women's oppression. As an activist in the radical science movement, the one thing I felt clear about was that science and technology – despite their claims to be 'neutral', 'objective' and 'above class, race and gender' – were, in actuality, much more like the less-than-neutral society that produced them (Rose and Rose, 1971). Together with Jalna Hanmer I wrote about the new reproductive technology (Rose and Hanmer, 1976). I think our hope/dream was that the women's liberation movement would see the advancing technological dangers for women and would use its energies to block them.

For some feminists the Utopian promise of Firestone's work was sufficient – she seemed to solve the problem central to radical feminist theory of how to guarantee the continuation of the species without needing men. Her bold project was to capture the imagination of science-fiction writers, fostering both the future post-gendered society of Mattapoissets envisaged by the socialist feminist Marge Piercy (1979) and the separatist feminist Wanderground of Sally Gearhardt (1985). For feminist theorists, particularly socialist feminists, the flawed premises of Firestone's analysis – that women's oppression lay in biology rather than in society – closed debate. Either way the feminist movement in the early seventies was not interested in the technological advances or their implication for women. The struggle for control over women's bodies, above all over fertility, was initially a struggle around birth-control and abortion, the right *not* to have a child. An almost simultaneous struggle was waged over the conditions of birthing; were women to be reduced always to patients, mere appendages to the high technology of delivery? It has only been much later that the right to *have* a child has been seen as an equally valid claim, so that rather than birth-control and abortion rights, feminism increasingly claims reproduction rights. It is from within this more complex way of thinking about our fertility and infertility that feminism now examines critically the new reproductive science and technology, above all in-vitro fertilization (IVF) and the prospect of genetic engineering. This chapter focuses on the new genetics and the social implications for would-be parents of its fast-developing technologies of mass genetic screening and gene therapy. It starts from the position that among the new reproductive technologies, the IVF cat is out of the bag, and – whatever else IVF does – it meets real needs for (some) real women. Consequently, a feminism that accepts the diversity of women's needs, must now work to limit IVF's imperialistic claims over women's bodies, and its associated claim to consume ever more of the health-care budget for high-tech, curative medicine. Limiting IVF is no small demand, not least when we consider the struggle to limit caesarian deliveries which, under the claim that they save life (manifestly true for some women) presently colonize women's bodies in their indiscriminating use. Because the new genetic technologies are likely to affect almost all would-be parents in Western countries (at least all of those with some sort of universalistic health-care provisions) the social implications are potentially more pervasive than those of IVF.

Louise Brown, the world's first test-tube baby, born in 1978, serves as a symbolic watershed of this deeply felt debate. Her existence and those of the other IVF children have changed the ground-rules. It is one thing to argue against a specific predictable technological development which is against the interest of women (if you like, to try to block or delay a future IVF programme): it is quite another to say to Lesley Brown (or any other infertile woman) that it was wrong for her to have Louise. Similarly, what we know about genetic and congenital impairments changes all the time, and our capacity to make choices changes; one thing that we can be confident about is that absolute rules (even feminist absolute rules) in a changing context don't work. To win control of the politics of reproduction we have to understand not only the changing balance of social forces but also how science and technology have developed and are likely to develop in the future.

How Science Grows

How science and technology grow is by no means self-evident. Within the field of the social studies of science, which includes historians, philosophers and sociologists together with a not insubstantial number of natural scientists (who like to keep control of how outsiders interpret their world) there are basically two positions in what has become a highly polarized debate. The first is known as 'internalism', the second as 'externalism'. As I shall try to make clear, neither the conservative 'internalism' nor even its radical opposition 'externalism' entirely encompasses women's experiences and neither therefore meets the demands of feminist theory. Yet we need to know the contours of this debate, not least because the increasing threat of reproductive science and technology to the autonomy of women's bodies means that we can neither afford to waste time reinventing quite useful theoretical wheels nor, (for that would be really counterproductive) elaborately reinventing a broken wheel. Understanding how science and technology grow is far too important to be left to men.

The dominant tradition – needless to say one that is both bourgeois and masculinist – of the history of science has been internalist; that is, it has told a story of cognitive transformation in the independent development of intellectual structures (Mendelsohn et al., 1977). Internalist accounts, above all of the new cosmology of Copernicus and Galileo and the new physics of Newton, see these advances within scientific culture as the birth of modern science, and together the most powerful influences in leaving medieval society, with its earth-centred universe patterned by God and His angels. Changing an explanation about how the natural world worked required nothing less than changing – in a deeply religious culture – the Divine purpose. The internalist account thus celebrates the scientist as hero. Defended only by truth, objectivity and the ex-perimental method, the hero opposes superstition and irrationality and clears the way for the birth of both modern science and modern society.

Thus science became synonymous with social progress. The understanding that this progress, with its move away from theology and towards objectivity, also entailed a move towards sharply patriarchal values, had to wait for the insights of feminist historiographers such as Donna Haraway (1979), Carolyn Merchant (1980), Ludi Jordanova (1980), and Evelyn Fox Keller (1985). Merchant's rereading of the founding fathers – above all of Francis Bacon – seventeenth-century statesman and ideologue for the new experimental method – seizes and reveals the central metaphor. For Bacon, 'Nature' was a woman and, as such, her secrets had to be wrested from her, she must be forcefully penetrated and mastered. But this critical rereading, which portrays the scientist as rapist rather than hero, does not appear until the third quarter of the twentieth century. Until that time the internalist account both reconstructed and celebrated the achievements of science and through this, explained its historical development. In this historical reconstruction, the scientists were almost entirely men. Those women who managed to contribute to science and even achieve some recognition in their lifetime were effortlessly erased (Alic, 1986). Hermetically sealed within their intellectual structures, the historical context in which the scientists work becomes mere background.

Against this dominant internalism stood an externalism that sought to explain the origins and growth of modern science in terms of the needs of a burgeoning capitalist society. In the pioneering work of the Soviet Marxist Boris Hessen (1971), Newton's studies of force and gravitation were determined, not by the autonomous cognitive development of physics, but by the economic base. The thesis presented at the international history of science meeting in London in 1931 enraged the conservative internalists and captured the imagination of young scientists increasingly attracted to Marxist theory (Needham, 1971; Bernal, 1939).

But even while the externalists emphasized class relations in the growth of science, they shared the progressivist ideology of science of the internalists. It has been left to feminists and historians sympathetic to the claims of women to draw out the gender-specific nature of that concept of progress. The gender of the scientists for both internalists and externalists lies outside the history of science. Women are silently agreed by both to be part of nature. While it would be wrong to suggest that no feminist voices opposed this erasure – there is, for example, Dora Russell's *Hypatia – or Women and Knowledge* (1925) – the dominant masculinist traditions remained sanguinely untouched.

Externalism in this Marxist form was largely a victim of history in which Stalinism and the cold war played major parts. In the West internalism reigned unquestioned until the publication of Thomas Kuhn's *The Structure of Scientific Revolutions* in 1970. Intensely debated and savagely criticized by the guardians of internalism (Lakatos and Musgrave, 1970) the text served as the catalyst to a renewed interest in the externalist account. Given political edge by the radical and counter-cultural movements of the sixties, the self-flattering claims of science to be above and independent from economic and social forces were thrown, once more, into increasing theoretical and political question (Rose and Rose, 1971). Science and technology were seen as neither neutral nor inevitable. Within a global capitalist system, an increasingly footloose capital aided by the internationalism of science and technology restructured both economy and society, penetrating areas of human existence hitherto relatively unexploited by market forces.

The New Critique of Science

The achievement of the externalist analysis of the growth and social functions of science was to turn the much-vaunted critical tools of science onto science itself. While much of science was too remote from everyday life to inspire this critical examination, certain areas thrust themselves into the political arena. Military technology, the high-tech delivery ward, arguments about the 'natural inferiority' of Black people and women demanded either capitulation or resistance. The challenges come in the form of both technological developments and scientific findings. Against that tradition which seeks to split modern science and technology – often trying to preserve science's 'purity' as against the everyday 'dirty' quality of technology – it is necessary to insist on their intimate connection. Modern science advances through technology; Rosalind Franklin had to be able to make the X-ray photographs for her work to be appropriated by the DNA theoreticians (Sayre, 1975). There is an action imperative built into modern science so that, regardless of the consciousness of the scientist, the technological application of the work is always present – evidenced not least by the last four decades of reproductive science. Modern science is action-oriented, it does not simply contemplate nature, but seeks to dominate and exploit it.

The new externalism also stimulated an exploration of the relationship between science and ideology (Rose and Rose, 1976). Nowhere perhaps can this be seen more clearly than in the recrudescence of biological determinism since the late 1960s. First IQ theory as a special case, then sociobiology more generally provided a renewed legitimacy to an unequal social order. By the early 1970s biology too was called into the service of a patriarchal society determined to resist the claims of the Women's Liberation movement. Invoking the mantle of an objective, neutral science only seeking after truth about the natural order the renewed biological determinism sought to demonstrate nothing less than the *Inevitability of Patriarchy* (Goldberg, 1977).

To note this is not to argue that externalism is merely a conspiracy theory of scientific development (though I would never rule out conspiracy theory as historical explanation, as conspiracies, while rarer than some imagine, are unquestionably a fact of life). It is simply that the IQ story and the attempt to renaturalize women are particularly graphic examples of the externalist thesis. For the new externalism takes as its programmatic position the view that science and society are not analytically distinct categories, but that society is present within science as much as science is present within society. Society being 'in' science is a deeper proposition than the kind of everyday argument that, without funds, science cannot advance or that the development of science is influenced by its environment. Instead the new externalism views social relations as constitutive of the logical structures of thought itself.

The Social Constructionist Account of Science

The new externalism or, as it is presently more commonly termed, the social constructionist analysis of science (Van den Daele, 1977) finds a good deal of support in the social studies of science. From R. M. Young (1977) we have, for example, the influential but contentious paper, 'Science *is* Social Relations'. In this he argues that the distinction between science and ideology can no longer hold because the dominant social relations are constitutive of science. In this thesis there is no space for an attack on, for example IQ theory from *within* science; the old distinction between science and ideology has been theoretically displaced and the distinction between 'good science' and 'bad science' made uninteresting. The only critique of IQ theory is to be made from a historical and sociological perspective.

In this way a strong version of the social constructionist programme ceases to be interested in the truth claims of science, for knowledge structures are reducible to the interest groups that produce them (Barnes, 1977). Social constructionism in the hands of men seems, at this point, to move into logical overdrive, adopting an extreme sociological reductionism. The knowledge of social relations is prioritized and becomes the ground from which other knowledge structures can be analysed. Put another way: the existence of social relations is implicitly accorded truth status, while at a formal level the possibility of truth claims are regarded as irrelevant. In the last analysis, social constructionism has no ground on which to stand, for everything, including its own propositions, is relativized away.

Feminism, Social Constructionism and Corporeal Reality

Feminist critiques of science have been profoundly attracted to the social constructionist programme but have, for the most part, been unwilling to swing into this logical overdrive; even where they have adopted the strong version theoretically they have eschewed the political price of extreme social constructionism. Thus, the historian Donna Haraway adopts an apparently similar theoretical stance to Young, in her recent paper 'Primatology is Politics by Other Means' (1986); nonetheless there are important differences which are more than the political good sense of not attacking one's own side, though the merits of that should not be entirely ignored. I think the 'more than' stems partly from the difference to which Harding (1986) draws our attention, between feminist empiricism and traditional or masculinist empiricism. At the core of traditional empiricism the social characteristics of the observer are irrelevant (it is to be taken for granted that this means the perspectives of white men). By contrast, what feminists from all kinds of theoretical and political standpoints insist upon, is the importance of their feminism – of the participating 'I' of the observer – to their observations.

Thus, substantial numbers of feminist natural scientists have criticized as 'bad science' or as 'ideology' work which claims that women's destiny is laid down within her biology, without themselves being criticized by other feminists for substaining the ideology of science.[1] Women's bodies and women's minds have thus been defended from within empirical science but – and the but is very important – from a science that is itself very consciously in the process of reconstruction.

A major dimension of the struggle for second-wave feminism has been about the control of women's bodies and women's minds. In this struggle we cannot abandon our corporeal identity and simply drift away in a cloud of disembodied social constructionism. Nowhere is this clearer than in the struggle for control of reproduction, as Rayna Rapp's (1984) scrupulously reported 'XYLO: A True Story' documents. From her experience of amniocentesis and a chosen abortion, she describes the closeness of her grief and that of

Mike, her partner – 'For two weeks Mike and I breathed as one person'. She reflects too on the ways in which her loss commanded widespread and loving support whereas his was culturally erased. She goes on to describe how Mike is able to throw off his grief whereas her body continues to remind her of her loss. As a feminist theoretician and as a woman experiencing a late abortion, she writes, 'Having spent fifteen years of my life arguing against biological determinism in my intellectual and political life, I'm compelled to recognise the material reality of this experience.' As a number of feminists (Sayers, 1982; Hartsock, 1983a; Harding, 1983; Rose, 1983) have argued, the dichotomy between essentialism – that is a view of women's nature as biologically determined – and social constructionism – that is a view of women's nature being socially constructed – is unhelpful to theory, and as poor theory is unhelpful to the interests of women.

Without wanting to go any deeper into the feminist debates about the growth of science – although there has been a tremendous wealth of writing in recent years – I want to suggest that there is a growing agreement that an adequate epistemology will require to take on board both the material reality of social relations and the material reality of nature, including our bodily selves (Harding, 1986). Such an epistemology provides feminism with a standpoint capable of acknowledging both the commonality and diversity of women's experiences. It is from this standpoint that we must consider the issues raised for women by the new reproductive technologies.

High Technology Futures and Fantasies

Given that women have been simultaneously shut out and socialized to shut themselves out of science, it is politically vital that we develop a realist appraisal of the new technologies – which are an immediate threat, and which are relatively remote or almost certainly not feasible? Certainly beyond IVF and the actual or potential gene therapies lies a scientific and technological horizon along which are ranged other possible reproductive interventions: would it be possible to rear a foetus from fertilization to independent 'birth' entirely in vitro (ectogenesis)? To clone identikit copies of individuals from single cells or 'gene libraries'? To rear a human embryo in the uterus of a non-human creature or even make human-non-human hybrids? Or to provide a technique that would enable women to give birth without the need for sperm to fertilize their eggs (parthenogenesis, a form of cloning)? Could men have babies? These prospects and others form the stuff of science-fantasy dreams, or serious dystopic concern and Utopian hopes amongst feminists[2] and of abstract moral theorizing among philosophers (Glover, 1984).

The Warnock Report (1985), dismisses some of these possibilities as beyond the range of presently envisageable science and technology (for instance, cloning); others it sees as feasible in principle but to be controlled by criminalizing or licensing (trans-species fertilization; ectogenesis). The focus of much of Warnock's attention was directed, therefore, to the control of human embryo research, and concluded (with some dissent) that the limit of the age to which human embryos should be kept alive in vitro was fourteen days. In all the predictable furore that followed this recommendation (and it is interesting that relatively little comment has been made on others of the technologies – such as hybrids – which might also seem close at hand), with Edwards and some other researchers and medical doctors urging the limit be lifted, and the Unborn Child (Protection) Bill and its supporters demanding a total ban – the fact that at present the fourteen-day limit is still beyond available technology tended to be ignored.

If we are to begin to find ways of controlling the new reproductive science and technology in the interests of women, it is important that we distinguish between those technologies of mainly ideological significance which serve to control through moral panic and those grounded in scientific and technological possibility. Not all that can be imagined is necessarily technically possible (like space-travel using anti-gravity machines, for instance). Powerful the new biological techniques may be, but they are not omnipotent.

The Need to Understand (and Control) the New Genetics

In its concern with the IVF debate and the speculation over the implications for women of such seemingly remote prospects as ectogenesis and parthenogenesis, feminism has paid less attention to the massive increase in genetic knowledge and to the capacity for direct intervention and manipulation that has accumulated on a mass base over the last decade and which shows no sign of slackening. So first, the new genetics.

From the moment of conception, of the fusion of egg and sperm, each individual carries two sets of genes, one inherited from each parent. As the embryo grows its cells divide over and over again and, at each division, new copies of each set of genes are made, so that each body cell of the foetus, and later of the child and adult, contains copies of the original genes which the fused egg and sperm inherited

– about 100,000 different genes in all. The genes are present in the form of long molecules of the 'genetic material' DNA, divided into a number of individual strands, called chromosomes. Normally humans have forty-six chromosomes in all, arranged in pairs. These are similar for males and females with one exception – females have two copies of the so-called X chromosome, whereas males have only one X, and one Y chromosome. This difference, as well as being involved in shaping the sex of the future child, is also important in a number of genetic disorders (for example colour-blindness and haemophilia) which can be carried by females but can only be expressed in males.

Genes carry the chemical code for the production of proteins, which are the chemicals of which cells and ultimately organisms are mainly constructed and which also do most of the day-to-day work of being alive. Just how a foetus and later a child develops depends on the interaction, during its development, of the unique set of genes that it has inherited and the unique environment in which it develops. The properties of a gene depend on its chemical composition – its DNA. If the DNA composition changes for any reason (such changes are called mutations and can be produced, for instance, by radiation) then the gene either cannot produce the protein it codes for, or makes a faulty protein, then the foetus is likely to miscarry. But if it is a relatively minor change, then the foetus will develop but may do so with characteristic abnormalities. Whether the abnormalities make any obvious difference depends in part on the fact that each foetus has two sets of each gene, one from either parent. If both parents have the same abnormal gene set, then the foetus is bound to inherit the genetic abnormality. But if only one parent has the abnormal gene then each conception carries only a statistically calculable chance of inheriting the problem. Some abnormal genes are dominant – that is, for the statistically unlucky conception even one copy of the gene is enough to affect the development of the foetus. Examples include such conditions as hypercholesterolaemia. Other genes, however, are recessive, which means that in the presence of a normal copy of the same gene, the foetus will develop more or less normally. The blood disorder sickle cell anaemia, common amongst Black people of African origin, or Thalassaemia amongst Mediterranean peoples are examples. However, the person with a single copy of a recessive gene remains a carrier for that gene and has a 50 per cent chance of transmitting it in turn to their own children.

It is important to be clear that whether or not a gene is actually deleterious depends in part on the environment in which the foetus, child and finally adult grows and lives – for instance, whilst the gene for sickle cell anaemia is regarded as deleterious in North America or Northern Europe, where people with two copies of the gene may suffer from problems resulting from not being able to get enough oxygen into their body tissues, a single copy of the gene seems to convey some immunity to malaria and is, therefore, an advantage in regions where malaria is common. Similarly, there is some evidence that short-sightedness is genetically inherited. This must have been a disadvantage in past human societies, but in societies where glasses are readily available it no longer matters very much. More dramatically phenylketonuria (PKU), a genetic abnormality that affects 1 in every 10,000 children born in Britain, used to lead to irreversible mental retardation, until effective dietary management was introduced which eliminated all the phenylalanine (in meat proteins for example) from the diet. Newborns are now routinely screened with a blood test, and dietary management introduced where the phenylalanine metabolism is abnormal. The example of PKU as a genetically transmitted abnormality whose outcome can be transformed through modifying the environment without changing the genes is a precious and rather rare example of a screening and intervention process with no losers, only winners.

All this genetic information seemed, only a few years ago, to belong in the realm of scientific knowledge without much immediate technological application. It did, however, make genetic counselling possible, as in the case of Thalassaemia – which has steadily been reduced in communities, of Greek Cypriots for example, where it was once common.[3] What has changed dramatically since the early 1970s has been the explosive growth of the new science of molecular biology and its application as biotechnology. Molecular biology opened up not mere abstract genetic knowledge but the power of manipulating genes. It became possible, for example, to develop methods for identifying genes – lengths of DNA – by means of specially synthesized molecular probes, to snip out the individual genes, from the DNA of human or other organisms, and to make multiple copies – or clones – of the genes. Even more remarkably, it became possible to take a gene, isolated and copied from humans, say, and insert it into bacteria, so that the bacteria would now begin to make the human protein – a technique now used to manufacture human insulin, the protein that diabetics cannot make for themselves.

Biotechnology took these molecular biological methods, coupled them with the techniques of chemical engineering originally developed by the brewing industry, and a multimillion-pound venture was born. In the early seventies, almost overawed by the potential of the new techniques, leading molecular biologists (such as the signatories to a letter initiated by the American molecular biologist Paul Berg) themselves pointed to the dangers of 'accidentally' making a potentially lethal organism that might escape control, and called for tight state regulation of the new laboratories. They seemed less perturbed at the potentially vast new profits that seemed to lie before them, as almost overnight academic molecular biologists became entrepreneurs, forming new companies with science-fiction-sounding names (Genentech, Celltech, Cetus and so on); bankrolled by big investors (not least the drug firms) they rapidly became paper millionaires as the biotechnology bandwagon began to roll (Yoxen, 1982). A decade later, some of the more wildly optimistic prophecies of what the new biotechnology might produce have begun to wear a little thin, and the same biologists who cautioned against the hazards of the new techniques are now arguing that the restrictions be lifted – but in the meantime biotechnology has opened a whole new framework within which the discussion about the new reproductive technologies must be set.

Preventive Screening or Coercion by Another Name?

Preventive screening for genetically transmitted or congenital disorders raised new problems which go well beyond the boundaries of science and medicine (Hubbard and Henifin, 1984). Because preventive medicine was seen as the socially progressive alternative to curative medicine, advocates of the new genetic screening have tended to argue that the gains to be made are unproblematic. Yet in the name of prevention, coercive practices are increasingly being introduced. Already available are methods for screening pregnancies by amniocentesis for a wide range of congenital and genetic conditions associated with disease or disability; soon likely to be added to amniocentesis, which cannot be carried out until the eighteenth to twentieth week of pregnancy, is chorionic villus sampling (CVS), which can be done as early as the eighth week. At present, the choices that can be offered to a pregnant woman as a result of these screening procedures revolve around the information that her foetus carries, or does not carry, any particular chromosomal or genetic condition. She can then, in principle, choose whether to have the pregnancy terminated. In this sense the new techniques increase the choices for women by offering the possibility of at least attempting a pregnancy with the option of not giving birth to an impaired child. Unfortunately, as Wendy Farrant's (1985) study shows, the majority of clinicians limit that choice by offering amniocentesis to women only if they agree in advance to have termination should the foetus show any abnormality. (Edwards drove this policy to its logical conclusion, requiring Lesley Brown to sign a written statement that she would agree to an abortion if the foetus was abnormal).

But genetic knowledge as well as screening technology continues to play a significant part in the decision whether or not to conceive. To take the most common form of congenital mental impairment, Down's syndrome, which accounts for 35 to 40 per cent of all children born with a severe mental impairment, 'at risk' women themselves take steps to reduce the chances of giving birth to impaired children. As it is widely recognized that one of the key factors in producing a Down's syndrome child is the age of the mother (and to a less clearly researched extent that of her partner) women over forty have, over the past ten years, increasingly eschewed conception. Of the 1,000 babies born each year with Downs' syndrome, only a quarter are born to older women. More research is needed to determine precisely what is happening here as women are increasingly caught in a time-trap, on the one hand pressured by the demands of their employment lives to postpone childbirth, on the other hand pressured by the correlational knowledge to have children before forty.

Those in the group most at risk who, by chance or choice, do conceive are more likely than younger women to be offered cytogenetic (screening) services. In the United States access to amniocentesis is not always covered by Medicaid and is controlled by income – in Britain the existence of National Health Service (NHS) does not appear to guarantee adequate provision. A study of North-east Thames Regional Health Authority revealed that rather less than half the women in the at-risk group for Downs' syndrome received amniocentesis (Murdrey and Slack, 1985). (Some of those not screened refused, for reasons varying from moral concern to unwillingness to accept the risk of miscarriage. For some the lack of information and language difficulties were a problem.) While the impact of genetic knowledge is evident, the effect of the availability of amniocentesis in terms of elected abortions is quite modest, as it appears that only 50 to 100 Down's syndrome conceptions are actually terminated over the course of a year. It is this modest actual figure which, despite the heroic claims for screening, has given rise to more radical proposals for non-invasive screening procedures for the entire pregnant population. Technical feasibility and the acceptability of the unit cost – rather than the acceptability to pregnant women – seem to be the two chief considerations in discussion of these proposals (Taylor et al., 1986). As Farrant (1985) points out, the emotional implications of screening are neglected in discussion

(Black Report, 1979, p. 35), and even more troublingly, no less than 25 per cent of the consultants she surveyed felt it was unnecessary to obtain the woman's consent to alphafetoprotein (AFP) screening.

But even where such screening programmes protect women's rights to choose, the problem for the intending parents is that while amniocentesis can provide reasonably accurate information about the presence or absence of Down's syndrome, or AFP screening about spina bifida, and perhaps Down's syndrome, what the tests cannot provide is any guidance as to the mildness or severity of the effects of the condition on the child. Would-be parents have, in the context of poor public services for mentally handicapped people, to assume the worst outcome and consider whether they can cope. As counselling services supporting screening programmes that might help parents in this difficult decision-making, are under-financed or non-existent, the would-be parents are forcibly reminded that they will be left to cope alone. In these circumstances the action imperative built into any screening test that can only generate either/or answers works strongly towards the abortion decision.

For this reason moves to non-invasive population-based screening for defects, even though they appear under the apparently benign banner of preventive medicine, are unacceptably coercive (Cooper and Schmidtke, 1986). The state regulation of reproduction in this way must be seen as the first step of a eugenicism which, while not codified by law as in Nazi policies, is increasingly codified in practice. Reproductive rights must mean the effective right to choose not to have a screening test as well as the effective right to choose to have one, and the issue of testing must be separated from choices about abortion.

Down's syndrome is a chromosomal abnormality, and has been recognizable by simple microscopic examination of cells for more than a century. The complexity of the issues opened by the newer genetic screening is much greater. What the molecular biology and genetics of the past decade has made possible, is the recognition of some 3,000 distinct 'conditions' which are transmitted from parent to child along straightforward genetic lines of inheritance (McKusick, 1983). These conditions include serious and relatively widespread disorders which result, apparently inexorably, in death early in life, such as Tay-Sachs disease, which occurs particularly amongst Jews of Eastern European origin and produces blindness, mental deficiency and then death in children, and very rare conditions like Lesch-Nyhan syndrome. Children born with this disorder, as they grow, develop a compulsive tendency to bite off their own fingers and tongue. Tay-Sachs and Lesch-Nyhan are conditions for which treatments are unknown, and may be beyond medical reach, but many more of the long list of known, common or rare, genetic disorders are relatively mild and their effects on a person born with them are not easily predictable. In fact, as genetic knowledge increases, and more and more human genes are studied, more and more potentially 'deleterious' genes are likely to be recognized. Indeed, it is already clear that all 'normal' people carry a proportion of such genes, without necessarily being in any way disabled.

Whilst the new genetics has theoretically identified the genes, the new molecular biology has opened the way to their detection by gene probes in tissue removed by amniocentesis or CVS. On the cards then is the possibility of detecting an increasing number of conditions during pregnancy which may or may not have disabling effects on the child or later on the adult. But the potential goes far beyond this.

Gene Therapy – the Imperfect Made Perfect?

Many molecular biologists now believe – and their belief is being backed by funding from drug companies and venture capital as part of the biotechnology boom – that is not sufficient merely to detect a potential genetic abnormality whilst the foetus is in the womb and to offer the choice of abortion. For now that it is possible to synthesize genes artificially, the way would seem, in principle, open to offer to 'correct' a faulty gene in an unborn child (French, 1984). The idea would be to diagnose the defect as soon after conception as possible and then to introduce the new genetic material in a form that could replace the faulty gene in all the body cells, thus ensuring normal development – this is so-called somatic cell therapy.[4] The second and even more ambitious objective seeks nothing less than modifying the human gene pool itself. By replacing the faulty genes both in the fertilized egg and in the sex cells, it is proposed to ensure not only that the fault is corrected but that it is eliminated from all subsequent offspring. In this eugenicist's dream the deficient gene is thus removed from the population.

Whilst these techniques are still both unproven (and indeed would be precluded in both Britain and the United States by therapeutic guidelines for patient care) there has been some success in inserting new genes into experimental animals. Mice, for instance, have had genes inserted for the production of growth hormone derived from humans or rats; the result has been the production of a certain number of extra-large super-mice, although it should be emphasized that the failure rate is very high in such experiments. Nonetheless, in

1980, an American scientist, Martin Cline, circumvented American guidelines on attempting somatic cell therapy in humans by moving his experiments abroad to Israel. The furore that followed led to the loss of his United States government grants, and eventually to his resignation from UCLA. The experiment also failed to work. But the fact that it was attempted at all is an indication of the pressure for this type of 'therapeutic' intervention. So we must assume that within the foreseeable future – unless research and treatment guide-lines specifically control or exclude them – these technologies will begin to become possible and available.

Mass Screening and Biomedicine's Perfect Body

In many ways the arguments for mass screening for genetic defects constitute a remarkable rerun of the history of mass biochemical screening in the sixties. Then all sorts of promises were made concerning the advantages of biochemical screening for the early identification and management of disease; the interests of the biochemical pathologists in extending their domain became as one with the sales talk of the firms selling huge auto-analyzers.[5] Medical insurance programmes in the United States pioneered the biochemical screening approach and the NHS trailed after. Problems thrown up then within health-care circles are echoed today by the much more public debates around genetic screening. Just what is the right course of action if a biochemical assay used in a screening programme unequivocally points to a number of people having diabetes even though some or all of them do not feel any 'diabetic' symptoms? What has happened to the concept of a normal measurement, and how do we understand these so-called abnormal findings? Just what is the right action if we know that we are carriers but do not know whether the condition in any offspring is likely to be mild or serious in form?

Basically, the political ploy of the would-be mass genetic screeners is to talk up the hard cases, such as Tay-Sachs, Lesch-Nyan and Thalassaemia, where the issues are so cruel that probably few women would choose to carry the foetus to full term. These genetic imperialists – though eugenicists would be the truer concept – then transfer this cruel clarity onto other areas of genetic impairment, without acknowledging that the issues are much more complex. Take even a hard case such as Huntington's chorea where in mid-life something rather similar to senile dementia develops irreversibly. Supposing would-be parents are carriers for Huntington's – as the offspring's life is without disability until around forty it could be a not unreasonable gamble that over that time-span medical science could effect control of the disorder. After all, for a long time now we have taken for granted that diabetes can be managed effectively through dietary control and the administration of insulin, yet in many of these cases diabetes is a genetically transmitted disorder which, untreated, leads to death. The point is that for real people, that is, people who live in the messy and confusing situation we call everyday life, even the geneticists' hard-won knowledge of the single gene transmission of a serious disorder does not lead to a single and inevitable choice. From the point of view of the person with the genetic impairment gene therapy is by no means necessarily the best or even the safest choice. In such a difficult situation, which confronts would-be parents, above all the women who will bear the children, it is they rather than any medical expert, who must be the best protectors of a child's interest.

The emphasis on identifying the transmission of genetic impairment or identifying genetically impaired foetuses also serves to devalue people with disabilities. Should they have been born? Were their parents – above all was their mother – failing in her duty by giving birth to a disabled child? Listening to some bioethicists (needless to say, men) one would certainly think so.For these moral mandarins, the fact that only such a small percentage (5 per cent) of those admitted to hospital for care as mentally handicapped patients have genetically transmitted problems is neither here nor there. The old and powerful mechanism of devaluing the victims and blaming mothers has been activated, and can run and run.

Sex Determination and the Problem with 'Femicide'

Screening has other implications. Feminist groups in India and elsewhere have raised a tremendous outcry against the use of both amniocentesis and chorionic villus tests to identify the sex of foetuses in order that male foetuses may be kept and female foetuses aborted. In India this negative trend is compounded; not only are tests used to determine sex and to abort female foetuses, but also at every stage of girls' and women's lives the death-rate is higher than that of boys and men, because their access to resources from food to medical care is seriously restricted compared with that of their male counterparts. The situation is so grave that there is a significant demographic imbalance in favour of men, reversing the usual sex ratio.[6]

But sex selection and sex determination are a growth industry and not only at the ideological level. A pre-conception technique to determine the sex of a foetus was recently reported by a group at Keio

University in Tokyo (Swinbank, 1986, p. 720). Using the differential density of X and Y chromosomes, they have centrifuged sperm and, using the X chromosome-rich fraction, artificially inseminated six women seeking girl children. When this news item was released on National Radio there was intense public criticism, scarcely diminished when the Sugiyama Clinic, also in Tokyo, revealed that they too were developing sex-selection techniques and were part of a world-wide network involving 770 groups. The Sugiyama group had similarly found the new centrifuging technique as more effective and had achieved a 90 per cent success rate in promoting the conception of girl babies in a group of twenty-four women. Sugiyama's statement that some women had sought the technique not to avoid hereditary disease such as haemophilia, but purely out of desire for a daughter, inflamed debate. What is interesting is the high passions that these reports aroused, compared with the relatively muted response to male sex selection. Selecting for female foetuses, it would seem, is far more controversial than selecting for males.

Feminists in many countries have become concerned about evidence of sex selection to the extent that some have argued that women who have amniocentesis should not be given the information about the sex of the foetus, lest internalized values or external pressure be placed upon them to abort female foetuses. Others oppose this position, and while acknowledging the risks, affirm that the choice of abortion remains a women's right. A woman might well choose to abort a foetus on sex-linked grounds. Where an impairment is, for example, carried by females but expressed in males, a woman who wishes for a child but feels that she cannot cope in this society with a seriously impaired child might wish to abort a damaged male foetus but keep an undamaged – but carrier – female foetus. Her daughter may, at the present state of knowledge be faced with an identical choice subsequently.

In the necessary attempt to draw attention to this fast-developing problem feminism has had the far-from-new problem of naming the phenomenon. There is a strong case for dropping one of the early terms used to describe the systematic destruction of female foetuses. Using the term 'femicide' to describe abortion is both theoretically loose and politically dangerous in that it elevates the foetus to the status of a person, and thus gives support to 'pro-lifers' in general. It also abets both the foetal rights litigation in the United States and moves in Britain such as the Powell Unborn Child (Protection) Bill. The proposal by ASH (the anti-smoking pressure group) to prosecute for neglect women who smoke while pregnant, and the current Californian case of a woman who had used drugs while pregnant being charged for neglect when her baby was stillborn are part of this dangerous trend.[7] Gena Corea's (1985a) alternative term of 'gynicide' – invoking the extermination of women and their culture – does not escape the problem.

Neither the concept of femicide, nor that of gynicide explains why a specific sex–gender system should seek to exterminate women. It may be in the interests of particular men to kill women and girls and to abort female foetuses, and for a patriarchal order to use terror to maintain control, but it does not follow that it is in the interests of a patriarchal order to eliminate such a useful source of labour, sexual servicing, etc. A society based on the domination of a subordinate group (even though in certain periods the dominant group may behave with immense savagery) does not exterminate that on which it relies. By analogy nineteenth-century capitalism in Britain came near – when the expectation of life in the Spitalfields area of London was seventeen – to destroying the work-force on which it relied. Without wishing to devalue the part played by workers' movements in their own defence, it was also the state as the logic of capital which acted to protect workers' lives – if necessary against the interests of individual capitalists.

Using the language of the holocaust may be dramatic, but whether it will help feminism grapple with the complex reality of the new reproductive technologies is dubious.

Conclusions: Victorian Values in the Test-Tube?

Unquestionably we are in the middle of a massive investment in research and development into the process of human reproduction. The economic and social forces which shape that development are those which have shaped the history of modern science and technology; what is new is the area of research activity and the level of investment and, therefore, the speed of technological change. The logic of a state that is both capitalist and patriarchal requires that there is continuous change but that the fundamental structures of power are left undisturbed. For the state, managing science and technology is always crisis management, as new knowledges and new technologies always offer – or seem to offer – the possibility of social change.

The impetus for the new developments in reproductive engineering come in part from their relevance not to human but to animal engineering – the search for innovation and profit in agriculture. Yet one of the keys to the new biological understanding is the similarity between the biologies of non-human animals and humans. Thus, reproductive engineering on animals achieves almost automatic, willy-nilly relevance to the prospect of intervention in humans. Despite the current unease about animal experimentation, working on animals was and remains for most scientists a conscious ethical choice. This has served to insulate advances in embryological and genetic research in other species from ethical and political debate. What was unthinkable about human beings became unthought. Science and scientists were thus free from the irritation of popular debate with all its misunderstandings – and understandings – and they escaped, not for the first time, popular and democratic accountability and control. In an interesting way the advent of the animal rights movement could – on an optimistic reading of its impact – help to close the ethical gap through which science escapes.

Nonetheless, however much discounted by the scientific establishment from the 1920s onwards, the new reproductive technology began to be considered in terms of its transferability to human beings. Today moral and media panic is generated around specific eye-catching technologies, some of which are at present fairly remote, to the extent that a supposedly serious weekly can publish an article on the possibility of men or transsexuals becoming pregnant, or feminists can suggest that all our troubles can be solved with parthenogenesis. At worst, such moral panic distracts from the very real dangers of screening under which the mass colonization of womens' bodies can proceed relatively unchecked.

IVF, for example, can be recognized, like other technologies discussed in this chapter, as a highly profitable enterprise. Now it is an almost routine technology, but during the early 1970s when the debate about the social implications of embryological research was firmly on the public agenda in the United States, public research funds for human embryological research were at a relatively low ebb. In the United States, government-controlled funds diminished, whilst in Britain the main source of public funds for medical research – the Medical Research Council – supported basic embryology in non-humans, such as amphibia and mice, but did not fund the Cambridge group of Robert Edwards and Patrick Steptoe for human IVF and embryo transfer. But Steptoe and Edwards were able to turn with success to private funding sources, and it was not long before they (and a group working in parallel in Melbourne, Australia, funded by Monash University) were able to announce the successful transfer of technology from animals to humans. The fact that their work, and the profuse flowering of clinical activity in IVF and embryo transfer work in the United States, could be sustained by venture capital points to the profitability of the programme. Indeed, as a surgical intervention, IVF and embryo transfer work meets all the criteria of highly profitable work whose control remains firmly in the hands of doctors and scientists.

For feminists, a central issue must be the way that with IVF the medical profession assumes increasing power to determine who shall mother and on what grounds. Thus when all the praises for the Warnock Report's clarity and reasoned reflections on the technical feasibility and ethical implications of embryological research are said, it nonetheless remains that not very far behind this rational mask and gender-sensitive language, lie entirely uninspected patriarchal values:

> However, notwithstanding our view that every patient is entitled to advice and investigation of his or her fertility, we can see occasions where the consultant may, after discussions with his or her colleagues, consider that there are valid reasons why infertility treatment would not be in the best interests of the patient, the child that may be born following the treatment, or the patient's immediate family. (Warnock, 1985, §2.12)

One of Warnock's strong claims is for reason and rationality yet the evidence that might support her Committee's conclusion that gynaecologists are suitable people to be trusted to act 'in the best interests of the patients' is in short supply. Indeed, the evidence of their performance in that other area of a comprehensive reproduction service, namely abortion, is that their conduct demonstrates a desire to deny not merely patients' interests, but even their legal rights. What definition of patients' 'best interests' can lead to the situation where consultants are able to deny abortion services to eight out of every ten women in the West Midlands legally entitled to a free NHS abortion?

IVF can provide a technological solution to the problems of an infertile woman but it does so at the price of strengthening the ideology of motherhood. Jan Brennan, who participated successfully in the Monash IVF programme, talking of the ways she coped with her infertility, said: 'There were times when I was depressed, feeling that somehow you weren't a real woman unless you were fertile.' What is interesting about the Brennan story, and it is echoed in a number of other accounts of IVF families, is that although the popular stereotype is of the childless couple, the actuality is frequently that one or even both partners have had children before. Len Brennan was already married when Jan met him, and the father of no less than six children. Obstetrician Walters and ethicist Singer (1982, chapter 2) are careful to provide a double legitimization for the

Brennans' need for IVF to provide them with a family: first, that the existing children 'spend little time in Melbourne' and, secondly, that 'Jan was more a sister to them than a mother.' The Brennan claim to share in the benefits of IVF motherhood is thus validated. The simple argument that Jan wanted a baby and could not have one is, by itself, inadequate; the successful 'Brennan Story' requires a heterosexual partner whose participation supports the legitimacy of the therapeutic intervention.

Now it is precisely this agreement (between obstetrician and ethicist) – that doctors naturally are the right profession to decide who is a suitable case for infertility treatment or gene therapy – that must be a major source of political and particularly feminist concern. A less mystified account would note that doctors in general and obstetricians in particular are unwilling to give up an inch of the power they wield over other people's – above all, women's – lives and bodies. They may be test-tube babies, but the values underlying the technology remain strictly Victorian. This pervasive conservatism lies at the heart of the debate about the so-called new challenges to ethics posed by the new science and technology of reproduction.

The problem for feminists is that we have to resist specific oppressive technologies while at the same time working to change nothing less than the values and structures of science. Thus our debates must be located within an understanding of the biologically determinist direction of modern science and medicine which contain within them fixed notions of woman's and man's natures. A determinist biology and medicine seek the causes of infertility and genetic imperfection, and their solutions, in the individual (not by chance primarily in the woman), rather than in an ecologically grounded concept of the individual in her or his natural and social contexts. This is why in infertility, biological determinism looks within the woman's womb (and, where it remembers, into the man's sperm-count)[8] in its efforts to cure a condition that it takes as given. The political demand that flows from this research orientation is for either more preventive or more curative medicine or both – more and more effective screening procedures, infertility clinics and gene therapies for imperfect organs or foetuses.

By contrast, the ecological approach asks first about the causes of infertility itself: is it our bodies, our life-styles or the result of environmental hazard? Or does it lie in the interaction between all three? If we focus our research attention on this socio-ecological domain the action imperative is transformed. No longer is the demand for more and more medicine, whether preventive or curative. Instead the demand must be for less toxic environments, safe contraception,[9] access to healthier life-styles and for conditions that actively promote health. This is not to say that new reproductive science and technology will have no part to play, just that feminism has to locate it in its proper place, serving as one, perhaps quite small, part of the research programme of a social vision that takes as one of its key objectives the well-being and – to use a not very twentieth-century expression – the happiness[10] of all its people.

9
Infertility – a Life Sentence? Women and the National Health Service

Lesley Doyal

Introduction

Infertility treatment in the British National Health Service (NHS) is currently receiving considerable public attention. New technologies such as in-vitro fertilization (IVF) are being hailed as the miracle solution for all those women who cannot conceive within their own bodies. At the same time, parliamentary questions have revealed very serious deficiencies in the more general provision of service for the infertile. These developments have led to a heated debate about future strategies for helping those unable to have children.

Vociferous opposition to the new reproductive technologies has come both from 'right to lifers' who are opposed to any interference with the foetus, and from some feminists who believe that these techniques are not in the interests of women. The latter argue that IVF is of little proven efficacy except as the means by which male doctors, embryologists and others can gain more prestige and greater financial rewards (Arditti, Duelli Klein and Minden, 1984). In the more long term, they see it having disastrous eugenic implications, making possible selective reproduction and even the involuntary use of poor women to 'breed' for richer ones (Corea, 1985a). Far from demanding the wider availability of these technologies, many feminists argue that they should be totally opposed.

However, many people who are themselves infertile (including of course some feminists) take a rather different view of the situation. They complain above all about the lack of services and the difficulties so many experience in trying to get sympathetic help. According to them, the debate about IVF often obscures the lack of basic facilities that infertile women need, and they see more generous funding and universal coverage (including some IVF provision) as the major priorities.

These very different approaches to infertility can best be understood by placing them in the wider context of the debate about the NHS. The problems of infertility services highlighted by these two groups of critics – quality and accountability on the one hand and access on the other – are not unique to this area of health care but reflect the broader failure of the NHS to meet women's needs and expectations. Feminist research has consistently shown health services for women to be insensitive and even sexist in their approach and inadequate in their coverage (Doyal, 1985). As we shall see, infertility provision suffers from these same deficiencies and both will need to be remedied if the needs of infertile women (and men) are to be met more effectively.

Does the National Health Service Care for Women?

Since its inception in 1948 the NHS has undoubtedly benefited the vast majority of British people. Above all, anxiety about the cost of medical care was removed by the provision of both general practitioner (GP) and hospital care free at source, making access to services more equal on both a geographical and a class basis. Women in particular were beneficiaries of the new system since married women outside the labour-market had been excluded from the earlier state health-insurance scheme set up in 1911. Moreover, their special needs connected with fertility and reproduction were difficult to meet without a nationally organized health-care system. Under the NHS women's access to health care improved considerably since services were made available to all irrespective of sex, marital status or contribution record, with the cost being met by a combination of general taxation, national insurance contributions and a smaller number of charges for specific items.

On the surface then, British women should be well pleased with the NHS. It has met many of their needs as users of services and has also become an important source of 'female' jobs with over 70 per cent of NHS workers being women. This success, however, has been only partial and as cuts in public expenditure have opened up the deficiencies of the service to wider scrutiny, the limitations of what it has achieved for women are becoming ever more obvious. While access has been improved for all, sharp inequalities remain between geographical areas, social classes and racial groups. If anything, the gap between social classes has widened; women who are married to semi-skilled and unskilled workers are now 70 per cent *more likely* to die prematurely than those who are married to men in professional and managerial groups (Office of Population Censuses and

Statistics, 1986a). Women in the lowest social class also suffer three times more long-standing illness than those in the highest (Doyal, 1985). Hence the NHS has not equalized either the life chances or the health status of British women.

One reason for this is the failure to equalize access to care. Women in the lowest social class use most services more frequently than their more affluent sisters, but not to the extent that their much greater health problems suggest that they should (Le Grand, 1982). Paradoxically, preventive services in particular are used least by those women who suffer most from the problems that preventive services are intended to forestall (Doyal, 1985). There is an especially marked social-class gradient in the use of services connected with fertility control; middle-class women are much more likely than working-class women to attend a family planning clinic or to discuss birth-control with their GP. There are also great variations in the availability of abortion services around the country and many women report considerable delays in obtaining an NHS termination (Clarke, Farrell and Beaumont, 1983). As a result, more than 50 per cent of abortions are still done outside the NHS in the commercial or charity sectors, making access dependent on the capacity to pay. The availability of health services for women has therefore improved with the introduction of the NHS but class inequalities persist (as do those associated with race, though little detailed information on this aspect of inequality is yet available). As we shall see, a similar pattern prevails in the case of infertility where the possibility of benefiting from the new technologies is almost entirely determined by the ability to pay.

As many feminists have pointed out, there is an additional problem in that those gains that women have made in access to medical care have not been wholly beneficial. This is because they have often been accompanied by an increase in the control that doctors are able to exert over women's lives (Riessman, 1983; Roberts, 1981). This is especially true in areas connected with reproduction. Doctors have the power to influence or even to determine womens' decisions about contraception, abortion or sterilization with moral and scientific decisions often being elided imperceptibly. In the area of mental illness too, doctors are often able to exert control over women at vulnerable times in their lives, reinforcing a particular model of femininity and a nuclear family life-style (Jordanova, 1981; Howell and Bayes, 1981; Penfold and Walker, 1984). Not surprisingly, similar criticisms have been made of infertility services – that doctors do not take womens' own needs and perceptions seriously, and accept only those who fit their own notions of the 'deserving parent'. Above all however, the NHS has been criticized for not being actively involved in the promotion of women's health. It has provided some services to treat them once they are ill but has done almost nothing to prevent their becoming sick in the first place.

In the main part of this chapter, I will look at these issues in more detail, exploring the ways in which the provision of infertility services reflects the broader failure of the NHS to meet women's needs and expectations. The chapter will show that infertility services are not yet available for all who need them; that the new high technology services are being introduced *despite* the lack of basic gynaecological and infertility care for all; that the emphasis on the more prestigious curative strategies has meant almost no attention being paid to the *prevention* of infertility, and above all, that women themselves have had far too little say in how the problem of infertility should be dealt with at a national, local or even individual level.

Assessing the Problem: the Invisibility of Infertility

Any attempt to assess the effectiveness of infertility services in Britain immediately founders on the lack of information. A national health service could reasonably be expected to collect a broad range of data, both on the health status of the population it serves and on the services it provides. In fact, the official data on health and health care in Britain are very limited and for a variety of reasons women are particularly badly served (Macfarlane, 1981; Oakley and Oakley, 1979). In areas like infertility which have traditionally received very little attention, the problem is, of course, even worse. Hence, we know very little indeed about how many women (or men) are infertile or about the facilities that are available to them.

Estimates vary but most commentators agree that at least one in ten couples are affected at some time in their lives. In Britain this means some 50,000 new cases of infertility each year (Pfeffer and Woollett, 1983). However, this is inevitably an underestimate of the problem since many people will not bring their difficulties into the medical arena and others will present themselves with different symptoms. Moreover, cases may go on for several years, leading to a cumulative total of between one and two million people in need at any one time. Indeed one very detailed study of a single District Health Authority recently concluded that at least one in six couples need specialist help at some time in their lives because of an average infertility of two and a half years (Hull et al., 1985).

Unfortunately, we have no information about the class or race distribution of those who are infertile, though as we shall see it seems likely that at least some of the known causes of infertility are more commonly found among the poorest groups. Nor do we know anything about the extent of infertility among single women – since it is normally heterosexual couples who are treated together. Most studies have shown that in about one-third of couples the problem lies with the woman, in about one-third with the man and in about one-third with both. In what follows, I will be concerned with the particular problems of women but of course many men will also be extremely distressed by infertility and the associated treatments.

Information about the provision of services should, in theory, be easier to obtain than information about the extent of infertility. However, a computerized search made in the preparation of this chapter threw up a large number of newspaper articles about 'test-tube babies' and surrogate motherhood but no estimates – official or unofficial – of the use or coverage of services. The authors of the Warnock Report have also commented on this lack of information and recommended that funding be allocated for the collection of relevant data (Warnock, 1985, p. 13). However, nothing has yet been done and a recent parliamentary question (*Hansard*, 11 March 1986) revealed that no information was available, even on the cost of infertility treatment to the NHS. It was this lack of knowledge that led Labour MP Frank Dobson to commission a survey of infertility services in all District Health Authorities (Mathieson, 1986). The results of this survey provide much of the data used in what follows.[1]

Inequality and Infertility

The most striking finding from the survey was the lack of attention paid to infertility within the NHS. No consistent policy has ever been formulated and as a result services are patchy and some regions and districts severely under-resourced. The Warnock Committee itself commented that the present organization of services was 'haphazard and unsatisfactory' (Warnock, 1985 p. 13) and this was confirmed in the survey. However, variations in provision are not random. Services are better overall in the South of England than in the Midlands, North or Wales, reflecting a traditional bias towards the more affluent parts of the country. But it is important to note that even in the best-provided regions in the South, some 40 per cent of District Health Authorities have little or no special provision for infertile people (Mathieson, 1986, p. 4).

It is extremely difficult to estimate the impact of these inequalities on potential parents. The few District Health Authorities who keep records report that many patients wait thirty weeks or more for their first visit to a clinic and can wait up to four years for eventual treatment. As Mathieson comments: 'Waiting is the most common experience for infertile people. Waiting to see their own doctor, waiting to be referred to a clinic, waiting for the outcome of tests and waiting to see whether the treatment has worked' (Mathieson, 1986, p. 5).

Those who can afford it may also have to travel long distances to get treatment. Finally, it is likely that those who live in the most under-provided districts will get less effective treatment. Even if they eventually reach a consultant she or he is less likely to have specialist knowledge and fewer facilities will be available. Frank Dobson's survey showed that only 96 out of 200 authorities were able to do ovarian scanning, only 86 provided microsurgery and only 70 offered a rapid radioimmune assay service for testing hormone levels. Experts agree that all three are essential for an effective infertility service, but only 40 District Health Authorities could offer them all (ibid., p. 4).

These inequalities are even more dramatic if we look at the techniques of assisted reproduction. Artificial insemination (AI) by donor (AID) and by husband (AIH) was the first of these techniques to be widely used. It has a long history but has never been properly integrated into the NHS (see chapter 4). It was first agreed that AID and AIH should be provided within the NHS in 1968 – if recommended on medical grounds. It was also decided in 1973 that there should be a system of accreditation for AI centres but this was never actually established (Warnock, 1985, p. 19). Since then the numbers requiring AI have risen continuously and in 1982 the Royal College of Obstetricians and Gynaecologists reported 1,000 conceptions and at least 780 live births (Warnock, 1985, p. 19).

NHS facilities for providing this service are still very limited, however. In East Anglia for instance, there is no service at all and none is planned, and very long waiting-lists of one to two years are common all over the country (Mathieson, 1986, p. 17). Moreover, even in those districts where services are provided, only three out of twenty-eight are completely free. In the other twenty-five authorities, most patients are asked to pay £10 – £15 per insemination (ibid.). While this is a fraction of the charges made in the private sector it is anomalous in the wider context of the NHS, since payment is not required for other surgical services. Above all it discriminates against those infertile people with lower incomes, since the shortage of NHS provision inevitably drives many of those people who can afford it into the private sector for artificial insemination. Twenty-five out of the fifty-three clinics providing this service in England and Wales are actually outside the NHS – seventeen of them commercial under-takings and eight of them charities. Thus, the situation with AI is very similar to that pertaining to abortions. That is to say, more than 90 per cent of patients actually end up in the private sector, reflecting a basic lack of commitment within the NHS to a woman's right to choose to have – or not to have – a child.

In the case of in-vitro fertilization, money – or the ability to borrow it – is an even more important determinant of who gets treated. IVF is a technique where an egg is fertilized in the laboratory and the resulting embryo is then implanted by a doctor in a woman's body. It is said to be appropriate for some 5 per cent of infertile couples but will certainly not be successful in all these cases. Hence, it will never be a general solution to the problem of infertility but could potentially benefit a small proportion of those who are currently unable to conceive. At present many of those who could try this technique are prevented from doing so by cost. The Warnock Report recommended the setting up of a Voluntary Licensing Authority to monitor the development of IVF in Britain. In its first report the members commented that:

> IVF is not considered by most health authorities to be a priority even by those who provide an infertility service. The opportunity for infer-tile couples for whom it is appropriate to have IVF treatment very much depends on whether they can afford to pay privately and have access to an IVF centre. (Medical Research Council and Royal College of Obstetricians and Gynaecologists, 1986, p. 15)

Only twelve of the fifteen NHS regions offer any IVF service at all and only one of these (North-west Regional Health Authority) has a clinic funded entirely by the NHS. St Mary's Hospital in Manchester does treat patients free of charge but has a four-year waiting-list for the first consultation and is unable to accept cases from outside the region (Mathieson, 1986, p. 20). The other (few) clinics providing a free service for NHS patients do so by running a private clinic and ploughing most of the fees back into the public sector. The first Report of the Voluntary Licensing Authority summarized this rather paradoxical situation with the comment that 'without the funds generated by private practice almost all NHS IVF centres would probably have to be closed or to restrict very severely their IVF services' (Medical Research Council and Royal College of Obstetricians and Gynaecologists, 1986, p. 12).

The end result of this situation is that most IVF treatments in the United Kingdom are at present carried out in private clinics in return for fees. The cost of this will vary and for most couples will include considerable travel costs and hotel bills as well as medical costs which are estimated to be £2,000 – £2,500 for in-patient IVF treatment. IVF is not, therefore, for the poor or the average wage-earner but only for the relatively affluent. Since private insurers such as BUPA have now removed it from their list of available benefits, only the rich and those single-minded enough and solvent enough to borrow a considerable sum will be able to try the possible benefits of IVF.

Thus, infertility treatment in general, and 'assisted reproduction' in particular, are not equally accessible to all in need. They are not an NHS priority and – like a number of other services – are increasingly being transferred to the private sector (Griffin and Rayner, 1985). Indeed, infertility is currently big business with Humana recently opening a private infertility centre in London, designed to deal with some 2,000 cases of infertility each year. However, money is not the only thing needed to ensure infertility treatment in Britain. You also need to be a 'suitable couple'.

Controlling the Infertile

Feminists have drawn attention to the stereotypical and often derogatory assumptions about women that underly much medical practice (Doyal and Elston, 1983; Fee, 1983; Oakley, 1980; Roberts, 1985). Women are generally seen as inferior to men – whatever their social and economic status. Their 'natural' function is assumed to be reproduction and this is seen as the central determining characteristic of their psychological and possibly even their physical being. Hence, motherhood is seen by most doctors (and many other health workers) as the real purpose of women's lives. It is 'good' for them to become pregnant and have babies – but at the same time this very process makes them different from and somehow inferior to men. This attitude is reflected in many different ways in medical encounters and very often the inherent – if often concealed – power of the doctor is used to 'persuade' women to behave in accordance with these wider social expectations.

When we look at these medical assumptions about women in the context of infertility, two rather obvious anomalies are immediately apparent. Despite the fact that women are assumed to desire motherhood above all else – indeed to be universally 'desperate' if they are unable to achieve it (see chapter 4) – very few NHS resources are allocated to help them. Lip-service is paid to the enormous importance of motherhood in women's lives but as we have seen, not enough facilities are available to solve the problems of the infertile. Even more illogically perhaps, the allegedly biological maternal instinct is assumed to affect only those heterosexual women who are married or enjoying a 'stable and happy relationship' with a man. Those who do not fit into this traditional nuclear family pattern are generally deemed unsuitable for treatment (Macintyre, 1977).

This ambivalence towards women who do not conform to doctor's expectations is manifested in several ways in the treatment or non-treatment of infertility. Lesbian and single heterosexual women wishing to obtain artificial insemination because they are not in a permanent relationship with a man have frequently reported problems in obtaining such services within the NHS. That is to say, non-medical criteria are clearly used in assessing who should receive AID. This is one of the reasons behind the recent increase in women attempting self-insemination with sperm either from friends or anonymous donors (Saffron, 1986; Lewin, 1985). Other women have sought more sympathetic treatment from charities such as British Pregnancy Advisory Service who are willing to consider all potential mothers for AID, whatever their marital status or sexual orientation. Judgemental attitudes of this kind are also experienced by those using infertility clinics and by those seeking IVF in particular, with only 'respectable' married couples being accepted for treatment. This represents clear discrimination on moral as well as financial grounds against those 'undeserving' women who have not chosen to live their lives in the way most doctors would consider normal but who still wish to enjoy the pleasures of motherhood.

This insensitivity of the NHS towards the needs of the infertile is not found only in the treatment of 'deviant' women. There is also an obvious failure in many clinics to take the more subjective and experiential needs of patients seriously. Infertility can be a devastating experience, colouring a woman's entire emotional existence.

> You can't plan. Nothing holds any interest for you. It's almost an obsessive desire. I became obsessed with pregnancy. I felt like a flower operating on two petals instead of five. Because I didn't think about anything else. I didn't seem to be living my life. I was too tensed up all the time. (Pfeffer and Woollett, 1983, p. 25)

The emotional significance of the situation, however, is often played down or ignored in the way services are delivered. This is very clear from women's own accounts of their experiences. Too often doctors treat them as sick patients rather than whole, otherwise healthy people who wish to have children but are not able to do so at that particular moment. One of the patients interviewed by Naomi Pfeffer and Anne Woollett commented:

It's like going through a battery team. You get about thirty seconds
with the doctor who doesn't really sit down. It's the practice nurses
who do most for you. They explain what's going on but each one has a
slightly different version. (ibid., p. 45)

The situation is often made worse by the fact that women are not able
to go to a separate infertility clinic but have to attend routine
gynaecological out-patient clinics. Hence, women seeking treatment
for infertility may be forced to join those wanting contraception or
abortion. Even more distressing perhaps, is the situation where out-
patient facilities are shared by an antenatal clinic. Again one of
Pfeffer and Woollett's interviewees commented:

You attend during the antenatal clinic. I am absolutely surrounded by
ladies delightfully pregnant. I don't think about it so much when I'm
out shopping or walking but I'm here because I'm infertile. I find it
extremely painful sitting with pregnant women with their little kids
side by side. (ibid., p. 43)

It is hard to imagine anything more certain to cause distress, but
Mathieson's study revealed that over the whole country only about a
third of District Health Authorities have special infertility clinics
separate from other gynaecological services, and in some regions,
especially in the North, the proportion is very much lower
(Mathieson, 1986, p. 6). This failure to prioritize infertility or to
respect it as a speciality in its own right is not only potentially
distressing to patients, but also means that the services themselves are
usually less effective with inadequate record-keeping, fewer facilities
and less-experienced staff. The authors of the Warnock Report were
vociferous in their recommendation that separate services should be
set up in all District Health Authorities and this has met with
considerable enthusiasm from the relevant professional bodies
(Royal College of Obstetricians and Gynaecologists, 1982). However,
there is currently little sign of moves in this direction.

Further evidence of the failure to meet patients' needs is to be
found in the dearth of either verbal or written information about the
cause and treatment of infertility and the almost complete absence of
counselling services. The inability to have an informed discussion
about their situation is something that many NHS patients complain
about. Reflecting the more general tenor of the Western medical
model, the service as a whole tends to concentrate on the body
without making adequate provision for the mind or spirit. In the case
of infertility this can be a particularly serious problem. While infertile patients do not have to face imminent death as do some whose

treatment has failed, the realization that they may not be able to have children will usually involve fundamental changes in women's perception of themselves and their plans for the future. Most women have been brought up to expect that motherhood will be the single most fulfilling aspect of their lives and coming to terms with the loss of this dream may well provoke a profound crisis, but few clinics provide any help in dealing with this situation. As Mathieson's study showed, less than one in four of the 200 District Health Authorities in the NHS provide either explanatory literature or non-medical counselling (Mathieson, 1986, p. 11). Hence, most women (and men) undertake the very lengthy and complex process of infertility treatment without adequate information or experienced help in dealing with accompanying emotional problems. The success of the treatment is measured only in terms of the physical achievement of a pregnancy. When treatment does not succeed many doctors do not discuss it with patients since they are unwilling or are unable to come to terms with their own failure. Yet the women involved will have to do just that. If sympathetic counselling is not available, too many end up enduring not only the terrible loss of their assumed fertility but also guilt about what they may feel is their own part in it.

The NHS therefore provides only a very partial service for infertile women. Despite a widespread belief that motherhood is a woman's 'destiny', little attention has been paid to those unable to carry out their 'natural function' unaided. Where services are provided, they tend to be firmly based on a mechanistic approach, emphasizing physiological repairs but ignoring more experiential considerations. The limitations of this narrow, curative approach become even more apparent if we consider strategies for prevention.

Infertility: Prevention or Panacea?

Most infertile women are unaware of their problem until they attempt to have children. Hence, they usually present themselves at a doctor's door when the condition is already long-standing. But could the problem not be prevented before it arose? Clearly there are some women for whom this would not be possible – those born with a congenital defect for instance. However, there are many others for whom the problem has arisen later in life, some of whom could have avoided it with the appropriate action. This was pointed out forcefully in the Warnock Report where attention was drawn to the need for more research into the causes of infertility. However a recent parliamentary question (*Hansard*, 25 March 1986) revealed that during the last three years the Department of Health and Social

Security had not funded any research into the causes of infertility 'among couples'.

Despite this lack of research, we do have some information about causes and once again this raises fundamental questions about the willingness of the NHS to take the needs of infertile women seriously. Pelvic inflammatory disease (PID) is known to be a significant cause of infertility, and the incidence of PID has risen by some 50 per cent over the past ten years. One attack of untreated PID produces tubal damage in 12 per cent of cases, two attacks produce damage in 40 per cent of cases and the figure rises to 80 per cent for three or more attacks. Many cases of PID develop from sexually transmitted diseases (STDs). In the past gonorrhoea was thought to be the main culprit and little was known about the other types of infections, often referred to as non-specific genital infections (NSGIs). However, recent research has shown that in women, some 80 per cent of these NSGIs are in fact caused by the chlamydia bacteria. In 1982 some 130,000 new cases of chlamydial infection were reported – three times more than the number of gonorrhoea cases and it is estimated that about 40 per cent of PID is now caused by the chlamydia bacteria (Phillips, 1985).

Pelvic infection is therefore a significant cause of infertility and chlamydia a major factor in PID. Yet there are very few facilities for screening or treatment. Gynaecologists dealing with PID rarely check for chlamydia and about 20 per cent of genito-urinary clinics still do not have appropriate screening facilities (ibid.). A new and simple test has just been developed but no extra resources have been provided to make it generally available. As a result many thousands of women are vulnerable to infertility in the future because current infections remain unidentified and untreated.

Another significant factor in the causation of PID and therefore of infertility is the use of an intra-uterine contraceptive device (IUD) (Vessey, Yeates, Flavel and McPherson, 1981). We know that many women become infertile after an infection caused by an IUD, yet these devices continue to be prescribed, in Britain, often without the recipients being properly informed about the risks (Roberts, 1981). The many recent cases of infection, infertility and even death caused by the Dalkon Shield provide adequate testimony to these problems. While this particular device is no longer marketed, there are others which can too often be the cause of chronic and potentially sterilizing infections. The development and continued use of these dangerous forms of contraception obviously have to be understood against the background of the predominantly male control of medical research and clinical practice. Effectiveness in preventing conception is too often pursued as the only goal with almost no regard for what are called 'side-effects' – in this case possible infertility (Pollock, 1984). Hence, NHS policies are not only unconcerned with the positive prevention of infertility but may actually be contributing to its incidence.

Fighting Back: a Feminist Strategy on Infertility

We have seen that women with fertility problems have not been treated as a priority by NHS planners. Indeed, they remained almost invisible until the advent of new reproductive technologies offered some doctors the possibility of improved professional status and financial rewards. Unfortunately many infertile women feel that feminists have not taken their problems very seriously either. Jo Pollentine recently wrote about her feelings in *Spare Rib*:

> I now feel the need to write this so that there will be more understanding and support from the women's movement for the many women who have fertility problems . . . infertility is a taboo subject and an infertile woman is an embarrassment. I am not treated as an ordinary woman even by feminists.

From the nineteenth century onwards, women have fought to ensure their right to contraception and abortion – to facilitate their choice *not* to have children. Fighting to ensure that they *can* have children has been less of a priority. This can partly be explained by the fact that infertility is a problem for only a relatively small number of women. However, it should also be acknowledged that the ambivalence of contemporary feminism towards motherhood has sometimes made it too easy to ignore the feelings of infertile women. It has been argued by some that the wish for children reflects little more than oppressive social conditioning and hence that women should not be encouraged to use up scarce resources in trying to achieve such dubious desires. This attitude has recently been reinforced by the growing campaign against reproductive technologies such as IVF which are seen as expensive and dangerous both for infertile women and for others (Arditti, Duelli Klein and Minden, 1984).

In response to this situation some infertile feminists are now 'coming out' in a way that they did not do in the past. Books like that of Naomi Pfeffer and Anne Woollett are making infertility visible and raising uncomfortable questions that need to be answered. As the feminist approach to motherhood becomes more complex it is surely important that the needs of infertile women be more openly discussed and incorporated as a campaigning issue (Dowrick and Grundberg, 1980). So what should feminists be fighting for in the area of infertility?

Most importantly, this cannot be an isolated fight but needs to be part of the broader campaign for a better health service in general and for the reproductive rights of women in particular. As the resources available to the NHS have diminished relative to need, all services have been stretched. Women have been affected especially badly since their use of health services is greater than that of men. Moreover, the so-called 'less-essential' services such as family planning and abortion have frequently been the target for cuts as desperate health administrators search for ways of keeping their budgets within cash limits. The current waiting-list for gynaecology in-patient treatment in Britain now stands at some 90,000 nation-wide and in this context it is not surprising that most infertility treatmeni has low priority. The broadly based campaign to save the NHS, in which women are already major participants, is therefore the backcloth against which attempts to improve infertility services will need to be set (Doyal, 1985). Unless expenditure on the NHS is increased, the current trend towards commercialization will continue and many more women will be forced to go without or to go outside the service for treatment. As a result, the gap between rich and poor will continue to widen, and the chance of a baby will become a 'commodity' available only to the prosperous infertile.

However, purely defensive campaigns that focus only on levels of expenditure have frequently been the focus of feminist concern (Doyal, 1985). As we have seen, the women's health movement has always been highly critical of Western medicine as practiced within the NHS and elsewhere. The sexism inherent in medical practice both at an individual and also a broader social level has been clearly identified and women are therefore anxious to campaign not just to defend what we already have but to change this for the better. Hence, it is argued, the struggle must be not just for the physical availability of services but for qualitative changes in how those services are provided. In the case of infertility treatment this means that much more attention will need to be paid to women's own wishes and desires. At the very least, infertile women themselves rather than doctors should be able to decide whether or not they are 'suitable' for motherhood – a choice that most fertile women can take for granted.

Successful services need to take the mind seriously as well as the body and to incorporate imaginative and humanitarian ways of dealing with those who are 'unsuccessful' as well as those who are 'successful' by orthodox medical criteria. Above all, women need the space and the support to explore their feelings about motherhood – the reasons why they want children and the ways in which they could restructure their lives if this proves to be impossible. Some will need help in investigating the non-biological alternatives for parenting while others may need help in mourning the loss of their fertility. Variants of grief counselling have proved useful for some while others have found lay theorists and self-help groups valuable. Above all, those who run services should seek feedback from users and make their arrangements accordingly.

Women therefore need to be involved in the planning of health services in general and infertility services in particular. They need the opportunity to make a more significant input into debates about how resources are to be spent, particularly when they affect women. This achievement of greater participation by women would require, among other things, an effective equal opportunities policy for NHS workers and the democratization of the NHS itself. Women are the majority of workers within the NHS, but they are severely under-represented at decision-making levels. The committees that make decisions about resource allocation and provision of services need to incorporate the expertise and experiences of women both as health-care providers and as consumers.

Increasing the participation of women in the running of the health service is particularly important in the case of a new technology such as IVF. As we have seen, some feminists are completely opposed to it both because of the lack of control women have over its use and also because the cost at present makes it available mainly to those who can afford to pay. They rightly emphasize the moral obscenity of a situation where some women can afford to pay huge sums to have children while attempts are made to bribe women in other countries with a sari or a few rupees to give up their fertility forever. Infertile women on the other hand emphasize what they see as a very real need in their lives, and are even prepared to put up with the stresses and indignities of IVF treatment if there is a chance of their greatest wish being realized. They sympathize with the fate of Third World women but argue that money *not* spent on IVF will not be sent to alleviate their poverty. How are these conflicting views to be reconciled?

The starting-point must surely be that at the very least the same services should be available to all women. Hence, *if* IVF is to be provided at all it should be available free on the NHS. However, the current cost is undoubtedly high and no health-care system can provide everything that is asked of it. Decisions about how much money – if any – should be put into IVF should be made not by individual clinicians or administrators but by a more representative group. Research has shown that doctors' own perceptions and interests may well be at odds with those of their female patients and a more open procedure would limit doctors' power (Farrant, 1985). Similarly, if IVF is to be available there should be greater public participation in deciding how the services are run and who is chosen to receive treatment since demand is always likely to exceed supply. Only if these more democratic procedures are adopted will there be any hope of using what benefits the technology has to offer for the interests of those most in need while not risking the health and well-being of others.

In the final analysis however, the debate about IVF may be largely a red herring, diverting attention away from the equally important problem of how to prevent infertility in the first place. IVF will only ever be a solution for a very small proportion of those who are infertile and prevention would be a much more cost-effective strategy. Yet the criticism that the NHS is a 'national sickness service' rather than a 'national health service' applies in the case of infertility in the same way that it does with other health problems. We have already seen that the level of infertility could be reduced by a more effective gynaecology service easily available to all women, with more priority given to chlamydia screening in both gynaecology clinics and those specializing in sexually transmitted disease. PID has always been a problem area in medical diagnosis, with many women suffering too long before being correctly diagnosed and effectively treated. Hence, medical services in this area should be more preventive than they are at present, with particular attention being paid to the potential health implications of contraceptives. This needs to be accompanied by more resources for the development of both male and female contraceptives that are effective *and* safe.

We also know that there are factors in the wider society that may be promoting infertility. Smoking, for instance, clearly reduces fertility though it is unlikely on its own to be the cause of infertility (Howe et al., 1985). There is also evidence that certain chemicals that are found mainly in the workplace can affect either male or female fertility or both (Elkington, 1986). Lead, anaesthetic gases, vinyl chloride, mercury and dioxin all fit into this category. Looking even more broadly there is also evidence, at least among animals, that stress can significantly reduce fertility. We need more information about these and other factors that affect fertility and we need to develop policies that could minimize their impact. These would range from more supportive health-education programmes to help people give up smoking, through more effective occupational and environmental regulation, to broader social and economic changes designed to minimize the stresses that many women currently experience in living up to the expectations that society has of them. The provision of more accessible and humane curative services therefore needs to be accompanied by wider preventive strategies that will not only reduce the incidence of infertility but promote the general health of all women.

Notes

Chapter 1   Reproductive Technologies and the Deconstruction of Motherhood

1 These examples are, of course, merely the tip of the iceberg. Campaigns against sterilization-abuse highlight many instances of coercive sterilization in the United States which tend to be concentrated among poor and ethnic minority women. Lower standards than those that apply in the West may govern the testing and marketing of contraceptive products in some Third World countries.

2 Women, Reproduction and Technology conference, organized by Robert King for the History Workshop Centre, Oxford, 14–15 February 1987.

3 Andrea Dworkin (1983) sketched out the idea of the 'reproductive brothel', as a metaphor for ways in which men attempt to exert standardized control over women's reproductive capacities. This notion has been applied to new reproductive technologies by several writers, including Ann Oakley in chapter 2, or Gena Corea (1985a and b). For a critique of this analogy, see Rayna Rapp (1985) and Juliette Zipper and Selma Sevehuijsen in chapter 6.

4 The writers who have been most influential in developing the approach to new technologies outlined in this paragraph include Gena Corea (1985a and 1985b); Renate Duelli Klein (1985); Jalna Hanmer (with Pat Allen 1980; 1981, 1985); Robyn Rowland (1984, 1985a and 1985b); Roberta Steinbacher (1983, and with Helen Holmes 1985) and Rita Arditti (et al., 1984; 1985).

5 In this context, it is interesting to note Jane Wilkie's (1984) argument that increases in infertility in the United States in recent years – which launch some women into a difficult search for motherhood against physiological odds – may be due in part precisely to the numbers of women who have been exercising new kinds of choices about their fertility. Pregnancies are more difficult to achieve for women in their late twenties and thirties, and the increasing number of women who have delayed child-bearing in order to pursue other avenues of identity is, Wilkie estimates, one of the major sources of fertility problems. The other major sources are chronic infections and the effects of infertility inducing contraceptive techniques.

6 Some writings on sociobiology take this furthest. In the claim that there is an innate urge to reproduce one's seed, an urge shared by tsetse flies and human beings, genetic transmission becomes not only a preference, but a species imperative. See the discussion in Fausto-Sterling (1985, chapter 6) or Sayers (1982).

7 In some of the accounts of children seeking out genetic parents, the desire to maintain blood ties becomes not a contingent matter – dependent upon a child's upbringing and the circumstances of its separation from genetic parents – but an inevitable one. Polly Toynbee, for example, interviewed a large number of adopted children, some of whom were indifferent to their genetic origins; this she discounts as the repression of painful desires (Toynbee, quoted by Janet Watts, *The Observer* 21 July, 1985, p. 43).

8 Ways of establishing relationships with children other than by genetic parenthood are often subject to strict surveillance and regulation. Adoption agencies, for example, are (rightly) rigorous about who may parent: but their policies and criteria of assessment are framed against a conventional notion of parenting – and particularly, of motherhood – which will deter many would-be parents. Adoption agencies in Britain may refuse (and often do) single women or those aged over thirty; may refuse (and usually do) those who are not heterosexual, whether married or not; may refuse (and sometimes do) women who have jobs, women who have had psychiatric referrals, women with disabilities, women whose unconventional life-styles cast doubt – for the social workers at least – on their suitability as mothers. They are also likely to refuse, in spite of the long and uncertain waiting period for adoption, women who intend to continue trying to achieve a pregnancy. For many would-be parents, particularly those who want their relationship with a child to begin while it is still in infancy or toddlerhood, the conceptive technologies are not so much about genetic transmission as about having a child at all.

9 In the lecture series on Human Reproductive Technologies, organized by the Department of History and Philosophy of Science, Cambridge University, 1986.

10 In the USA, the first major report on in-vitro fertilization and related techniques, prepared by the Ethics Advisory Board of the Department of Health, Education and Welfare (1979) recommended the restriction of in-vitro fertilization to married couples. Robert Murray, a member of that Board, later explained that 'the Board said that the government has an interest in fostering marriage and in discouraging illegitimacy however defined' (in Holmes, Hoskins and Gross, eds, 1981, p. 278). Given the contradictions in the Warnock Committee's reasoning on the question of access, I'm inclined to think that Murray's position is the more honest one. Governmental inquiries such as Warnock and the Ethics Advisory Board have won a degree of acceptance for the new technologies, but only by attempting to reincorporate them within the confines of the conventional family.

11 According to *Newsweek* (11 August 1986) pp. 48–9, Marie Odette Henderson went into a coma in hospital when she was twenty-six weeks pregnant. Her parents, as next-of-kin, ordered the respirator to be turned off. Derek Poole, her lover, contested the order in court, and was named the guardian of the unborn child. Marie was kept on a respirator for fifty-three days, until doctors were ready to deliver by caesarian a baby girl. When Donna Paizzi was pronounced dead in hospital, her husband Robert asked for life support to be withdrawn. David Haddon opposed the move in court, and eventually the judge ruled that life support should be maintained until the baby could be delivered by caesarian section. *Newsweek* estimates that there have been over a dozen births to brain-dead mothers in the United States.

12 Naomi Pfeffer, chapter 4, p. 93, quotes *The Sunday Despatch* of November 1945 on artificial insemination by donor: 'a super-race of test-tube babies will become the guardians of atom-bomb secrets . . . Fathers will be chosen by eugenic experts of the United Nations. The mothers will be hand-picked on their health and beauty records.'

13 See, for example, Corea (1985a), Minden (1985), Hubbard (1985) and for an assessment of some of these concerns, Rose (in chapter 8).

14 And, as individual women facing this decision, we must develop the courage not to echo the language of eugenics. For the sake of reproductive freedoms, and for the sake of our own and other 'imperfect' selves, we must learn to say – when we feel unable to continue with a suspect pregnancy – that it is because of our own 'dreams of mothering', and not 'for the sake of the child' (Fine and Asch, 1985, p. 9).

15 Two types are envisaged. The first, and by far the more feasible, somatic-cell therapy, would replace 'faulty' cells with normal ones soon after conception, so that – hopefully – an infant would show no signs of the disorder it carried previously. The second, purely speculative prospect, would involve similar manipulations on reproductive cells, so that the improvement in the human gene pool would be transmitted from one generation to the next (see chapter 8).

16 The President's Commission for the Study of Ethical Problems in Medicine and Biomedical and Behavioural Research (1982) identified four steps involved in genetic engineering, from cloning a normal gene to ensuring that the host cells of a patient are not harmed by its introduction. The Commission concluded that 'Only the first step – cloning a normal counterpart of a defective gene – is a straightforward matter with current knowledge and technology' (Kevles, 1986, p. 297).

17 Lecture series on Human Reproductive Technologies, organized by the Department of History and Philosophy of Science, Cambridge University, 1986.

18 Or take another example: in-vitro fertilization. The success rate for in-vitro fertilization procedures is fearfully low, with only 10 to 15 per cent of treatments in British clinics resulting in live births. Feminist researchers have pointed out that female patients sometimes have an

inflated idea of chances of success, and that information which they
need in order to make a realistic appraisal of their options is in some
cases being withheld (Crow, 1985; Rowland, 1985a). However, it should
not be suggested that if infertile women had details of the success rate,
they would shun in-vitro fertilization like the plague. On the contrary,
armed with this information, a woman might well say: I have only
thirteen chances in a hundred to give birth using this technique. But that
is infinitely greater than the chance that I would have if I refused in-vitro
fertilization. Accurate technical information is one of the prerequisites
for informed choice. Such information does not foreclose decision-
making.

19 Duelli Klein, 1985, p. 65.

Chapter 2 From Walking Wombs to Test-tube Babies

1 For a detailed history of the application of both X-rays and ultrasound
to pregnancy see Oakley (1984), *The Captured Womb*.

Chapter 3 Foetal Images: the Power of Visual Culture in the Politics of Reproduction

1 *City of Akron* v. *Akron Center for Reproductive Health*, 426 US 416
(1983); and *Thornburgh* v. *American College of Obstetricians and
Gynecologists*, 54 *Law Week*, 4618 (10 June, 1986). From a pro-choice
perspective, the significance of these decisions is mixed. While the
court's majority opinion has become if anything more liberal and more
feminist in its protection of women's 'individual dignity and autonomy',
this majority has grown steadily narrower. Whereas in 1973 it was 7–2,
in 1983 it shrank to 6–3 and then in 1986 to a bare 5–4, while the
growing minority becomes ever more conservative and anti-feminist.

2 Cf. Hubert Danisch: 'the photographic image does not belong to the
natural world. It is a product of human labor, a cultural object whose
being . . . cannot be dissociated precisely from its historical meaning
and from the necessarily datable project in which it originates' (in
Trachtenberg, 1980, p. 288).

3 In her dissenting opinion in the *Akron* case, Justice Sandra Day
O'Connor argued that *Roe* v. *Wade* was 'on a collision course with itself
because technology was pushing the point of viability indefinitely
backward. (In *Roe* the court had defined 'viability' as the point at which
the foetus is 'potentially able to live outside the mother's womb, albeit
with artificial aid'; after that point, it said, the state could restrict
abortion except when bringing the foetus to term would jeopardize the
woman's life or health; cf. Rhoden, 1985). Meanwhile, a popular weekly
television programme, *Hill Street Blues*, in March 1985 aired a
dramatization of abortion clinic harassment in which a pregnant woman
seeking an abortion miscarries and gives birth to an extremely premature

foetus/baby, which soon dies. Numerous newspaper accounts of 'heroic' efforts to save premature newborns have made front-page headlines.

4 Rayna Rapp has advised me, based on her field research, that another response of women who have suffered difficult pregnancy histories to such diagnostic techniques may be denial – simply not wanting to know. This too, however, may be seen as a tactic to gain control over information, by censoring bad news.

5 Coercive, invasive uses of foetal images, masked as 'informed consent', have been a prime strategy of anti-abortion forces for some years. They have been opposed by pro-choice litigators in the courts, resulting in the United States Supreme Court's repudiation on two different occasions of specious 'informed consent' regulations as an unconstitutional form of harassment and denial of women's rights (*Akron*, 1983; *Thornburgh*, 1986).

6 I obtained this information from interviews with Maria Tapia-Birch, administrator in the Maternal and Child Services Division of the New York City Department of Health; and Jeanine Michaels, social worker; Lisa Milstein, nurse-practitioner and Jeffrey Karaban, sonographer; at the Eastern Women's Health Clinic in New York, who kindly shared their clinical experience with me.

Chapter 4 Artificial Insemination, In-vitro Fertilization and the Stigma of Infertility

1 The source of this information is the job columns of the *New Scientist* from 1983 to the end of 1986. Of course, this list may not be complete; there may be other programmes investigating different problems of human fertility. Details are available on all research programmes that rely on the manipulation of human embryos and are published in the Report of the Voluntary Licensing Authority set up by the Medical Research Council and Royal College of Obstetricians and Gynaecologists.

2 Gynaecologists are not the only professionals who stand to gain from these new techniques; embryologists have had a key role in their development and proliferation. Like artificial insemination using donor semen, in-vitro fertilization and embryo transfer had long been practised on animals before their use of human beings in a clinical setting, and in both cases, the idea to use these techniques on human beings came from a scientist. Working on animals in their laboratory away from patients, scientists appear able to contemplate new procedures which those tempered by clinical practice may hesitate to suggest. As Patrick Steptoe, a gynaecologist, observed of his collaborator the embryologist Robert Edwards, 'I felt his scientific approach to infertility was harder, more penetrating than those of the practising gynaecologist' (Steptoe and Edwards, 1980, p. 77) – and it was Edwards who contacted Steptoe to gain access to patients.

There is no clear career structure for embryologists; they are dependent on short-term funding for their research. But finding solutions to the technical problems posed by IVF and embryo transfer has offered embryologists a route to international repute. There is a shortage of competent scientists experienced in this increasingly competitive area; and centres looking for embryologists with clinical experience are forced to advertise abroad, to countries where pioneering work has been done. The job columns of the *New Scientist*, for example, a British publication which does not have a wide international readership, has had job adverts seeking trained embryologists placed by centres in Germany and Australia.

3 This list gives a flavour of the many official and semi-official reports that examined artificial insemination using donor semen. The Ministry of Health conducted its own internal enquiries but these files are closed for 100 years. I have not included the many reports prepared by the churches and by voluntary and campaigning organizations for submission to these committees:

1947　*Artificial Human Insemination*. Report of a conference held in London under the auspices of the Public Morality Council (London: Heinemann).

1948　*Artificial Human Insemination: The Report of a Commission appointed by His Grace the Archbishop of Canterbury* (London: SPCK).

1949　Pope Pius XII, *Votre présence autour*, (Address, 29 September), ActApS, 41, pp. 557–61).

1951　Pope Pius XII, *Vegliare con sollectudine*, (Address, 29 October), Act ApS, 43, pp. 835–54.

1958　*Royal Commission on Marriage and Divorce*, 1958, Cmnd 9678 (London: HMSO).

1960　*Report of Departmental Committee on Human Artificial Insemination* (The Earl of Feversham's Report), Cmnd 1105, (London: HMSO).

1973　*Law and Ethics of AID and Embryo Transfer*, CIBA Foundation Symposium 17 (new series)(London: Associated Book Publishers).

1973　*Annual Report of the Council. Appendix V: Report of the Panel on Human Artificial Insemination*, (Peel Committee). British Medical Association, *British Medical Journal*, 2 (suppl.) pp. 3–5.

1976　*Artificial Insemination*, Proceedings of the Fourth Study Group of the Royal College of Obstetricians and Gynaecologists (London: RCOG)

1977　*Confidential Enquiry into Extent to which Artificial Insemination by a Donor (AID) is practised in the United Kingdom (up to the End of 1977)* (London: Royal College of Obstetricians and Gynaecologists).

1979　*Artificial Insemination* (London: Royal College of Obstetricians and Gynaecologists).

1984 *Report of the Committee of Inquiry into Human Fertilisation and Embryology* (the Warnock Report), Cmnd 9314 (London: HMSO).

4 For an analysis of legal opinion on the paternity of children born through artificial insemination by donor since Feversham, see Carol Smart, chapter 5.

5 Lesley Doyal examines in detail the shortcomings of infertility services in Britain, and inequalities of access, in chapter 9.

Chapter 7   Human Embryos and the Law

1 Australia's Waller Commission, appointed to consider such issues, recommended that the Rios embryos be thawed but not implanted. The Provincial Parliament in Victoria later voted that the embryos *should* be implanted in one of the many volunteers who had come forward as a result of the massive publicity (*Boston Globe*, 24 October 1984). However, the legislation involved has proved so complicated and difficult to interpret that no action had been taken by the fall of 1986 (personal communication with Dr Margot Somerville, McGill University, 24 September 1986). Doctors think a successful implantation and pregnancy unlikely, since the freezing was done at a very early stage in the technical development of cryopreservation (*New York Times*, 24 June 1984).

2 Sexuality and reproduction, it seems, are to be treated as reserved spheres of the 'natural', guarded from purposeful human intervention by the watchfulness of celibate male clerics. For a trenchant critique of this view and a proposal for re-envisioning procreation along lines more in keeping with feminist and liberation theologies, see Harrison (1983, pp. 57–118).

3 Lay Catholics in Australia, however, parted company with the clergy on this issue. Polls revealed strong support for IVF among Catholics and individual Catholics sought out the procedure in roughly the same numbers as other Australians (Singer and Wells, 1984, pp. 28,33).

4 For a sympathetic, but not uncritical description of the infertility treatments, see Andrews, (1984).

5 Interestingly enough in this regard, the Warnock Committee Report recommended adoption of legislation that would provide that 'any child born by AIH [artificial insemination by husband] who was not *in utero* at the date of the death of its father shall be disregarded for the purposes of succession to and inheritance from the latter' (Warnock, 1985, §.10.9). It also recommended that 'for the purposes of establishing primogeniture the date and time of birth, and not the date of fertilization, shall be the determining factor' (ibid., §.10.14).

6 The Warnock Committee, while not proposing any absolute bar to single people's access to infertility treatments, had earlier declared that 'as a general rule it is better for children to be born into a two-parent family, with both father and mother' (Warnock, 1985. §.2.11).

7 Embryos stored for over ten years, or whose progenitors had died or disagreed, would become subject to the 'use or disposal' of a national 'storage authority' (Warnock, 1985, §.10.10–13). Prof. George Annas, an American legal commentator, rejects the concept of ownership of embryos but suggests that frozen embryos be destroyed when the specific purpose for freezing them has been fulfilled or when both gamete donors have died (Annas, 1984, pp. 51–2). Reproductive technology expert Lori Andrews also argues that progenitors should have the right to control disposition of gametes and embryos, including the right to have them removed from storage and allowed to expire (Andrews, 1986).

8 No criminal law sanctions were proposed for violation of this recommendation, however, and its force was further undermined by addition of the phrase 'Whenever this is possible' (Warnock, 1985, §.11.24).

9 Concerns about embryonic pain are far-fetched. In 1985, amidst uproar occasioned by a 'pro-life' film's claim that a twelve-week foetus would experience pain and fear during an abortion, the American College of Obstetricians and Gynecologists issued a 'Statement on Pain of the Fetus' declaring:

> We know of no legitimate scientific information that supports the statement that a fetus experiences pain early in pregnancy.
>
> We do know that the cerebellum attains its final configuration in the seventh month and that mylenization (or covering of the spinal cord and the brain) begins between the 20th and 40th weeks of pregnancy. These, as well as other neurological developments, would have to be in place for the fetus to perceive pain.
>
> To feel pain, a fetus needs neurotransmitted hormones. In animals, these complex chemicals develop in the last third of gestation. We know of no evidence that humans are different. (Quoted in *Planned Parenthood Federation of America* (n.d.) p. 3)

10 Historian Allen Hunter observes:

> Like the family, the fetus is a condensed symbol. The fetus simultaneously stands for the desire to regain traditional society, and for hostility to feminism and freer sexuality which threaten that world. . . . Further, the desire to protect the fetus – itself thematized as a miraculous meeting of nature and God – is connected with the view that the world is changing in ominous and threatening ways, ways that even deny life itself the opportunity to come into being. (Hunter, 1981, p. 132)

Nineteenth-century manifestations of such uneasiness also tended to cluster around sexual and reproductive issues (Gordon, 1977; Smith-Rosenberg, 1985).

11 As George Annas has noted, 'We need not, of course, consider it a person to afford it legally recognized protection, any more than we need consider a dog a person to protect it against cruelty, or a dolphin a person to protect it against destruction, or a national park a person to protect it against loggers' (Annas, 1984, p. 51). Lori Andrews's proposal

that progenitors retain decision-making power over gametes and embryos could be expected to serve as a brake on at least some research abuses (Andrews, 1986).

The American Fertility Society's Ethics Committee has called for voluntary interim guide-lines while national discussion of the research issue proceeds. It has urged that programmes offering medical assistance in reproduction 'develop and announce to candidate couples explicit policies on the options of transfer, donation, pre-embryo research, storage and discard. . . . Program policies on these issues should be reviewed in advance by Institutional Review Boards or other authorized and legitimate authorities' (American Fertility Society, 1986, p. 31S).

Chapter 8   Victorian Values in the Test-tube: the Politics of Reproductive Science and Technology

1 The critique of biological determinism by feminist scientists has been mounted with energy. A selection from a rich array of writing would include:– Tobach, E. and Rossoff, B. (eds) *Genes and Gender* (New York: Gordian 1978); Lowe, M. and Hubbard, R. *Women's Nature, Rationalisations of Inequality* (Oxford: Pergamon 1983), Athene series; Leibowitz, L. *Males, Females and Families: A Biosocial Approach* (Cambridge, MA: Duxbury 1978); Brighton Women and Science Group *Alice Through the Microscope* (London: Virago, 1980).

2 Thus Hanmer and Allen (1980) envisage the elimination of women in their final solution scenario, while at the same time encouraging hopes for a male-less future through parthenogenesis – a misplaced hope in that all the genes would be duplicated, including the problem ones, so that a resulting baby would show all the problems contained in the woman's egg (Hubbard and Stanford, 1985).

3 The history is by no means uncomplicated. Geneticists who introduced knowledge of the transmission of Thalassaemia to the village of Orchemenos produced the unintended and negative effect of carriers being excluded as potential marriage partners. A later and better thought-out initiative sought instead to give community, including religious, support to would-be parents in their screening and abortion choices.

4 The 1986 British Association meeting devoted a morning to somatic gene therapy. The subsequent media coverage by television provided a paradigmatic example of a scientist – in this case the molecular geneticist Professor Bob Williamson – talking up the potential for somatic therapy for human treatment. The cautious note sounded by a review of research by Marx, J. 'Gene Therapy – So Near and Yet So Far Away', *Science*, 232 (16 May 1986), pp. 924–5, went unheard.

5 Three examples of the commercial interest in the new screening procedures:

1 Approximately half the laboratories undertaking AFP analysis are using commercially produced kits, yet these are criticized by the Clinical Genetics Society for their expense and unreliability. (At the same time the research laboratories are urging the case for reliable testing equipment because routine testing is driving out research (*Nature*, 321, 5 (June 1986), p. 557)).

2 The ultrasound market is 'among the fastest growing medical instrumentation markets of all time', (Farrant, 1985, p. 102).

3 'With the marked increase in infertility, the surrogate mother business looks to have a bright future', *International Herald Tribune* (29 August 1986).

6 The demographic situation in India is so exceptional and horrific that it may be the one country where it begins to be appropriate to speak of a growing femicide.

7 Janet Gallagher discusses the foetal rights movement in chapter 7.

8 In a recent television documentary the gynaecologist and obstetrician Robert Winston spoke of the situation in which, when a couple presented with the problem of infertility, the woman had received tubal surgery – cost to the NHS £1,500 to say nothing of the distress to the woman – when the man had not even had a sperm count – cost to the NHS £2!

9 While all the interest focuses on infertility the old research battle to find safe contraception is under-funded. See *UN Report on the International Conference on Population*, E/Conf. (New York: UN, 1984); and a letter to *Nature* from the European Medical Research Council, drawing attention to the *decrease* in funding, *Nature*, 322 (2 July 1986), p. 24.

10 The debate on new reproductive technology began with a speech by Lord Brabazon, in a wartime debate concerning the use of artificial insemination (AI) in animal husbandry, in which he reflected on its human implications:

'It is our duty . . . to know the problems that are about to face us (AI) and in our wisdom to do the best that in us lies, so as to direct these new forces that they will result in bringing happiness and good into the world' H.L. Debate, 1943, Vol. 128, c 823). Brabazon's 'happiness and good' offered a breadth of moral vision from which alas the debate (and Brabazon) all too quickly retreated to the current narrow concern that in Warnock seems to be about the transmission of property rights and the preservation of masculinist and professional power.

Chapter 9   Infertility – a Life Sentence? Women and the National Health Service

1 A short questionnaire was sent to all 200 District Health Authorities in England and Wales: 170 of the authorities responded. Detailed results are obtainable from Frank Dobson, House of Commons, London.

Bibliography

ACOG (American College of Obstetricians and Gynecologists) (1982) 'Diagnostic Ultrasound in Obstetrics and Gynecology', in D. Young (ed.) *Women and Health*, 7, (New York: Haworth Press), (reprinted from ACOG, *Technical Bulletin*, 63 [October 1981]).

Albury, R. (1984) 'Who Owns the Embryo?', in Arditti et al., (eds) *Test-Tube Women*, pp. 54–67.

Albury, R. (1986) 'Frozen Embryo Babies: Australian Media Tells'. Unpublished paper, Department of Sociology, University of Wollongong.

Alic, M. (1984) *Hypatia's Heritage: The History of Women's Science* (London: The Women's Press).

American Fertility Society (1986) 'Ethical Considerations of the New Reproductive Technologies', *Fertility and Sterility*, 46, 3, Supplement 1.

'America's Abortion Dilemma', (1985) *Newsweek*, 105, Special Report (14 January) pp. 20–9.

Andrews, L. (1984) *New Conceptions* (New York: St Martin's Press).

Andrews, L. (1986) 'The Legal Status of the Embryo', *Loyola Law Review*, 32, 2 (Summer), pp. 357–409.

Annas, G. F. (1984) 'Redefining Parenthood and Protecting Embryos: Why We Need Laws', *Hastings Center Report*, (October) pp. 50–2.

Archbishop of Canterbury (1948) *Artificial Human Insemination: The Report of a Commission Appointed by His Grace the Archbishop of Canterbury* (London: SPCK).

Arditti, R. (1985) 'Reducing Women to Matter', *Women's Studies International Forum*, pp. 577–82.

Arditti, R., Duelli Klein, R. and Minden, S. (eds) (1984) *Test-Tube Women: What Future for Motherhood?* (London: Pandora Press).

Arms, S. (1975) *Immaculate Deception* (New York: Houghton Mifflin).

Arney, W. R. (1982) *Power and the Profession of Obstetrics* (London: University of Chicago Press).

Arnold, B. and Vogt, C. (1986) 'Kinderwunsch, Kinderlösigkeit und Weibliche Identität' in Brockskothen et al. (eds) *Frauen gegen Gentechnik und Reproduktionstechnik*.

Association for Improvements in the Maternity Services (AIMS) (1983) *Quarterly Newsletter*, (Summer).

'Babies Before Birth' (1962) *Look*, 26, pp. 19–23.

Badinter, E. (1980) *L'Amour en plus. Histoire de l'amour maternel XVIIe–XXe siècle* (Paris: Flammarion).

Barnes, B. (1977) *Interest and the Growth of Knowledge* (London and Boston: Routledge and Kegan Paul).

Barrett, M. and McIntosh, M. (1982) *The Anti-Social Family* (London: Verso).

Barrett, M. and Roberts, H. (1978) 'Doctors and their Patients: The Social Control of Women in General Practice', in C. Smart and B. Smart (eds) *Women, Sexuality and Social Control* (London: Routledge and Kegan Paul).

Barthes, R. (1982) 'The Photographic Message', in S. Sontag (ed.) *A Barthes Reader* (New York: Hill and Wang).

Barton, M., Walker, K. and Weisner, B. P. (1945) 'Artificial Insemination', *British Medical Journal*, (13 January) pp. 40–3.

Bates, B. and Turner, A. N. (1985) 'Imagery and Symbolism in the Birth Practices of Traditional Cultures', *Birth*, 12, pp. 33–8.

Bazin, A. (1980) 'The Ontology of the Photographic Image', in A. Trachtenberg (ed.) *Classic Essays on Photography*, pp. 237–44.

Behrman, S. J. and Kistner, R. (eds) (1975) *Progress in Infertility*, 2nd edn (Boston: Little Brown and Co.).

Benda-bericht: see *In-Vitro-Fertilisation, Genomanalyse und Gentherapie*.

Bendit, L. J. (1943) *British Medical Journal*, (25 September) p. 404.

Benjamin, J. (1983) 'Master and Slave: The Fantasy of Erotic Domination', in A. Snitow, C. Stansell and S. Thompson (eds) *Powers of Desire* (New York: Monthly Review Press).

Berger, B. and Berger, P. (1983) *The War over the Family: Capturing the Middle Ground* (London: Hutchinson).

Berger, J. (1980) *About Looking* (New York: Pantheon).

Bernal, J. D. (1939) *The Social Functions of Science* (London: Routledge and Kegan Paul).

Biggers, J. D. (1981) 'In Vitro Fertilization and Embryo Transfer in Human Beings', *New England Journal of Medicine*, pp.304–39.

Bijzondere wijzen van voortplanting, draagmoederschap en de juridische problematiek (1985) *Vereniging voor Familie en Jeugdrecht*.

Black Report (1979) *Report by the Working Group on Screening for Neural Tube Defect* (London: DHSS), cited in Farrant 'Who's for Amniocentesis?'.

Blundell, J. (1834) *The Principles and Practice of Obstetry* (London: ECOX).

Booth, The Hon. Mrs Justice (1985) *Report of the Matrimonial Causes Procedure Committee* (London: HMSO).

Boston Globe (1984) 'Law may Save Dead Couple's Frozen Embryos' (24 October).

Breen, D. (1975) *The Birth of a First Child* (London: Tavistock).

Brockskothen, M. et al., (eds) (1986) *Frauen gegen Gentechnik und Reproduktionstechnik. Dokumentation zum Kongress* (19–21 April),

Bonn (Köln: Die Grünen im Bundestag, AK Frauenpolitik und Sozialwissenschaftliche Forschung und Praxis für Frauen e.V., Köln).

Brophy, J. (1985) 'Child Care and the Growth of Power: The Status of Mothers in Custody Disputes', in Brophy and Smart (eds) *Women in Law*.

Brophy, J. and Smart, C. (1981) 'From Disregard to Disrepute: The Position of Women in Family Law', *Feminist Review*, 9.

Brophy, J. and Smart, C. (eds) (1985) *Women in Law* (London: Routledge and Kegan Paul).

Brophy, K. (1981) 'A Surrogate Mother Contract to Bear a Child', *Journal of Family Law*, 20, pp. 263–91.

Browne, F. J. (1935) *Antenatal and Postnatal Care* (London: J. A. Churchill). New editions 1937, 1939, 1942, 1944, 1946, 1951, 1955 (authors F. J. Browne and J. C. McC. Browne); 1960, 1970, 1978 (authors F. J. Browne, J. C. McC. Browne and G. Dixon).

Bullough, V. and Bullough, B. (1977) *Sin, Sickness and Sanity: A History of Sexual Attitudes* (New York: Meridian).

Bunkle, P. (1984) 'Calling the Shots? The International Politics of Depo-Provera', in Arditti et al., (eds) *Test-Tube Women*.

Burgin, V. (ed.) (1982) *Thinking Photography* (London: Macmillan).

Campbell, J. M. (1927) *The Protection of Motherhood* (London: HMSO), Reports on Public Health and Medical Subjects, 48, Ministry of Health.

Campbell, S. and Little, D. J. (1980) 'Clinical Potential of Real-Time Ultrasound', in Bennett, M. J. and Campbell, S. (eds) *Real-time Ultrasound in Obstetrics* (Oxford: Blackwell Scientific Publications).

Capron, A. M. (1984) 'The New Reproductive Possibilities: seeking a Basis for Concerted Action in a Pluralistic Society', *Law, Medicine and Health Care*, (October), pp. 192–8.

Carmichael, J. H. E. and Berry, R. J. (1978) 'Diagnostic X-Rays in Late Pregnancy Neonate', *Lancet*, 1, pp. 351–2.

Cartwright, A. (1967) *Patients and their Doctors* (London: Routledge and Kegan Paul).

Central Statistical Office (1986) *Social Trends* (London: HMSO).

Central Statistical Office (1987) *Social Trends 17*, 1987 edition (London: HMSO).

Chamberlain, M. (1981) *Old Wives' Tales* (London: Virago).

Christiaens, M., van der Weel, C. and Rolies, J. J. (1985) 'Draagmoederschap; Ethische Overwegingen', *Justitiële Verkenningen*, 5, pp. 65–93, Den Haag: Ministerie Van Justitie, W.O.D.C.

Cixous, H. (1981) 'Sorties', in E. Marks and I. de Courtivron (eds) *New French Feminisms* (New York: Schocken).

Clarke, L., Farrell, C. and Beaumont, B. (1983) *Camden Abortion Study*, available from British Pregnancy Advisory Service (BPAS), Austy Manor, Wooton Wawen, Solihull, W. Midlands, B95 6BX.

Coleman, J. S., Katz, E. and Menzel, H. (1966) *Medical Innovations: A Diffusion Study* (New York: Bobbs-Merrill).

Cooper, D. N. and Schmidtke, J. K. (1986) 'Diagnostics of Genetics, Disease Using Recombinant DNA', *Human Genetics*, 73, pp. 1–11.

Corea, G. (1977) *The Hidden Malpractice* (New York: Harper and Row).

Corea, G. (1985a) *The Mother Machine: Reproductive Technologies from Artificial Insemination to Artificial Wombs* (New York: Harper and Row).

Corea, G. (1985b) 'The Reproductive Brothel', in Corea et al., *Man-Made Women*.

Corea, G. (1985c) 'How the New Reproductive Technologies could be Used to Apply the Brothel Model of Social Control Over Women', *Women's Studies International Forum*, 8, 4, pp. 299–305.

Corea, G., Duelli Klein, R. et al., (1985) *Man-Made Women: How New Reproductive Technologies Affect Women* (London: Hutchinson).

Cortese, A. and Feldmann, A. (1984) 'Leihmutterschaft – die neue Heimarbeit?', *Streit*, 4, pp. 123–30.

Council for Science and Society (1984) *Expensive Medical Techniques* (London: Council for Science and Society).

Council of Europe, *Ad hoc* Committee of Experts on Progress in the Biomedical Sciences (1986) *Provisional Principles on the Techniques of Human Artificial Procreation* (Strasbourg: CE).

Cranbrook Committee (1959) *Report of the Maternity Services Committee* (London: HMSO).

Crowe, C. (1985) ' "Women Want It": In-vitro Fertilization and Women's Motivations for Participation', *Women's Studies International Forum*, 8, 6, pp. 547–52.

Damisch, H. (1980) 'Notes for a Phenomenology of the Photographic Image', in Trachtenberg (ed.) *Classic Essays on Photography*.

Däubler-Gmelin, H. (1986) 'Fortpflanzung und Gentechnologie: erprobung des Gesetzgebers', *Demokratie und Recht*, 2, pp. 143–51.

David, M. (1985) 'Motherhood, Child Care and the New Right'. Paper presented to the British Association for the Advancement of Science, . August 1985.

Davis, A. (1982) *Women, Race and Class* (London: The Women's Press).

Donnison, J. (1977) *Midwives and Medical Men* (London: Heinemann).

Dorland, W. A. N. and Hubeny, M. J. (1926) *The X-Ray in Embryology and Obstetrics* (London: Henry Kimpton).

Dowrick, S. and Grundberg, S. (eds) (1980) *Why Children?* (London: The Women's Press).

Doyal, L. (1985) 'Women and the National Health Service: The Carers and the Careless' in E. Lewin and V. Olesen (eds) *Women, Health and Healing* (London: Tavistock).

Doyal, L. and Elston, M. (1983) *Medicine and Health* (Milton Keynes: Open University), Unit 14, Course U221, 'The Changing Experience of Women'.

Dreifus, C. (ed.) (1978) *Seizing our Bodies. The Politics of Women's Health* (New York: Vintage Books).

DuBois, E. C. and Gordon, L. (1984) 'Seeking Ecstasy on the Battlefield: Danger and Pleasure in Nineteenth-Century Feminist Sexual Thought', in C. S. Vance (ed.) *Pleasure and Danger. Exploring Female Sexuality* (Boston: Routledge and Kegan Paul).

Duelli Klein, R. (1985) 'What's "New" about the "New" Reproductive Technologies?', in Corea et al., *Man-Made Women*.

Duelli Klein, R. (1986) 'The Crucial Role of In-Vitro-Fertilisation as a Means of the Social Control of Women', *Documentation: Women's Hearing on Genetic and Reproductive Technology*, (6–7 March), Brussels, European Parliament.

Dworkin, A. (1974) *Woman Hating* (New York: E. P. Hutton).

Dworkin, A. (1983) *Right-Wing Women* (New York: Perigee Books).

Eastlake, Lady E. (1980) 'Photography', in Trachtenberg (ed.) *Classic Essays on Photography*.

Echols, A. (1984) 'The Taming of the Id: Feminist Sexual Politics, 1968–83', in Vance (ed.) *Pleasure and Danger*.

Edholm, F. (1982) 'The Unnatural Family', in E. Whitelegg et al., (eds) *The Changing Experience of Women* (Oxford: Martin Robertson).

Editorial (1945) 'Doctors in Hot Print', *British Medical Journal*, (10 March) p. 339.

Eekelaar, J. and Clive, E. (1977) *Custody After Divorce* (Oxford: Centre for Socio-legal Studies).

Ehrenreich, B. and English, D. (1979) *For Her Own Good: 150 Years of the Experts' Advice to Women* (London: Pluto Press).

Elkington, J. (1986) *The Poisoned Womb: Human Reproduction in a Polluted World* (Harmondsworth: Pelican).

Elliott, J. P. and Flaherty, J. (1983) 'The Use of Breast Stimulation to Ripen the Cervix in Term Pregnancies', *American Journal of Obstetrics and Gynaecology*, 1 (March), pp. 553–6.

Enkin, M. and Chalmers, I. (eds) (1982) *Effectiveness and Satisfaction in Antenatal Care* (London: Spastics International Medical Publications).

Erickson, P. D. (1985) *Reagan Speaks: The Making of an American Myth* (New York: New York University Press).

Ethics Advisory Board (1979) *HEW Support of Research Involving In Vitro Fertilization and Embryo Transfer* (Washington, DC: Department of Health, Education and Welfare).

Evans, W. (1978) 'Changing a Child's Name After Re-marriage', *Family Law*, 8.

Ewen, S. (1984) 'The Political Elements of Style', in J. Bucholtz and D. B. Monk (eds) *Beyond Style: Precis 5* (New York: Columbia University Graduate School of Architecture and Planning/Rizzoli), pp. 125–33.

Ewen, S. and Ewen, E. (1982) *Channels of Desire: Mass Images and the Shaping of American Consciousness* (New York: McGraw-Hill).

Farrant, W. (1985) 'Who's for Amniocentesis? The Politics of Prenatal Screening', in H. Homans (ed.) *The Sexual Politics of Reproduction* (Aldershot: Gower).

Faulder, C. (1985) *Whose Body Is It?* (London: Virago).

Fausto-Sterling, A. (1985) *Myths of Gender: Biological Theories about Women and Men* (New York: Basic Books).

Fee, E. (1983) *Women and Health: The Politics of Sex and Medicine* (Farmingdale, N.Y.: Baywood).

Ferriman, A. (1985) 'Embryo Doctors Hit Back', *The Observer* (10 November), p. 3.

Feversham, the Earl of (1960) *Report of the Departmental Committee on Human Artificial Insemination*, Cmnd. 1105 (London: HMSO).

Fine, M. and Asch, A. (1985) 'Who Owns the Womb?', *Women's Review of Books*, II, 8 (May), pp. 8–10.

Finnrrage (1985) *Network News*, (Spring).

Firestone, S. (1970; 1971) *The Dialectic of Sex* (New York: William Morrow and Co.; London: Jonathan Cape).

Flanagan, G. L. (1962) *The First Nine Months of Life* (New York: Simon and Schuster).

Fletcher, J. (1981) 'The Fetus as Patient: Ethical Issues', *Journal of the American Medical Association*, 246, pp. 772–3.

Fletcher, J. C. and Evans, M. I. (1983) 'Maternal Bonding in Early Fetal Ultrasound Examinations', *New England Journal of Medicine*, 308, pp. 282–93.

Fortin, J. (1980) 'The Nature of the Right to Select a Child's Surname', *Family Law*, 10, 2.

Fowkes, F. G. R., Catford, J. C. and Logan, R. F. L. (1979) 'Abortion and the NHS: The First Decades', *British Medical Journal* (27 January), pp. 217–19.

Francis, H. H. (1985) 'Obstetrics: A Consumer Orientated Service? The Case Against', *Maternal and Child Health*, (March), pp. 69–72.

French, A. W. (1984) 'Prospects for Gene Therapy', *Science*, 226 (24 October), pp. 401–9.

Gallagher, J. (1979) 'Abortion rights: critical issue for women's freedom', *WIN* (8 March), pp. 9–11, 24–6.

Gallagher, J. (1984) 'The Fetus and the Law', *Ms*, (September), pp. 62–6, 134–5.

Gallagher, J. (1985) 'Fetal Personhood and Women's Policy', in V. Sapiro (ed.) *Women, Biology and Public Policy* (Beverley Hills: Sage).

Gallagher, J. (1987) 'Prenatal Invasions and Interventions: What's Wrong with Fetal Rights'. *Harvard Women's Law Journal*, 10 (Spring), pp. 9–58.

Gearhardt, S. (1985) *The Wanderground: Stories of the Hill Women* (London: The Women's Press).

Gezondheidsraad: see *Interimadvies inzake in vitro fertilsatie*.

Gieve, K. (1987) 'Rethinking Feminist Attitudes Towards Mothering', *Feminist Review*, 25 (Spring), pp. 38–45.

Gilman, C. P. (1903) *The Home: Its Work and Influence* (New York: McClure Phillips and Co.).

Glover, J. (1984) *What Sort of People Should There Be?* (Harmondsworth: Penguin).

Gold, R. B. (1984) 'Ultrasound Imaging During Pregnancy', *Family Planning Perspectives*, 16, pp. 240–3.

Goldberg, S. (1977) *The Inevitability of Patriarchy* (London: Maurice Temple Smith).

Goldstein, J., Freud, A. and Solnit, A. J. (1980) *Beyond the Best Interests of the Child* (London: Burnett Books).

Gordon, L. (1977) *Woman's Body, Woman's Right* (Harmondsworth: Penguin).

Gorovitz, S. (1982) 'Introduction: The Ethical Issues', in D. Young (ed.) *Women and Health* (New York: Haworth Press), vol. 7: *Obstetrical Intervention and Technology in the 1980s.*

Graham, D. (1982) 'Ultrasound in Clinical Obstetrics', in Young (ed) *Women and Health*, 7.

Graham, H. (1984) *Women, Health and the Family* (Brighton: Wheatsheaf).

Green, M. (1976) *Goodbye Father* (London: Routledge and Kegan Paul).

Griffin, B. and Rayner, G. (1985) *Commercial Medicine in London* (London: Greater London Council).

Grimes, D. (1984) 'Second-Trimester Abortions in the United States', *Family Planning Perspectives*, 16, pp. 260–5.

Grobstein, C. (1981) *From Chance to Purpose: An Appraisal of External Human Fertilization* (Reading, MA: Addison-Wesley).

Gullick, D. (1972) 'Sorcerers' Apprentices', *British Medical Journal*, (8 April), p. 111.

Hanmer, J. (1981) 'Sex Predetermination, Artificial Insemination and the Maintenance of Male-Dominated Culture', in Roberts (ed.) *Women, Health and Reproduction.*

Hanmer, J. (1985) 'Transforming Consciousness: Women and the New Reproductive Technologies', in Corea et al. *Man-Made Women.*

Hanmer, J. and Allen, P. (1980) 'Reproductive Engineering: The Final Solution?', in Brighton Women and Science Group (eds) (1980) *Alice Through the Microscope* (London: Virago).

Haraway, D. (1979) 'The Biological Enterprise: Sex, Mind and Profit from Human Engineering to Sociobiology', *Radical History Review*, 20, pp. 206–37.

Haraway, D. (1985) 'A Manifesto for Cyborgs: Science, Technology and Socialist Feminism in the 1980s', *Socialist Review*, 80, pp. 65–107.

Haraway, D. (1986) 'Primatology is Politics by Other Means', in R. Bleier (ed.) *Feminist Approaches to Science* (Oxford: Pergamon), Athene series.

Harding, S. (1983) 'Why has the SexGender System become Visible Only Now?', in S. Harding and M. Hintikka (eds) *Discovering Reality: Feminist Perspectives on Epistemology, Metaphysics, Methodology and the Philosophy of Science* (Dordrecht: Reidel).

Harding, S. (1986) *The Science Question in Feminism* (Milton Keynes: Open University Press).

Harrison, R. et al. (1981) 'Management of the Fetus with a Correctable Congenital Defect', *Journal of the American Medical Association*, 246, pp. 774.

Harrison, B. (1983) *Our Right to Choose* (Boston: Beacon Press).

Hartsock, N. (1983a) 'The Feminist Standpoint' in Harding and Hintikka (eds) *Discovering Reality.*

Hartsock, N. (1983b) *Money, Sex and Power* (Boston: Northeastern University Press).

Haverkamp, A. D. and Orleans, M. (1982) 'An Assessment of Electronic Fetal Monitoring', in Young (ed.) *Women and Health*, 7, pp. 126–34.

Heida, A. (1984) 'Juridische perikelen rond het draagmoederschap', *Weekblad voor Publiek en Notariëel Recht*, 5716, pp. 649–54.

Hellegers, A. E. and McCormick, R. A. (1978) 'Unanswered Questions on Test-Tube Life', *America*, 139.

Henshaw, S. K. et al. (1985) 'A Portrait of American Women who Obtain Abortions', *Family Planning Perspectives*, 17, pp. 90–6.

Hessen, B. (1971) 'The Social and Economic Roots of Newton's *Principia*', in J. Needham (ed.) *Science at the Crossroads* (London: Cass).

Himes, N. E. (1963) *Medical History of Contraception* (New York: Gaunt Press).

Hoggett, B. (1981) *Parents and Children* (London: Sweet and Maxwell).

Hohler, C. W. and Platt, L. D. (1984) American College of Obstetrics and Gynaecology, Office Ultrasound Survey. Personal communication. Quoted in National Institutes of Health, Consensus Development Conference 'The Use of Diagnostic Ultrasound Imaging in Pregnancy' (6–8 February) Washington, DC.

Hollinger, J. H. (1985) 'From Coitus to Commerce: Legal and Social Consequences of Non-Coital Reproduction', *Journal of Law Reform*, 18.

Holmes, H., Hoskins, B. and Gross, M. (eds) (1981) *The Custom-Made Child?* (Clifton, NJ: Humana Press).

Holtrust, N. (1985) 'Moederzorg en vaderrecht', *Nederlands Juristenblad*, pp. 201–7.

Holtrust, N. and de Hondt, I. (1985) 'Kunstmatige bevruchting', *Nemesis*, 2, 2 (1985–6) pp. 72–3.

Holtrust, N. and De Hondt, I. (1986) 'Draagmoederschap: Morele paniek waarover?' *Nemesis*, 2, 3 (1985–6) pp. 117–19.

Holtrust, N. and Sevenhuijsen, S. (1986) 'Nieuw wetsvoorstel omgangsrecht', *Nederlands Juristenblad*, 61, 18, pp. 545–9.

Holtrust, N., Sevenhuijsen, S. and Verbraken, A. (1986) 'Rights for Fathers and the State. Recent Political Developments in the Netherlands Around Custody'. Paper, University of Amsterdam, Department of Political Theory.

Home Office and Scottish Department (1960): see Feversham, the Earl of.

Hondt, I. De and Holtrust, N. (1986) 'The European Convention and the "Marckx-Judgement Effect"', *International Journal of Law*, (November).

House of Commons Debates (Unborn Child Protection Bill) (1984–5), 73 columns, 633–700.

Howe, G., et al. (1985) 'Effects of Age, Cigarette Smoking and Other Factors on Fertility', *British Medical Journal*, 290 (8 June) pp. 1697–1700.

Howell, E. and Bayes, M. (1981) *Women and Mental Health* (New York: Basic Books).

Hubbard, R. (1982) 'Some Legal and Policy Implications of Recent Advances in Prenatal Diagnosis and Fetal Therapy', *Women's Rights Law Reporter*, 7 (Spring 1982), pp. 201–18.

Hubbard, R. (1984) 'Personal Courage is not Enough: Some Hazards of Childbearing in the 1980s', in Arditti et al. (eds) *Test-Tube Women*.

Hubbard, R. (1985) 'Prenatal Diagnosis and Eugenic Ideology', *Women's Studies International Forum*, 8, 6, pp. 567–76.

Hubbard, R. and Henifin, M. S. (1984) 'Genetic Screening of Prospective Parents and of Workers', in J. M. Humber and R. T. Almeder (eds) *Biomedical Ethics Review* (New Jersey: Humana).

Hubbard, R. and Stanford, W. (1985) 'The New Reproductive Technology', in Boston Women's Health Collective, *The New Our Bodies Our Selves* (Greenville, N. C.: S & S) pp. 317–26.

Hull, M. G. R. et al. (1985) 'Population Study of Causes, Treatment and Outcome of Infertility', *British Medical Journal*, (14 December).

Hunter, A. (1981) 'In the Wings: New Right Organization and Ideology', *Radical America*, 15 (Spring), pp. 113–38.

Illich, I. (1975) *Medical Nemesis* (London: Calder and Boyars).

In-Vitro-Fertilisation, Genomanalyse und Gentherapie (1985) Bundesministerium für Forschung und Technologie, Bonn (Benda-bericht).

Ince, S. (1984) 'Inside the Surrogate Industry', in Arditti et al. (eds.) *Test-Tube Women*.

Interdepartmental Committee on the Physical Deterioration of the Population (1904) *Report* (London: HMSO).

Interimadvies Inzake In Vitro Fertilsatie (1984) (Den Haag: Gezondheidsraad).

Irigaray, L. (1981) 'Ce sexe qui n'en est pas un', in Marks and de Courtivron (eds) *New French Feminisms* (New York: Schocken).

Isaacs, S. (1948) *Childhood and After* (London: Routledge and Kegan Paul).

Johnston, M., Shaw, R. and Bird, D. (1984) 'Expectation of Success and Stress Associated with In Vitro Fertilisation and Embryo Transfer'. Unpublished paper, London: Royal Free Hospital.

Jordanova, L. (1980) 'Natural Facts: A Historical Perspective on Science and Sexuality', in C. MacCormack and M. Strathern (eds) *Nature, Culture and Gender* (Cambridge: Cambridge University Press).

Jordanova, L. (1981) 'Mental Illness, Mental Health: Changing Norms and Expectations', in Cambridge Women's Studies Group *Women in Society* (London: Virago).

Kalter, J. (1985) 'TV News and Religion', *TV Guide*, 33 (9, 16 November).

Kaplan, E. A. (1983) 'Is the Gaze Male?', in Snitow, Stansell and Thompson (eds) *Powers of Desire*.

Kaufert, P. and McKinlay, S. (1985) 'Estrogen-Replacement Therapy: The Production of Medical Knowledge and the Emergence of Policy', in Lewin and Olesen (eds) *Women, Health and Healing* (London: Tavistock).

Keane, N. and Breo, D. (1981) *The Surrogate Mother* (New York: Everest House).

Keller, E. Fox (1985) *Reflections on Gender and Science* (New Haven, CT: Yale University Press).

Keller, E. Fox and Grontkowski, C. R. (1983) 'The Mind's Eye', in Harding and Hintikka (eds) *Discovering Reality*.

Kern, P. A. and Ridolfi, K. M. (1982) 'The Fourteenth Amendment Protection of a Woman's Right to be a Single Parent Through Artificial Insemination by Donor', *Women's Rights Law Reporter*, 7, 3, pp. 251–84.

Kevles, D. (1986) *In the Name of Eugenics* (Harmondsworth: Penguin).

Kilian, G. M. (1985) 'Draagmoeders en Draagmoederschap in Nederland, een Kennismaking', *Justitiële Verkenningen*, 5, pp. 94–123, Den Haag: Ministerie van Justitie, W.O.D.C.

King, P. (1979) 'The Juridical Status of the Fetus: A Proposal for Legal Protection of the Unborn', *Michigan Law Review*, 77, pp. 1647–87.

Kitzinger, S. and Davies, J. A. (eds) (1978) *The Place of Birth* (Oxford: Oxford University Press).

Kontos, S. (1986) 'Wider die Dämoniserung medizinischer Technik', in Brockskothen et al. (eds) *Frauen gegen Gentechnik und Reproduktionstechnik*.

Kramer, M. (1985) 'Last-Chance Babies: The Wonders of In Vitro Fertilisation', *New York*, (12 August).

Kuhn, A. (1982) *Women's Pictures: Feminism and Cinema* (London: Routledge and Kegan Paul).

Kuhn, T. (1970) *The Structure of Scientific Revolutions* (Chicago: Chicago University Press).

Lakatos, I. and Musgrave, A. (eds) (1970) *Criticism and the Growth of Knowledge* (New York and Cambridge: Cambridge University Press).

Lancet, (1934) 'Antenatal Care on Trial', Notes and Comments, 2, p. 1204.

Law Commission (1979) *Family Law: Illegitimacy* (London: HMSO), Working Paper 74.

Law Commission (1982) *Report on Illegitmacy* (London: HMSO), No. 118.

League of Nations (1927) *Report of the Special Body of Experts on Traffic in Women and Children* (Geneva: League of Nations).

Le Grand, J. (1982) *The Strategy of Equality* (London: George Allen and Unwin).

Lewin, E. (1985) 'By Design: Reproductive Strategies and the Meaning of Motherhood', in Homans (ed.) *The Sexual Politics of Reproduction*.

Lewis, J. (1980) *The Politics of Motherhood: Child and Maternal Welfare in England, 1900–1939* (London: Croom Helm).

Lifton, R. J. (1986) *The Nazi Doctors: Medical Killings and the Psychology of Genocide* (Basingstoke: Macmillan).

Lindsay, K. (1985) 'Do we Reject Technology too Quickly?', *Sojourner*, (July).

Lokhorst, E. van (1929) *Vrouwen* (Amsterdam: Querido's Uitgeversmaatschappij).

Luker, K. (1984) *Abortion and the Politics of Motherhood* (Berkeley and London: University of California Press).

MacFarlane, A. (1981) 'Women and Health: Official Statistics on Women and Aspects of Health and Illness', *Equal Opportunities Commission Research Bulletin* (Manchester: EOC).

MacFarlane, A. and Mugford, M. (1984) *Birth Counts: Statistics of Pregnancy and Childbirth* (London: HMSO).

Macintyre, S. (1976) ' "Who Wants Babies?" The Social Construction of Instincts', in D. L. Barker and S. Allen (eds) *Sexual Divisions and Society* (London: Tavistock).

Macintyre, S. (1977) *Single and Pregnant* (London: Croom Helm).

MacLennan v. *MacLennan* 1958, Scottish Courts, 105.

Mackinnon, C. A. (1982) 'Feminism, Marxism, Method and the State', *Signs*, 7, 3, pp. 515–44.

Mackinnon, C. A. (1983) 'Feminism, Marxism, Method and the State: Towards Feminist Jurisprudence', *Signs*, 8, 4, pp. 635–58.

Margolick, D. (1985) 'Damages Rejected in Death of Fetus', *New York Times*, (16 June), p. 26.

Marsden, D. (1969) *Mothers Alone* (London: Allen Lane).

Mathieson, D. (1986) *Infertility Services in the NHS: What's Going on?*, a report prepared for Frank Dobson, MP. Available from Frank Dobson, House of Commons, London.

Mayo, M. M. (1976) 'Legitimacy for the AID Child', *Family Law*, 6.

McCormick, R. A. (1985) 'Therapy or Tampering? The Ethics of Reproductive Technology', *America*, (December), pp. 396–403.

McGilvray, D. B. (1982) 'Sexual Power and Fertility in Sri Lanka', in C. P. MacCormack (ed.) *Ethnography of Fertility and Birth* (London: Academic Press).

McKinlay, J. B. (1981) 'From "Promising Report" to "Standard Procedure" – Seven Stages in the Career of a Medical Innovation', *Milbank Memorial Fund Quarterly*, 59, 3, pp. 374–411.

McKusick, V. A. (1983) *Mendelian Inheritance in Man*, 6th edn (Baltimore: Johns Hopkins Press).

McLaren, A. (1978) *Birth Control in Nineteenth Century England* (London: Croom Helm).

McLaren, A. (1984) *Reproductive Rituals* (London: Methuen).

McNally, F. (1979) *Women for Hire* (London: Macmillan).

Mead, M. (1962) *Male and Female* (Harmondsworth: Penguin).

Medical Notes in Parliament (1943) *British Medical Journal*, (4 August), p. 219.

Medical Research Council (1975–6) *Annual Report* (London: HMSO).

Medical Research Council (MRC) and Royal College of Obstetricians and Gynaecologists (RCOG) (1986) *First Report of Voluntary Licensing Authority for Human In Vitro Fertilisation and Embryology* (London: MRC/RCOG).

Mellown, D. (1985) 'An Incomplete Picture: The Debate about Surrogate Motherhood', *Harvard Women's Law Journal*, pp. 231–47.

Mendelsohn, E., Weingart, P. and Whitley, R. (eds) (1977) *The Social Reproduction of Scientific Knowledge* (Dordrecht: Reidel).

Merchant, C. (1980) *The Death of Nature: Women, Ecology and the Scientific Revolution* (New York: Harper and Row).

Mies, M. (1985) '"Why do we Need all this?" A Call Against Genetic Engineering and Reproductive Technology', *Women's Studies International Forum*, 8, 6, pp. 553–60.

Mies, M. (1986) 'Argumente wider den Bio-Krieg', in Brockskothen et al. (eds) *Frauen gegen Gentechnik und Reproduktionstechnik*, pp. 114–19.

Miller, S. (1986) *The Good Mother* (New York: Harper and Row).

Minden, S. (1985) 'Patriarchal Designs: The Genetic Engineering of Human Embryos', *Women's Studies International Forum*, 8, 6, pp. 561–66.

Modell, B. (1983) 'Implications of Fetal Diagnosis', in C. H. Rodeck and K. H. Nicolaides (eds) *Prenatal Diagnosis* (London: Royal College of Obstetricians and Gynaecologists).

Mohr, J. (1978) *Abortion in America* (Oxford and New York: Oxford University Press).

Morgan, D. (1985) 'Making Motherhood Male: Surrogacy and the Moral Economy of Women', *Journal of Law and Society*, 12,.pp. 219–38.

Morton, Lord (1956) *Report of the Royal Commission on Marriage and Divorce*, Cmnd. 9678 (London: HMSO).

Mulvey, L. (1975) 'Visual Pleasure and Narrative Cinema', *Screen*, 16, pp. 6–18.

Murdrey, V. and Slack, J. (1985) 'Screening for Down's Syndrome in the N.E. Thames Region', *British Medical Journal*, 291, pp. 1315–28.

Needham, J. (ed.) (1971) *Science at the Crossroads* (London: Cass).

New York Times (1984) 'Frozen Embryos in Legal Limbo', (24 June).

New York Times (1986a) 'Concerns on Surrogate Motherhood', (9 September).

New York Times (1986b) 'Dead Baby's Mother Faces Criminal Charges on Acts in Pregnancy', (9 October).

Nilsson, A. (1985) 'FINNRET/FINRRAGE Emergency Conference on the New Reproductive Technologies, Vällinge, Sweden (July)', *Women's Studies International Forum*, 8, 6, pp. ii–iv, Feminist Forum.

Oakley, A. (1976) 'Wisewoman and Medicine Man: Changes in the Management of Childbirth', in J. Mitchell and A. Oakley (eds) *The Rights and Wrongs of Women* (Harmondsworth: Penguin).

Oakley, A. (1980) *Women Confined: Towards a Sociology of Childbirth* (Oxford: Martin Robertson; New York: Schocken).

Oakley, A. (1984) *The Captured Womb: A History of the Medical Care of Pregnant Women* (Oxford: Basil Blackwell).

Oakley, A. and Oakley, R. (1979) 'Sexism in Official Statistics', in J. Irvine, J. Miles and J. Evans (eds) *Demystifying Social Statistics* (London: Pluto Press).

O'Brien, M. (1983) *The Politics of Reproduction* (London: Routledge and Kegan Paul).

Office of Population Censuses and Statistics (1985) *General Household Survey 1983* (London: HMSO).

Office of Population Censuses and Statistics (1986a) *Occupational Mortality: December Supplement England and Wales 1979–80* (London: HMSO).

Office of Population Censuses and Statistics (1986b) *Birth Statistics 1985* (London: HMSO).

Owens, D. and Read, M. W. (1979) *The Provision, Use and Evaluation of Medical Services for the Subfertile: An Analysis Based on the Experience of Involuntarily Childless Couples* (Cardiff: University of Cardiff), SRU Working Paper, 4).

Paltrow, L. (1985) 'Book Review: *Test-Tube Women*', *Women's Rights Law Reporter*, 8 (Fall), pp. 303ff.

Paltrow, L. (1986) 'Amicus Brief: *Richard Thornburgh* v. *American College of Obstetricians and Gynecologists*', *Women's Rights Law Reporter*, 9, pp. 3–24.

Parker, P. J. (1982) 'Surrogate Motherhood: The Interaction of Litigation, Legislation and Psychiatry', *International Journal of Law and Psychiatry*, pp. 341–54.

Parry, M. L. (1978) 'Changing a Child's Name after Re-Marriage – A Reply', *Family Law*, 8.

Penfold, P. and Walker, G. (1984) *Women and the Psychiatric Paradox* (Milton Keynes: Open University Press).

Pepperell, R. J., Hudson, B. and Wood, C. (1980) *The Infertile Couple* (London: Churchill Livingstone).

Petchesky, R. P. (1981) 'Reproductive Freedom: Beyond "A Woman's Right to Choose"', in C. R. Stimpson and E. S. Person (eds) *Women, Sex and Sexuality* (Chicago: University of Chicago Press). Originally in *Signs*, (Summer 1980).

Petchesky, R. P. (1985; 1986) *Abortion and Woman's Choice: The State, Sexuality and Reproductive Freedom* (Boston: Northeastern University Press; London: Verso).

Pfeffer, N. and Woollett, A. (1983) *The Experience of Infertility* (London: Virago).

Pfeufer Kahn, R. (1984) 'The Reform of Childbirth', *The Women's Review of Books* II, 3 (December), pp. 15–16.

Phillipp, E. E. (1973) in CIBA Foundation *Symposium* 17 (new series) (Amsterdam: Elsevier), p. 66.

Phillips, A. (1985) 'A Crippling VD Doctors Miss', *Observer*, (10 November).

Piercy, M. (1979) *Woman on the Edge of Time* (London: The Women's Press).

Planned Parenthood Federation of America (n.d.) *The Facts Speak Louder: Planned Parenthood's Critique of 'The Silent Scream'* (New York: Planned Parenthood Federation of America).

Playfair, W. S. (1898) *A Treatise on the Science and Practice of Midwifery* (London: Smith, Elder and Co).

Polikoff, N. (1982) 'Why are Mothers Losing: A Brief Analysis of Criteria Used in Child Custody Determinations', *Women's Rights Law Reporter*, 7 (Spring), pp. 235–43.

Pollock, S. (1984) 'Refusing to take Women Seriously: Side Effects and the Politics of Contraception', in Arditti et al. (eds) *Test-Tube Women*.

Porter, M. (1984) 'Infertility: The Extent of the Problem', *Biology and Society*, 1, pp. 128–35.

Public Morality Council (1947) *Artificial Insemination: Report of a Conference Held in London under the auspices of the Public Morality Council* (London: Wm. Heinemann Medical Books).

Radcliffe, W. (1967) *Milestones in Midwifery* (Bristol: John Wright and Sons).

Rakusen, J. (1981) 'Depo-Provera: The Extent of the Problem', in Roberts (ed.) *Women, Health and Reproduction*.

Rapp, R. (1984) 'XYLO: A True Story', in Arditti et al. (eds) *Test-Tube Women*.

Rapp, R. (1985) 'Feminists and Pharmacrats', *The Women's Review of Books*, II, 10 (July), pp. 3–4.

Raymond, J. (1985) 'Preface', in Corea et al. *Man-Made Women*.

Reece, L. N. (1935) 'The Estimation of Fetal Maturity by a New Method of X-Ray Cephalometry: Its Bearing on Clinical Midwifery', *Proceedings of the Royal Society of Medicine*, (18 January), pp. 489–504.

Reiser, S. J. (1978) *Medicine and the Reign of Technology* (Cambridge: Cambridge University Press).

Report of the Committee on Homosexual Offences and Prostitution 1956–57 (Wolfenden Report), Cmnd. 247 (London: HMSO).

Rhoden, N. K. (1985) 'Late Abortion and Technological Advances in Fetal Viability: Some Legal Considerations', *Family Planning Perspectives*, 17, pp. 160–1.

Rich, A. (1976) *Of Woman Born: Motherhood as Experience and Institution* (New York: W. W. Norton).

Riessman, C. K. (1983) 'Women and Medicalization: A New Perspective', *Social Policy*, (Summer).

Rights of Women Family Law Subgroup (1985) 'Campaigning Around Family Law: Politics and Practice', in Brophy and Smart (eds) *Women in Law*.

Riley, D. (1983) *War in the Nursery: Theories of the Child and Mother* (London: Virago).

Rimmer, L. and Popay, J. (1982) 'The Family at Work', *Employment Gazette*, (June), pp. 255–60.

Roberts, H. (1985) *The Patient Patients: Women and their Doctors* (London: Pandora Press).

Roberts, H. (ed.) (1981) *Women, Health and Reproduction* (London: Routledge and Kegan Paul).

Rodeck, C. H. and Nicolaides, K. H. (eds) (1983) *Prenatal Diagnosis: Proceedings of the Eleventh Study Group of the Royal College of Obstetricians and Gynaecologists* (London: RCOG).

Romein-Verschoor, A. (1935; 1977) *Vrouwenspiegel. De Nederlandse Romanschrijfster na 1880* (Nijmegen: SUN).

Rood-de Boer, M. (1984) 'Rechtsvragen met Betrekking tot Moederschap', *Familie en Jeugdrecht*, 6–8, pp. 232–8.

Rood-de Boer, M. (1986) 'Moderne Methoden van Voortplanting: Wetgeving of Niet?', *Socialisme en Democratie*, 7/8, pp. 218–22.

Rose, H. (1983) 'Hand, Brain and Heart: Towards a Feminist Epistemology for the Natural Sciences', *Signs*, 9, 1 (Fall), pp. 73–90.

Rose, H. and Hanmer, J. (1976) 'Women's Liberation, Reproduction and the Technological Fix', in Barker and Allen (eds) *Sexual Divisions and Society*.

Rose, H. and Rose, S. (eds) (1976) *Ideology of/in the Natural Sciences* (Boston: Schenkman).

Rose. S. and Rose, H. (1971) 'The Myth of the Neutrality of Science', in *Impact of Science on Society* (Paris: UNESCO); reprinted R. Arditti et al. (eds) *Science and Liberation* (Boston: South End Press).

Rothman, B. K. (1982) *In Labour: Women and Power in the Birthplace* (New York and London: W. W. Norton).

Rothman, B. K. (1984) 'The Meanings of Choice in Reproductive Technology', in Arditti et al. (eds) *Test-Tube Women*.

Rothman, B. K. (1986) *The Tentative Pregnancy* (New York: Viking).

Rowland, R. (1984) 'Reproductive Technologies. Of Woman Born – but for How Long?'. Paper given to the 'Woman in Society' course, SPS, Cambridge University (6 November).

Rowland, R. (1985a) 'A Child at Any Price?', *Women's Studies International Forum*, 8, 6, pp. 539–46.

Rowland, R. (1985b) 'Motherhood, Patriarchal Power, Alienation and the Issue of "Choice" in Sex Preselection', in Corea et al. *Man-Made Women*.

Royal College of Obstetricians and Gynaecologists (RCOG) (1982) *Report of the RCOG Working Party on Further Specialisation within Obstetrics and Gynaecology* (London: RCOG).

Russell, D. (1925) *Hypatia – or Women and Knowledge* (London: Kegan Paul, Trench and Trubner).

Russell, Lord Justice (1966) *Report of the Committee on the Law of Succession in Relation to Illegitimate Persons*, Cmnd. 3051 (London: HMSO).

Saffron, L. (1986) *Getting Pregnant our own Way: A Guide to Alternative Insemination*. Available from Women's Health Information Centre, 52 Featherstone St, London, EC1.

Sayers, J. (1982) *Biological Politics* (London: Tavistock).

Sayre, A. (1975) *Rosalind Franklin and DNA: A Vivid View of what it is Like to be a Gifted Woman in an Especially Male Profession* (New York: W. W. Norton).

Schapiro, R. (1985) 'Britain's Sexual Counter-Revolutionaries', *Marxism Today*, 29, 2 (February), pp. 7–10.

Sekula, A. (1982) 'On the Invention of Photographic Meaning', in Burgin (ed.) *Thinking Photography*.

Sevenhuijsen, S. (1986a) *Feminism, Illegitimacy and Filiation Law in the Netherlands, 1900–1940* (Madison: University of Wisconsin, Institute for Legal Studies).

Sevenhuijsen, S. (1986b) 'De Waarheid, Sex en Spruitjes', *Katijif*, 3, pp. 30–4.

Sevenhuijsen, S. and de Vries, P. (1984) 'The Women's Movement and Motherhood' in A. Meulenbelt et al. (eds) *A Creative Tension* (London: Pluto).

Shaw, M. and Damme, L. (1980) 'The Legal Status of the Fetus', in A. Milunsky and G. J. Annas (eds) *Genetics and the Law II* (New York: Plenum).

Shearer, M. H. (1984) 'Revelations: A Summary and Analysis of the NIH Consensus Development Conference on Ultrasound Imaging in Pregnancy', *Birth*, 11, pp. 23–6.

Sheehan, K. H. (1985) 'Abnormal Labor: Cesarians in the U.S.', *The Network News*, 10, National Women's Health Network, (July–August), p. 1, 3.

Short Report (Second Report from the Social Services Committee) (1980) *Perinatal and Neonatal Mortality* (London: HMSO).

Singer, P. and Wells, D. (1984) *The Reproduction Revolution: New Ways of Making Babies* (Oxford: Oxford University Press).

Smart, C. (1984) *The Ties That Bind: Law, Marriage and the Reproduction of Patriarchal Relations* (London: Routledge Kegan Paul).

Smith, G. P. (1978) 'A Close Encounter of the First Kind: Artificial Insemination and an Enlightened Judiciary', *Journal of Family Law*, 17, 1, pp. 41–7.

Smith-Rosenberg, C. (1985) *Disorderly Conduct: Visions of Gender in Victorian America* (New York: Alfred A. Knopf).

Sofia, Z. (1984) 'Exterminating Fetuses: Abortion, Disarmament, and the Sexo-Semiotics of Extraterrestrialism', *Diacritics*, 14, pp. 47–59.

'Sonar Look at an Unborn Baby, A' (1965) *Life*, 58, pp. 45–6.

Sontag, S. (1973) *On Photography* (New York: Delta).

Sontag, S. (ed.) (1982) *A Barthes Reader* (New York: Hill and Wang).

Stack, C. (1974) *All our Kin* (New York: Harper and Row).

Steinbacher, R. (1983) 'Sex Preselection: From Here to Fraternity', in C. Gould (ed.) *Beyond Domination: New Perspectives on Women and Philosophy* (Towota, NJ: Rowman and Allenheld).

Steinbacher, R. and Holmes, H. B. (1985) 'Sex Choice: Survival and Sisterhood' in Corea et al. *Man–Made Women*.

Steptoe, P. and Edwards, R. (1980) *A Matter of Life* (London: Hutchinson).

Stewart, A. et al. (1956) 'Malignant Disease in Childhood and Diagnostic Irradiation in Utero', *Lancet*, 2, p. 447.

Stimsom, G. V. (1975) 'Obeying Doctor's Orders: A View from the Other Side', *Social Science and Medicine*, 8, pp. 97–104.

Strachey, R. (1978) *The Cause: A Short History of the Women's Movement in Great Britain* (London: Virago).

Struck, G. (1986) 'Der Benda-Bericht zur Gentechnologie – Diskussion ohne Neuland', *Demokratie und Recht*, 14, 2, pp. 123–6.

Swinbank, D. (1986) 'Japanese Gynaecology: Gender Selection Sparks Row', *Nature*, 321 (June), p. 19.
Taylor, J. et al. (1986) *Mental Handicap Partnership in the Community* (London: Office of Health Economics).
Thacker, S. B. and Banta, H. D. (1982) 'Benefits and Risks of Episiotomy', in Young (ed.) *Women and Health*, vol. 7, pp. 173–81.
Titmuss, R. M. (1958) *Essays on the Welfare State* (London: George Allen and Unwin).
Townsend, P. and Davidson, N. (1982) *Inequalities in Health: the Black Report* (Harmondsworth: Penguin).
Trachtenberg, A. (ed.) (1980) *Classic Essays on Photography* (New Haven, CT: Leete's Island Books).
Tyler Smith, W. (1858) *A Manual of Obstetrics* (London: John Churchill).
Tyson, J. E. et al. (1983) 'An Evaluation of the Quality of Therapeutic Studies in Perinatal Medicine', *Journal of Pediatrics*, 102, pp. 10–13.
Van den Daele, W. (1977) 'The Social Construction of Science', in Mendelsohn et al. (eds) *The Social Reproduction of Scientific Knowledge*.
Veevers, J. (1980) *Childless by Choice* (Toronto: Butterworth).
Vega, J. (1986) 'Dwang en Instemming. Klassiek Liberale Koncepten in Teksten over Seksueel Geweld', *Tijdschrift voor vrouwenstudies*, 26, 2, pp. 179–95.
Verbraken, A. (1981) 'Wordt Vaders wil Wet?', in S. Sevenhuijsen et al. (eds) *Socialisties-Feministiese Teksten*, (Amsterdam: Sara), vol. 6, pp. 17–43.
Versluysen, M. (1981) 'Midwives, Medical Men and "Poor Women Labouring of Child": Lying-In Hospitals in Eighteenth Century London', in Roberts (ed.) *Women, Health and Reproduction*.
Vessey, M. P. et al. (1981) 'Pelvic Inflammatory Disease and the IUD: Findings from a Large Cohort Study', *British Medical Journal*, 282 (14 March).
Waller, L. (1984) *Report on the Disposition of Embryos Produced by In Vitro Fertilization*.
Wallerstein, J. and Kelly, J. (1980) *Surviving the Breakup: How Children and Parents Cope with Divorce* (London: Grant McIntyre).
Walters, W. and Singer, P. (eds) (1982) *Test-Tube Babies* (Oxford, Melbourne, New York: Oxford University Press).
Warnock, M. (1985) *A Question of Life: The Warnock Report on Human Fertilisation and Embryology* (Oxford: Basil Blackwell). Originally (1984) *Report of the Committee of Inquiry into Human Fertilisation and Embryology*, Cmnd. 9314 (London: HMSO).
Weideger, P. (1978) *Female Cycles* (London: The Women's Press).
Weir, L. and Casey, L. (1984) 'Subverting Power to Sexuality', *Socialist Review*, 14, pp. 139–57.
Wertz, D. (1983) 'What Birth has done for Doctors', *Women and Health*, 8, pp. 7–24.
Wilkie, J. R. (1984) 'Involuntary Childlessness in the United States', *Boldt*

Verlag Boppard Zeitschrift fur Bevolkerungswissenschaft, 10, 1, pp. 37–52.

Williamson, N. E. (1976) 'Sex Preferences, Sex Control and the Effects on Women', *Signs,* 1, pp. 1096–01.

Willis, E. (1983) 'The Politics of Abortion', *In These Times,* (15–28 June), pp. 12–13.

Wolfenden Report: see *Report of the Committee on Homosexual Offences and Prostitution 1956–57.*

Woollett, A. (1985) 'Childlessness: Strategies for Coping with Infertility', *International Journal for Behavioral Development,* 8, pp. 473–82.

World Health Organization (WHO) (1985) *Having a Baby in Europe* (Copenhagen: WHO Regional Office for Europe).

Wortman, S. F. M. (1985) 'Juridische Aspecten van Kunstmatige Bevruchting en Draagmoederschap', *Justitiële Verkenningen,* 5, pp. 41–64, (Den Haag: Ministerie van Justitie, W.O.D.C.).

WRRIC (1986) *Women's Reproductive Rights Information Centre Newsletter,* (June–July). Available from 52–54 Featherstone Street, London EC1.

Young, R. M. (1977) 'Science *is* Social Relations', *Radical Science Journal,* 5, pp. 65–131.

Yoxen, E. (1982; 1983) *The Gene Business* (London: Crucible; Pan).

Zimmerman, P. (1986) 'The Amateur, the Avant-Garde, and Ideologies of Art', *Journal of Film and Video,* 38, pp. 63–85.

Zipper, J. (1986a) 'Geboortetechnologie: Over Medici, Meesters en Moeders' in S. Sevenhuijsen et al. (eds) *Socialisties-Feministiese Teksten* (Baarn: Ambo), vol. 9, pp. 35–53.

Zipper, J. (1986b) *Het Zaad der Twijfel. Politieke Debatten over Kunstmatige Inseminatie in de Jaren '50–'65* (Amsterdam: Universiteit van Amsterdam, Subfaculteit der Algemene Politieke en Sociale Wetenschappen).

Zipper, J. (1986c) 'Kind, Kind waar Moet dat Heen? Feministische Opvattingen over Voortplantingstechnologie', *Katijf,* 32, pp. 36–9.

Zola, I. K. (1977) 'Healthism and Disabling Medicalisation', in I. Illich et al. (eds) *The Disabling Professions* (London: Marion Boyars).

Notes on Contributors

Lesley Doyal is Head of the Department of Nursing, Health and Applied Social Studies at Bristol Polytechnic and was previously co-ordinator of the Women's Studies Unit at the Polytechnic of North London. She is the author of *The Political Economy of Health*, and has written extensively on women's health issues. She was one of the founders of the Women's Health Information Centre in London and is currently working on a book on what makes women sick.

Janet Gallagher is an Attorney affiliated with the Civil Liberties and Public Policy Program of Hampshire College, Amherst, Massachusetts. She was a founding member of the New York City Committee for Abortion Rights and Against Sterilization Abuse, and serves on the National Board of Catholics for Free Choice and the Bioethics Advisory Committee of the Planned Parenthood Federation of America. She has written and lectured extensively on bioethical topics, especially those involving reproduction.

Ann Oakley is a sociologist who has researched and written widely in the areas of women's situation, the sociology of gender and the family, and the sociology and history of health care. Her books include *The Sociology of Housework, Taking it Like a Woman* and *The Captured Womb*. She is currently Deputy Director of the Thomas Coram Research Unit, University of London, is doing research on social support and pregnancy and is working on a novel tentatively entitled *The Men's Room*.

Ros Petchesky is Professor of Political Science and Coordinator of Women's Studies at Hunter College, City University of New York. She has written widely on reproductive issues, including the award-winning book *Abortion and Woman's Choice*. She lives in New York City, where she has been active in the feminist movement for reproductive rights.

Naomi Pfeffer's current research examines the history of population, medicine and sterility in the twentieth century. She is co-author of a recent report, advocating improvements in the treatment of infertility which do not involve high-technology medicine, for the Greater London Association of Community Health Councils. Among her other publications is *The Experience of Infertility* (co-authored with Anne Woollett).

Hilary Rose is Professor of Social Policy and Director of the West Yorkshire Centre for Research on Women, at the University of Bradford. She was a founding member of the British Sociological Association's Women's Caucus and sometime chairperson of the Standing Committee for Equality between the Sexes. She has been researching and writing about the politics and social relations of science for twenty years. Her recent publications include: 'Beyond Masculinist Realities: a Feminist Epistemology for the Sciences', in Ruth Bleier (ed.) *Feminist Approaches to Science;* 'Women's Work: Women's Knowledge' in Juliet Mitchell and Ann Oakley (eds) *What is Feminism?*; and 'Hand, Brain and Heart', in Sandra Harding and Jean O'Barr (eds) *Sex and Scientific Inquiry.*

Selma Sevenhuijsen is Assistant Professor of Political Science at the University of Amsterdam. She has published on feminism, gender relations and the state, and on political and legal aspects of motherhood and fatherhood. At the moment she is working on a research project on the political history of family law, with special attention to feminist involvement in this field.

Carol Smart is Lecturer in Sociology at the University of Warwick. Formerly she was Director of the National Council for One-Parent Families, and she has carried out research at the University of Sheffield and the Institute of Psychiatry, London. Her recent publications include *The Ties that Bind* and *Women in Law*, which was co-edited with Julia Brophy. She has also written widely in the field of feminism and criminology. Carol now lives in Leamington Spa and is working on a book on feminist perspectives on law.

Michelle Stanworth is Senior Lecturer in Sociology at Cambridgeshire College of Arts and Technology, and Editor of the Feminist Perspectives series for Polity Press. Her publications include *Gender and Schooling* and *Women and the Public Sphere* (with Janet Siltanen). She is currently continuing research on reproductive technologies.

Juliette Zipper works in the Department of Political Theory at the University of Amsterdam. She has published on the politics of reproductive technology and is currently doing research in that area for her Ph.D.

Index